Unveiling Glory

Visions of Christ's
Transforming Presence

"*The theme of* Unveiling Glory *is that the incarnational knife cuts both ways. God became flesh. But he did so in the hope that flesh might become god-like. Childers and Aquino cut into the life of Christ to discover things profound and practical for shaping our own lives and the communities of faith in which we live.*

"*This is a wonderful book, contemplating vast themes from a practical perspective. Like the incarnation itself (a particular focus of this work),* Unveiling Glory *keeps shifting our attention from the glorious to the mundane, from the eternal to the intensely personal. That's as it should be for a book written to jars of clay who—improbably—contain heavenly treasures within themselves.*

"*In a religious milieu where great heat is often generated over the minute and peripheral, it is wonderful to read a book reminding us that the only legitimate and life-giving heat radiates from the Son at the center.* Unveiling Glory *sits us in front of Jesus and allows us to warm ourselves in his glow.*"

TIM WOODROOF
TEACHING MINISTER, OTTER CREEK CHURCH OF CHRIST

UNVEILING GLORY

VISIONS
OF
CHRIST'S
TRANSFORMING
PRESENCE

JEFF W. CHILDERS · FREDERICK D. AQUINO

STUDY GUIDE BY
JEANENE REESE

A·C·U
PRESS

UNVEILING GLORY:
Visions of Christ's Transforming Presence

The Heart of the Restoration, Volume 3
Douglas A. Foster, Series Editor

A·C·U
PRESS

Acu Box 29138
Abilene, TX 79699
www.acu.edu/acupress

Volume Editors · Sherry Rankin & William Rankin
Study Guide · Jeanene Reese
Cover · Sarah Bales
Author Photo · Steve Butman Photography
Book design & typesetting · William Rankin
This book is set in Adobe® Minion Pro 11.5/13, a font drawn by Robert Slimbach
and originally issued in 1990. This book was composed in Adobe® InDesign®.

ISBN 0-89112-038-6

LCCN 2003109465

❡ 10 9 8 7 6 5 4 3 2 1

Permissions

The scenario "Service or Sacrifice" (pp. 200–202) was adapted from a case by the same title in Introduction to Christianity: A Case Method Approach (Atlanta: Westminster/John Knox, 1977). Used by permission. All rights reserved.

The case "Not in My Back Yard" (pp. 207–210) was adapted from one by the same title written by Warren L. Dennis of New Brunswick Theological Seminary (17 Seminary Place, New Brunswick, NJ 08091). Copyright© Case Study Institute, 1998. Distributed by Yale University Divinity School Library (409 Prospect Street, New Haven, CT 06511). Used by permission of the Association for Case Teaching, Abilene Christian University, ACU Box 29443, Abilene, TX 79699. All rights reserved.

The case "Peace Child" (pp. 214–219) was adapted from a book by the same title written by Don Richardson (Gospel Light Publishing, 1974). Professor Jack Bartlett Rogers of Fuller Theological Seminary adapted this as a case and published it in Christian Theology: A Case Method Approach, edited by Robert A. Evans and Thomas D. Parker. Minor revisions have been made to fit the context of Unveiling Glory. Used by permission of the author and editor. All rights reserved.

To B. Shelburne
who taught me what it means to be a disciple of Jesus

J C

To Michelle Aquino
who embodies the spirit of this book

F A

Contents

Acknowledgments

We have benefited from the help and encouragement of many people in writing this book. First of all, we're thankful for the constant support and advice of the *Heart of the Restoration* series directors, Doug Foster, Jack Reese, and Royce Money. They and our other Salado Group colleagues engaged us in fruitful conversations about the subject matter of this book, making many excellent suggestions for improving the manuscript. To Ken Cukrowski, Mark Hamilton, Randy Harris, Mark Love, Tim Sensing, Charles Siburt, James Thompson, and David Wray, we offer heartfelt thanks.

We are especially indebted to one of our Salado colleagues: Carroll Osburn. From the beginning of this project, he invested an enormous amount of time and energy as our collaborator and advisor, working closely with us in the development of this book's material. His commitment to the biblical text and his long experience serving among Churches of Christ have left an imprint upon us and upon this book.

Stacy Obenhaus and Kris Southward have been worthy critics. We thank them for reading the manuscript and offering many helpful recommendations. Thanks also to Jason Bridges and Kevin Wells, who assisted us in preparing the manuscript.

Thanks to our colleagues at ACU Press, Thom Lemmons and Karen Cukrowski. They not only helped us with the manuscript, but they also exhibited great patience in waiting for us to finish—beyond one deadline after another. A special thanks to our editors, Bill and Sherry Rankin. Their gifts with language have immeasurably enhanced the quality of our writing. With great skill and in constant friendship, they guided us through some difficult passages in the process of completing the manuscript, becoming crucial partners during the closing months of this project. Their help has been invaluable.

We're very grateful for our families. Their companionship is precious to us every day, and their encouragement to us during the writing of this book has been a constant source of refreshment. They have had to carry some heavy loads so that we could finish. For Michelle, David, and Elizabeth Aquino (who joined the Aquino team during the writing of this book), along with Linda, Rebekah, Amara, and Joel Childers, we reserve our deep gratitude and appreciation.

Most of all, we thank God, the Father of our Lord and Savior Jesus Christ. We honor him as the source of all good things, and it is to him that we entrust our labors.

Jeff W. Childers
Frederick D. Aquino
September 2003

Preface to the Series

From its beginning in 1906, Abilene Christian University has existed as an institution of higher education to serve the fellowship of the Churches of Christ. While we welcome students and supporters from a variety of Christian traditions who are sympathetic with our Christ-centered focus, we know who our primary constituents are. ACU's Bible Department, now the College of Biblical Studies, has for almost a century been a guiding light for our fellowship through its contributions in Christian scholarship and ministry. Thousands of missionaries, ministers, elders, teachers, and Christian servants have come under the positive influence of these godly professors. They have steadfastly upheld the lordship of Christ, the authority of the Scriptures, and the necessity of living a life of Christian service through the church.

Abilene Christian University, in conjunction with its ACU Press, launched the *Heart of the Restoration* series with *The Crux of the Matter* in 2001 and now continues it with the third volume, *Unveiling Glory*. We pray that this series will help stimulate discussion and make a meaningful contribution to the fellowship of the Churches of Christ and beyond. This volume deals with christology—the way Christ continues to shape and transform his people. Subsequent volumes will address topics such as the Church and worship. The authors are all faculty members in ACU's College of Biblical Studies. In these volumes, they will model a biblical spirit of unity in Christ, with individual perspectives on the details of the gospel message. Above all, they are committed to the lordship of Jesus Christ and to his church, and they are committed to restoring the spirit of the Christian faith "once for all delivered to the saints."

My special thanks go to Dr. Jack Reese who shared the dream of this series with me from the beginning. Dr. Doug Foster, as the editor of the series, has made the dream into a reality. My thanks go also to our benefactors, who believed that the project would result in a clearer articulation of our faith and identity in Churches of Christ at the dawning of a new century.

> Now to him who is able to do immeasurably more than all we ask or imagine, according to his power that is at work within us, to him be glory in the church and in Christ Jesus throughout all generations, for ever and ever! Amen.
>
> *Ephesians 3:20–21*
>
> *Royce Money, President*
> *Abilene Christian University*

Introduction: If Jesus is the Answer...
What's the Question?

"Say, do you love Jesus?"
  "Oh, yes we love Jesus!"
"Do you really love Jesus?"
  "Yes, we really love Jesus,"
  "Because he first loved me!"

Like enthusiastic fans lifting up a rousing cheer, the children stand and answer the question in spirited echoes, over and over again, imprinting the message on everyone's heart: *"Oh, yes we love Jesus!"* Some of the first songs the kids in our churches learn are those about loving Jesus. They write out their love in crayon captions to the finger paint portraits of Jesus decorating our refrigerator doors. From a very early age, kids raised in our churches are imparted with the instinct to love him. And it isn't just the kids. The grown-ups are in on it, too. Many of our oldest and most cherished hymns speak of our love for Jesus Christ, songs like "Jesus is Lord, My Redeemer" and "All Hail the Power of Jesus' Name." Contemporary songs carry on the celebration, with new favorites such as "Jesus, You're My Firm Foundation" and "You are My All in All."

In fact, there are signs of love for Jesus almost any-where you look—bumper stickers, calendars, Bible covers, bookmarks, t-shirts, and web-sites. In words and songs, in pictures, with snappy red heart logos, people are declaring that they love Jesus. We see it in other ways, too. Families come to church every Sunday. High school youth groups spend their vacation time on campaigns to help under-privileged kids in developing nations. Middle-aged housewives dedicate hours every week to Bible study. College students decide to make a career of full-time ministry. Business people in various communities covenant together to uphold Christian practices. Praise nights are happening more frequently and lasting for hours. All for the sake of loving Jesus.

But who is Jesus? That many people claim to love him is undeniable. That many are deeply sincere in their love for him we do not question. It encourages our hearts to hear the children exclaiming their love. We know that every time they intone, "*Yes, we really love Jesus!*" they are laying a plank in the foundation of a lifetime of discipleship. All this love for Jesus can only be a good thing. Yet we wonder, who is this person Jesus we all love so much?

Jesus is a real person, after all—a Jewish carpenter, a teacher, the Messiah of God. First-century Galilee was his home. He taught certain things; he stood for certain things. He died on a cross and was raised to life. He is Lord.

It is inspiring to see so much excitement about Jesus these days, and we only want to see the ardor grow hotter, yet the person Jesus cannot be reduced merely to an intense feeling in our hearts. We do not mean to say that passionate emotions are unimportant—they are essential, a part of true love. Genuine relationships between real people involve all sorts of emotions, matters of heart

A Story that Transforms...

Beyond all question, the mystery of godliness is great:
He appeared in the flesh,
    was vindicated by the Spirit,
    was seen by angels,
    was preached among the nations,
    was believed on in the world,
    was taken up in glory.

1 Timothy 3:16

and soul. The same is true for any good relationship with Jesus Christ. True love transcends the brain. Yet true love also desires to know the beloved truly.

In the case of Jesus, only the love of heart, soul, mind, and strength will do. Bracketing out the mental part of love for the sake of experiencing only its passion does not produce discipleship. Two newlyweds or even good friends may have great affection for one another, but their relationship cannot deepen unless they learn some basic facts about each other. Thoughtful reflection about who Jesus is and what he means to us does not contradict love; rather, it celebrates and shares love. At the same time, being content just to get all the facts about Jesus straight in our heads makes for an anemic piety because Jesus is not merely a historical figure of interest. And, though accurate head knowledge is important and heartfelt emotions are crucial, neither of them will excuse us from getting our hands dirty in the actual work Jesus gives us to do because Jesus is an active, working presence in our daily Christian walk.

True love for Jesus demands our all. Jesus wants us to put everything we have into our relationship with him, not just once, but over and over in a lifetime of growth. This is why Christians should welcome the chance to do some hard thinking and have some serious discussions about Jesus. Devoted disciples are never content to stop learning and growing, because the relationship offers so much. Careful study of our faith in Jesus Christ is nothing to fear—unless we are so devoted to our own cherished image of Jesus that we will let nothing challenge it, not even a confrontation with the actual person and presence of Jesus. Then there is reason to fear, but all the more reason to invite the Lord to lead us deeper into the truth about him so we can mature.

3

A Lens for Reflection

This is a book on christology. Simply put, "christology" is the study of Jesus Christ. Every Christian does christology, though he or she may not always call it that. To be Christian is to meditate on Jesus Christ, to ponder who he is, what he says, what it all means. The Christian life is one of reflecting on the story of Jesus and living a life of discipleship consistent with that story. Without thoughtful reflection and faithful conversation about Jesus, we tend to find in him what we want to find or to overlook something important. Even his earliest disciples tended to misunderstand him, so he spoke to them in parables, using a teaching strategy that required them to ponder and reflect. The mystery of the kingdom was a great treasure, but they would have to dig for it. He wanted them to invest themselves in the chore of seeking understanding so that by their humble commitment they might glimpse "the knowledge of the secrets of the kingdom of heaven" (Matthew 13:10–17).

Our churches are seeking the same kingdom knowledge today. Churches of Christ face a number of challenges. It is a time of great opportunity for people who hold out the gospel in a lost world, yet for many it is also a time of anxiety and uncertainty. Numerous questions loom in the minds of church leaders—questions about worship, the nature of proper leadership, tradition, the church's mission, how to relate to culture, and a host of other things. The problems seem overwhelming, as they do in every age. Situations can be difficult, and the way forward is often unclear. The stakes are high. In order to negotiate the tricky terrain before them, churches need to follow the lead of their Shepherd, the Lord Jesus Christ. This is not just a pious-sounding sentiment. By undertaking the discipline of reflecting seriously on the significance of Jesus Christ for faith and life, Christians acquire a "christological lens" through which they can look at the problems they face, finding God's resources for help.

4 Take worship, for example. Many of our churches are struggling with questions about proper worship. Should we use a traditional style of music or something more contemporary? Are hand-clapping and hand-raising appropriate? What about bringing in

different elements, such as personal testimony? How long should the sermon be, and for whom is it written? What yardstick should we use to measure good worship—accuracy, liveliness, or outreach potential? In many places, conflict erupts over questions like these. Each faction draws its lines and divisions occur. A congregation torn by worship issues may decide to create two services, each with its own style, or even to split into two churches. A church that has made certain worship choices may criticize congregations that have made different choices.

In the heat of conflict over something incendiary like worship, we get confused about what the problem really is. The problem is not just one of clashing styles, or of differences between the generations, or of disagreements regarding the church's mission, or how to interpret New Testament instructions about worship. The problem includes the business of how we understand Jesus. The other issues are important, but it is our *christological* foundation that will determine how we approach all the other matters. And it is our grounding in Jesus that will determine whether our solutions are sound.

To be sure, Christians will not always find direct answers to their worship questions in Jesus' teaching or example. Jesus issued no commands about whether we ought to worship in church buildings or in homes. Nor do his own synagogue practices give us any clues as to whether the best worship style is contemporary, traditional, or blended. But what if the people in a church kept studying Jesus' teaching and example so much that they all got into the habit of imitating him? A church full of people who take up their crosses daily, constantly aware of the risen Christ's active presence and keeping love for God and love for neighbor as core values, will be able to work out their conflicts.

5

What if a community of believers paid such close attention to the meaning of Jesus' coming into the world that they were gripped by the mission of God? They would have a guiding vision, a driving purpose that helps them make decisions fitting their sense of destiny. What if a preacher helped his church meditate on the deeper mysteries about Jesus, such as the significance of his being both human and divine? That church might develop some new attitudes about such things as diversity in the church or the place of tradition. What if a church's leaders regularly talked together about the Apostles' teachings on Christ? They might get excited about the Apostles' basic aim of transformation into Christlikeness. This is a clear agenda, a Christ-centered ideal they could use to measure ministry decisions. They would look for worship policies that helped form a church environment that nurtures spiritual growth and maturity.

Christological reflection carries a payoff, but not in the form of quick and easy answers to every problem. Christology is not so much a procedure of looking for fill-in-the-blank answers as it is a process of asking questions about what Jesus' life, death, and resurrection actually mean for the Christian life. That process forms a kind of lens through which we look. Jesus and the Apostles did not give us a specific teaching or example for every subject that we deal with today. But when we reflect carefully on a subject—like worship—in light of the meaning of Christ, we can come to see it in Christ-centered ways, to talk about it in Christ-focused language, and to keep our conclusions about it grounded in the central matters of the gospel.

Ultimately then, the aim of christology is the same as that of our salvation: transformation. Done well, it forms us into the image of Jesus, and the power of that transformation in the lives of people presents churches with opportunities they cannot even imagine. More than techniques and strategies, the issues facing Churches of Christ today require leadership that is Christlike in character. The writers hope this book will help people as they think about and embrace this character—as they are transformed into the image of Jesus.

God is up to something in our churches. He is up to something in the world. His glory is being unveiled right in front of us. But in order to see and understand what he is up to, we need a lens to look through. Jesus Christ supplies that lens; giving deliberate attention to the meaning of Christ puts the lens into our hands. Looking through that lens changes the way we see things. It changes us. Not only do we end up seeing the problems that face our churches in a different way, but we come to see the world in a new way, too. Jesus is the answer to the problems facing Churches of Christ precisely because he is the answer to some much larger problems facing the whole world. We must be wary of devoting all our study and discussion to our pet insider issues, however important they may seem, for in today's world, we need to get clear on something much more basic and profound—the way that the Christian belief in a divine and human Son of God sets people on a distinctive course of life amidst the wreckage of a broken world.

Unveiling God's Vision of Peace

Young children and the evening news do not go well together. We want our children to be informed about world events, but the content of most evening newscasts is disturbing. As adults, we grow numb to the tragedies that saturate leading news stories—floods, terrorism, sexual abuse, starvation, school shootings, warfare. Our senses are deadened, and we learn to cope. But very young children find their first exposure to the world's horrors, professionally hyped

> "There is much that is bad and meaningless in the universe, and the universe contains men who know that much is bad and meaningless. The Christian answer is that this is a good world gone wrong, but with a memory of what it should have been."
>
> *Kathryn Lindskoog (1973)*

and in graphic color, unsettling. "Reality," as we sometimes call it, gives their naïve and impressionable little systems a jolt. They find the news difficult to swallow, nearly impossible to choke down, and they pass this indigestion on to their parents in the form of troubled dreams and troubling questions. When young children experience atrocity for the first time—perhaps on the television screen, perhaps more directly—the simple anguish of their puzzled "Why?" reminds us that every catastrophe, on any scale, rings out like a shot and shatters the peace of what should be—a world in which all creation enjoys harmony within itself and with its Creator.

Muslims crave *salaam*. Hindus seek the universal *brahman*, the ultimate experience of unity and wholeness. Buddhists aspire to the peaceful quiet of *nirvana*. Taoists suggest that we should wisely surrender to the unstoppable flow of *yin* and *yang* in the *tao*. Everywhere human beings show their brokenness and reveal their longing for peace. The world is not right. Things are not as they should be. *Shalom* has been dashed into a thousand pieces, in ten thousand ways. Yet it has left a sweet residue on the wrecked fragments of our world. Like an aroma that invokes a vivid recollection from childhood, we sense the memory of peace, and we long to get it back somehow. We crave good relationships with one other, with our world, and with our God.

Christians are not alone in the spiritual quest for wholeness and reconciliation. However, Christians profess the God who is One—the God of Abraham, Isaac, and Jacob, the Father of Jesus Christ. The world may be fractured, but he is One. He created the universe whole and meaningful. He blessed it with wonderful relationships, joining the elements of creation together like a composer crafting beautiful harmonies. Yet now the melody is broken, and we hear only echoes of it, distorted and distant. Because of human selfishness and self-worship, the sins of past and present, creation's wholeness has disintegrated into disharmony and discord. Things are not as they should be. This is true in the world and also true in churches.

> "You have made us for yourself, and our heart is restless until it comes to rest in you...."
>
> *Augustine of Hippo (c. 400)*

Christianity does not shrink from facing the world's brokenness. But Christians also believe that God has unveiled a vision of peace restored: Jesus Christ. In other words, God's solution to the world's problems is to offer himself. Revealing himself in Christ, he invites people to enter a relationship with him so that they may find in that relationship healing, a redirected purpose, and the power to live it out. In Christ, God has revealed not only himself, but he has also shown us a glorious picture of what we are to become. In Jesus, we see the fullness of the Father and the perfect human, intact and whole. Yet in the presence of such an ideal Son of God, we must come to grips with the painful truth of our own sin and helplessness. We need more than insight. We need a solution. As important as the facts about Jesus are, we also need something more. Humanity needs an unveiling that is not merely informative, but also transformative.

In the first century, the church at Corinth fell victim to the world's fragmenting forces, prompting the writing of 2 Corinthians. Some self-involved teachers, whom Paul ironically dubs "super-apostles," seem to have captured the hearts of people in the church. They were promoting themselves by advertising impressive credentials and displaying elocutionary polish. In Paul's absence, they tried to enhance their own authority by belittling his skills and pedigree and by fostering doubts about his sincerity. The values by which they operated were foreign to the gospel, but they apparently had so many people buying into them that the church's integrity was dissolving due to the corrosive effects of its own delusions about what really mattered.

In 2 Corinthians, Paul defends and explains himself in various ways, but one theme running through much of the book has to do with the place of humble sacrifice and genuine service in proving a minister's worth. More than defending himself, he wants to refocus the church's values, by redirecting its adoration to the image of Christ as servant leader. Paul insists that what makes ministry of the gospel authentic, and even superior to Moses' ministry, has nothing to do with the minister's own glory, but with the surpassing glory of Jesus Christ that

9

the ministry reveals. The quality of a gospel ministry is not to be graded by counterfeit measurements like those of the "super-apostles," but by its effects in transforming people into the image of the Lord, as Paul suggests in 2 Corinthians 3:18:

> And we, who with unveiled faces all reflect the Lord's glory, are being transformed into his likeness with ever-increasing glory, which comes from the Lord, who is the Spirit.

By focusing on the Lord and submitting themselves to his work of transforming them into his likeness, the Corinthians would discover the solution to their problems.

Paul's picture of unveiling glory supplies the guiding metaphor for this book. It is a visual metaphor, a dynamic picture of the transforming relationship that can exist when the Lord's people are so attentive to him that they begin to reflect his character. Those who have chosen to fix their gaze upon Jesus have had the veil separating them from the Father lifted from their eyes. It falls away when we are "in Christ." Due to our faith in him, he recreates us by his Spirit. "To all who received him, to all who believed in his name, he gave the right to become God's children" (John 1:12). Adopted back into the family through our brother Jesus, we enjoy the firstfruits of God's salvation as he works to bring his creation back to himself.

The key to peace in the world is reunion with God, and it is towards that end that he is working. Christians believe that Jesus Christ is the door leading to that peace. When Christians confess that "Jesus is Lord," they are accepting his claim of being the Way, the Truth, and the Life, and that no one comes to the Father except through him (John 14:6). By inviting us into his Son, God has invited us to share his own life, the abundant life that we were designed

> "The Trinity is an attempt to affirm that God is a thoroughly relational being. The doctrine of the Trinity accents this truth by claiming that God not only forms relationships but that He is a relationship."
>
> C. Leonard Allen & Danny G. Swick (2001)

for and that only happens in a relationship with Father, Son, and Spirit—the life of God (John 10:10).

The picture that God unveils to us is no museum exhibit. A masterpiece it may be, but it is not roped off from human contact, shielded by bulletproof glass and infrared alarms to keep people away. The picture is a hands-on piece, a work of interactive art, inviting full contact. It is a picture in which we become involved. God is fixing his world by unveiling himself in Jesus and drawing the world into that picture. As we peer into its glory, it captures us, involving our lives in its project, changing us into its own image and making us like Jesus.

We know this because of our own experience as Jesus' disciples. The saving event of Jesus' life, death, and resurrection is not just a far-off moment in time or a mechanical fix to some remote technical problem with the world. The Jesus-event is breaking news. It is happening around us and within us, rescuing what was lost and restoring what was broken. We see it in our families, and we experience it in our churches. Jesus is alive and well, reigning at the right hand of the Father. Our relationship with him is vital and active. Baptism connects us to him, and the Lord's Supper renews the connection constantly. In the church, we find our places within his living body. The church and its members are on a journey of ever-increasing Christlikeness, and with each step of progress, the world regains a measure of peace. On the day that he returns, everything will finally submit to his Lordship and the restoration of God's peace will be complete.

In short, the church's answer to the world's problems is Jesus Christ.

An Invitation to Gaze upon Jesus

Approaching Christ with transformation in mind has not always been a key element in the preaching of our heritage. Yet we are convinced that whenever scripture is allowed to speak with its full voice, the notion of Christianity as transformation into the image of Christ becomes inescapable. Even 150 years ago, this subject dominated the thinking of Restoration leader and biographer of Alexander Campbell, Robert Richardson:

> It is the contemplation of infinite excellence that exalts, as it is the society of the good and the noble that inspires nobility of soul.... It is while we contemplate the glory of the Lord in the brilliant mirror in which his perfections are revealed that we are "changed into the same image from glory to glory, as by the Spirit of the Lord."

In our book, the authors invite the reader to explore with them the significance of Jesus Christ for belief and life. Some parts of this exploration will seem familiar and comfortable. Other parts may be strange and unusual. The authors do not presume to offer a full unveiling of Jesus, nor do they presume that the reader does not already enjoy an intimate relationship with the Lord. They simply want to invite the reader to join them in cultivating disciplined habits of meditating on Jesus' significance, and in so doing to find wisdom, experience transformation, and enjoy an ever-deepening relationship with the Lord. The authors are confident that the reader shares their enthusiasm for opportunities to grow.

The church that is engaged in healthy reflection on the significance of Christ is providing the kind of ecology necessary for transformation and growth to occur. Growing plants or animals need a healthy environment; the same is true for spiritual growth. Healthy spiritual living involves matters of right thinking along with good habits and practices. Within a healthy environment, Christians will mature and churches can make sound decisions. One of the basic principles of *The Heart of the Restoration* series is that individuals and congregations must make their own decisions and apply scripture to their own situations. The series is meant to stimulate conversation and provide resources to aid people who are seeking to serve the Lord where they are, but the purpose of this book is not to prescribe specific strategies. The ideas and principles in this book naturally lead to concrete application, but good strategies can be constructed only in the context of a local church. The Study Guide is designed to help readers grapple with the book's implications and apply them to their own situations. Yet rather than dictating definite programs, the authors hope instead to offer some guidance in how to reflect on the significance of Jesus for Christian belief and living.

The story of Jesus Christ is the core of our faith, its center of gravity. Although this book is not a "Life of Jesus," it is organized according to the basic narrative pattern of Jesus' life as presented in the Gospels. So, in a sense, this book is an explanation of the gospel, a retelling of the Good News. Specific moments in Jesus' story function like windows, providing opportunities to look in on various topics that give us insight into his significance for our lives. Chapter 1 introduces the concept of the incarnation. When Jesus came into the world,

> **The Gospel Defined**
>
> "The mission of Christ for man's redemption is the Gospel; and the Gospel is Christ's mission, work, suffering, sorrow, death, burial, resurrection and ascension for the redemption of the world from the dominion of sin and death."
>
> *David Lipscomb (1869)*

both sides of that union were stepping into something new. The history of humankind and even God's story took a major turn. Mysterious as it is, the doctrine of the incarnation is more than an interesting fact or curious dogma of Christian tradition. Grappling with the incarnation in its linking of divine and human opens us up to experience the full unveiling of God's glory, bringing into focus his plan for the world and leading us to discover who we really are. Chapter 2 looks specifically at the event of Jesus' birth. At the manger, we're privileged to peer into the heart of a humble God, one who gently invites us into his presence and is committed to a collaborative relationship with us. Moreover, he invites us to practice the humble glory of the nativity in our own lives.

Chapter 3 treats Jesus' baptism and his call to discipleship. At the Jordan river, we catch a glimpse of the

Father, Son, and Spirit conversing together, sharing the life that is our birthright, too. By answering Jesus' radical call to discipleship, we find ourselves immersed into a new world, one in which we learn to live according to the redemptive rhythm of death and new life. Chapter 4 travels with Jesus during his ministry. His works of service help clarify God's program for treating the world's ills, imparting a vision of God's kingdom that continues to inspire and direct the church. Chapter 5 considers Jesus' role as teacher and his disciples' place as students. While conforming to earthly expectations for teachers in some ways, Christ shattered expectations as well, revealing himself to be not just a teacher, but *the* Teacher, the One who imparts knowledge while at the same time enfleshing the very subject matter he teaches.

Chapter 6 explores the atonement and Jesus' role in our salvation. Though the Christian symbol most consistently associated with salvation is the cross, the atonement is actually bound up in the entire Jesus story, everything that Jesus is and does. We will examine different images Christians have used to capture the meaning of the atonement, attempting to gather them all up into a broad vision of salvation as the dynamic process of transformation that we experience each day. Chapter 7 deals with Jesus' resurrection. For centuries, people have made pilgrimages to Jerusalem to see an empty tomb. In a world of broken dreams and shattered hopes, where promises ring hollow and the scars from yesterday's mistakes are slow to heal, the chance for a fresh start is very appealing. Jesus' resurrection speaks to us of renewal and second chances. It also clearly depicts the goal of the Christian life, providing Christians and churches with a means of determining whether they're on the right track. The concluding chapter, Chapter 8, follows the risen Christ through his ascension and beyond. On this side of Jesus' ascension, the open doorway of the empty tomb is like a window through which we look at the Christian life. We peer into the opening from both sides. From the outside, we look in to catch a hopeful glimpse of our eternal destiny. From within the tomb, we look out as people who have been with Christ in death and have already begun to taste resurrection power. We experience the Christian life as an ongoing journey that shapes us into the image of Christ through the power of the one who ascended and yet remains present and active among us.

This book is not comprehensive. It will not address every question about Jesus. Nor is it a book for specialists. Some classic items of christology will be left to one side. This book does not survey christological titles or attempt to prove and define Jesus' divinity or establish his historicity. Instead, presuming the truth of scripture's testimony about Christ, the authors devote themselves to a constructive discussion of what it all means, tracing out some key implications for our faith and practice today. The authors hope the discussion will acquaint the reader with a particular way of thinking and of practicing faith, one that is intentionally christological. This type of reflection is valuable, and the reader is encouraged to pursue the subject further and to continue cultivating his or her own habits of meditating on Jesus. To this end, the Annotated Bibliography at the end of the book will guide the reader in finding further resources for exploring and developing christology. The cultivation of individual meditation and response is not the only purpose here, however. Another vital function of this book is to serve the practical purpose of guiding congregations as they seek productive ways to negotiate the challenges facing Churches of Christ today. The Study Guide is designed to help congregations think through and apply the principles of Christlikeness discussed in the book and to help them.

Unveilings are dramatic occurrences. A suspenseful hush falls on the crowd gathered at an art museum to see a new work of art revealed. As the authors of this book have meditated afresh on Jesus' life and teachings and his ongoing deeds of resurrection power, a sense of hush has fallen upon their hearts also. They have been reminded how incomplete their understanding is. They are made aware of how much farther they have to go before they see the image of Jesus perfectly reflected in their own lives. The Apostle Paul beheld the radiant glory of the risen Lord on his journey to Damascus, and afterwards he could see nothing at all.

So it is with some hesitation that the authors explore with you the significance of Jesus Christ for faith and life, not as masters of the subject but as those who would come alongside the reader to witness God's unveiling together. It is the authors' conviction that God has provided his church with all the resources it needs for discernment: the scriptures first of all, along with its living faith, its experience, and the guiding Spirit abiding within. Far from attempting to utter the last word, the authors' desire is to prompt more conversation within the body. They are convinced that churches that talk more and more about their Lord Jesus Christ are churches in possession of a great hope—a hope for their own bright futures as congregations and a living hope that they may offer for the healing of a broken world.

Together we invite the Lord to unveil our faces anew.

1

Beholding the New Humanity

As a child, I remember my parents emphasizing the importance of enjoying life to its fullest. They encouraged me to engage in many different activities involving school, church, and sports. They refused to isolate one aspect of life to the neglect of other parts. I accepted their encouragement as part of what parents do, but I never saw the religious side of what they were doing because they never explicitly mentioned any religious ties. However, as I look back on my childhood, I realize that church, school, and play were wonderfully integrated into a seamless fabric of life.

My parents' robust understanding of creation refused to separate faith from the world. Through their example, I gradually came to understand deep down that life, in its varied expressions, was to be celebrated and appreciated. My parents' wisdom has shaped me tremendously, especially as I have come to realize that the example of Jesus Christ calls us to an integrated life, a way of living that embraces all the different pieces of what it means to live in the world God created. Upon reflection, I realized that my parents' integrative strategy, though not explicitly motivated by the story of Christ, has wonderful implications for thinking about the relevance of christology. The urge to sever the divine from the human is one that strays from the life of Christ.

Frederick

17

What is the relevance of Jesus Christ for everyday life? The answer to that question depends on how one answers another question: Who is Jesus Christ? The New Testament insists that Jesus is the Son of God, human and divine, but what exactly does that mean? This is about as satisfying as having a question answered with a riddle. The relationship of Jesus' humanity and divinity is hardly a simple business. Over the years, the church has struggled to understand and explain it. He is human and he is divine, but how do the human and divine relate in the life of Christ? The historic affirmation of Jesus as fully divine and fully human is a basic part of Christian faith, grounded in scripture; but often this belief seems to be more of an abstract idea or a formula that doesn't translate into a visible Christian practice. Given its complexities and difficulties, why is this doctrine so important? What difference does it make, and why should this be the starting point for our discussion of Christ? One could conclude that the notion of *incarnation* is a theological abstraction largely irrelevant to everyday faith, complex and confusing. In reality, beholding God's glory in the doctrine of the incarnation furnishes Christians with a lens for viewing everyday life that transforms everything.

Much of our traditional preaching has focused on our heavenly reward in a way that severs salvation from creation, making it hard for us to see the connections between many basic Christian beliefs and everyday life.

The Nicene Summary of Faith

One early attempt to summarize the Incarnation:

"We believe...in one Lord Jesus Christ, the only-begotten Son of God, begotten from the father before all time, Light from Light, true God from true God, begotten not created, of the same essence as the Father, through whom all things were made, who for us people and for our salvation came down from heaven, and was incarnate by the Holy Spirit and the Virgin Mary and became human. He was crucified for us under Pontius Pilate, and suffered and was buried, and rose on the third day, according to the scriptures, and ascended to heaven, and sits on the right hand of the Father, and will come again with glory to judge the living and the dead. His kingdom shall have no end."

Council of Nicea (325)

The assumption is that being saved means being rescued out of the world. In contrast, the incarnation connects salvation and creation. It joins heavenly realities with the mundane affairs of the here and now. By becoming one of us, the Son of God reaffirmed the original goodness and purpose of creation. The surprising truth of the incarnation is that our fleshly condition, with all its flaws and weaknesses, is not so worthless and contemptible that God is above becoming flesh himself. In fact, in Jesus, he takes on our everyday human condition as the very means through which God reclaims us as his own.

The aim and goal of the incarnation is to offer a fuller vision of humanity and to redirect our steps accordingly. We are sinners, but when we sin, we are prone to say, "I'm only human." Yet to sin is not to be merely human—it is to be less than human. We cannot excuse ourselves from God's call to be changed in Christ, cannot allow ourselves to grow comfortable in our imperfection, shirking our responsibility to be transformed by his glory and grace. We have self-destructive tendencies, but we are redeemable. Yet we might also be tempted to think that God has called us to something different than our own humanity. This misunderstanding leads some to defame everything human and earthly as sad and worthless. Others misunderstand the call to be Christlike as a call to become superhuman. Each of these responses reflects a flawed and narrow view of the incarnation.

The incarnation—the union of the divine and human in Jesus Christ—unfolds a wonderful mystery, redirecting us to our divinely created purpose. It is as basic to the Christian life as the person of Jesus. The incarnation enables us to understand why God has made us, empowering us to reclaim that purpose and to live the full lives that God intends for his children. In essence, the coming of the Son of God in the person of Jesus focuses on the central question of what it means to be human. Yet it also draws our attention to the nature and character of God. It tells of our magnificent potential and the true beauty of human life, but it also confronts us with our own ugliness and the world's stubborn injustice. The existence of human and divine in Jesus sets up difficult tensions, but the tensions are no more difficult than the problems of everyday life. The doctrine of the incarnation respects these complexities, involving us in a lifestyle of discipleship that gets its direction and potency for effective living from the energy generated by the tensions present within Jesus himself.

A Tense Situation: Jesus' Attitude Toward the World

God visited the earth as a human being, a full-bodied participant in the world. Yet he called people to disconnect from the world they knew and seek a higher road. These two attitudes seem contradictory, yet they met in Jesus, creating a tension that knocked people off balance. Sometimes Jesus offended people. For example, he did not always make the most enjoyable dinner guest. In the middle of the meal, he was likely to do or say something unpleasant, something bound to offend the other guests (or even the host). As the people at Simon's dinner party discovered, there was something deeply annoying about Jesus—and something deeply appealing (Luke 7:36–50). Perhaps the two qualities were really the same thing. This man who patiently welcomed sinners could also be ruthlessly confrontational and harsh. There was a simplicity about him, a single-mindedness that was compelling yet could also cut like a sharp knife. He was uncompromising and radical. Søren Kierkagaard observed that "purity of heart is to will one thing." By this standard, Jesus' heart had the iridescent purity of a finely-cut diamond, and was just as unyielding.

In his teaching and his behavior, Jesus struck the pose of a prophet of old, penetrating and harsh. He proclaimed the coming justice of God upon a corrupt world, justice that was terrifying to the wicked but offered the oppressed a glimmer of fresh hope. Jesus' forerunner, John the Baptist, had also warned people of the "coming wrath." He exhorted them to show repentance by sharing

20

their food and clothing with the needy and by changing their habits of greed and extortion (Luke 3:7–14). Like John—and Amos and Isaiah and Zechariah before him—Jesus had come to share a vision with his Father, a vision of the world as it should be. "The kingdom is near," he insisted, picturing the advent of a holy society in which people were at peace with God, generously shared their tunics, and even loved their enemies (Matthew 5:40, 44). He believed in the vision, preached the vision, acted out the vision. In fact, he was its best likeness.

In other words, God's Messiah envisioned a world that was truly home, yet one so different from the world as it actually is that, to those who did not share his vision, it did not appear homey at all, but unfamiliar and even hostile. Jesus proclaimed a double-edged message, revealing a deeply complex attitude towards the world. On the one hand, his preaching has elements that are strongly world-affirming. His investment in regular people and in the concerns of everyday life was total. His head was not in the clouds, and he did not teach people to treat our earthly phase of existence as some kind of distraction from the real goal of heaven. He attended dinner parties and even made high quality wine for the guests to drink (John 2:1–11). He worked with materials like fish and bread, spit and mud (Mark 6:30–44; John 9:6). He entertained children, intervened in everyday conflicts, and had compassion on mothers mourning their dead sons (Matthew 19:13–15; Luke 10:38–42; 7:11–17). He was constantly instructing people on how to live in heaven's kingdom, yet his "otherworldly" instructions were for the here and now, not the afterlife (see Matthew 5–7; John 14–16). He saw the kingdom of heaven breaking into the world in his own ministry, and he fully expected it to bear its fruit in this world. Jesus, like his Father, was world-affirming.

Yet Jesus' mission also had a world-rejecting side, a call to deny the world, take up a cross, and embrace the dawn of a new order, one that will be fully realized only after the Son of Man leads his angels in a harvest of final judgment (Mark 13:26–27; Matthew 13:47–50). By

21

spurning even a place to lay his head, the Son of Man declared his rejection of the corruption infecting the world and modeled adherence to higher values. "Don't worry about your life," he said, "what you will eat or drink…but seek first his kingdom" (Matthew 6:20, 25, 33). He counseled people to store up treasures in heaven. Jesus did not marry or settle down. He did not live out his days as an honest, hard-working citizen of an average Jewish community.

In fact, Jesus and his Apostles believed that God's plans for humankind went far beyond anything this world could offer. They taught that God will accomplish his full and final will for the world only after a massive break with the normal order has occurred. The Day of the Lord will come and the heavens will disappear and the elements will be destroyed by fire, making way for a new heaven and new earth (2 Peter 3:10, 13). Meanwhile, the creation groans in painful anticipation and the victims of injustice cry out, "How long, Sovereign Lord?" (Romans 8:19–22; Revelation 6:10). This picture of the world's antagonism and coming destruction permeates the New Testament. For Paul, terms like "flesh" and "world" represent dangerous categories. Disciples ought to make their choices in life, he says, knowing that "the world in its present form is passing away" (1 Corinthians 7:31).

"My kingdom is not of this world," Jesus remarked to Pilate (John 18:36). Yet he also believed that the kingdom's presence could be seen and felt and lived in this world: "if I drive out demons by the finger of God, the kingdom of God has come to you" (Luke 11:20). By manifesting these tensions, Christ unveils for us the heart of God's own attitude toward the world. It remains the good work of his hands, but it has also fallen from its original perfection. God's response mirrors the complexity of this situation; it has world-affirming and world-rejecting elements. Holding both of these impulses at the same time is difficult, yet they help us see why the eternal God undertook the amazing task of becoming human.

22

Why Did God Become Human?

Churches of Christ have traditionally tended to lean towards Jesus' world-rejecting side, presenting him as a person concerned primarily about heavenly existence. We have normally presumed that God became human in order to forgive us of our sins and to give us a place in heaven. Though this assumption contains some truth, it also contributes to a "pie-in-the-sky" theology, one that lets the destination (heaven) trump the journey (a walk with Jesus everyday). The hope of heaven is precious to us, but focusing exclusively on our future inheritance diminishes the value of the present, driving a wedge between our "spiritual" and "earthly" lives, as if the two were incompatible.

Traditionally, much of our preaching echoed this impression that salvation involves a radical separation from the world, calling people to convert to Jesus by renouncing the physical world and focusing on heavenly

> **Longing for Heaven**
>
> "This world is not my home, I'm just a passing through. My treasures are laid up somewhere beyond the blue....And I can't feel at home in this world anymore."
>
> *Traditional*

reward. The incarnation shows us another way to view the relationship between the physical and the spiritual. One does not count more than the other. Viewed properly, the incarnation corrects a lopsided understanding of salvation as redemption from the physical world. Jesus shows us that reaching the heavenly destination involves a rich journey in the here and now, filled with life-transforming experiences. In fact, the now (everyday life) and the not-yet (the full manifestation of salvation) fit together, sharing continuity, direction, and purpose. Experiencing Jesus in the here and now is a foretaste of the new humanity toward which we are growing.

The incarnation offers a concrete portrait of the nature and activity of both God and humanity. In its stark presentation of God's full holiness and goodness, it

23

exposes our tragic tendencies, declaring a rejection of our world. Yet it also affirms life in this world by furnishing fresh insights into the nature, meaning, and purpose of life. On the one hand, the incarnation reveals our self-destructive tendencies, reminding us that the habits we picked up in the Garden of Eden die hard. For the sake of being our own masters, we seem only too eager to refuse God's love and helpful gifts, even if it means eking out a subsistence living of thorns by our own sweat and pain. Humanity's rejection of Jesus is a case in point. The Son of God was "in the world, and the world came into being through him; yet the world did not know him. He came to what was his own, and his own people did not accept him" (John 1:10–11). Jesus' teaching about religion was designed to help people rediscover the whole point of religion—connecting our lives to God's life. Yet he challenged many prevailing religious notions, inflaming the religious establishment with such indictments as the prophet's words, "These people honor me with their lips, but their hearts are far from me. They worship in vain" (Matthew 15:8–9). In his ministry, he showed people how to repair and nurture human relationships by imitating God's mercy and doing "unto others as you would have them do unto you." Yet this meant living by the principle of self-denial, giving up status, money, and privilege. Jesus' teaching continually called people to embrace both this world and the next, but rather than accepting this cross, people chose to crucify him.

Without God, we form habits that are detrimental to our own well-being. Left to our own logic and devices, we exchange "the glory of the immortal God" for idols of our own making and the reduced quality of life that comes with them (Romans 1:23). Jesus offered people God's solutions, but they rejected him. Some people thought Jesus was a lunatic or demon-possessed, and still today he is rebuffed by doubtful and stubborn hearts—even among those who follow him. Part of the reason he has been so difficult to accept is his unflinching call to holiness. By revealing to us God's goodness, Jesus forces us to peer

24

into the darkness of our own depravity, inviting us to join him in rejecting the ways of this world.

In addition to showing us our own need, though, God became human in order to show us a better way of living as humans in the world. God's liberation of humanity from the power of sin and death in Christ is a restoration of human dignity and a loving correction of our misguided desires. Looking through the lens of the incarnation, God calls us to a new kind of earthly life. In other words, Jesus Christ fleshes out what it means to be created in "the image" and "likeness of God" since he is "the reflection of God's glory and exact imprint of God's being" (Hebrews 1:3). He came not only to save us from our sins but also to show us what it means to be truly human, as humans were intended to be. Jesus illustrates through his life and teaching how God intends for us to commune with him and with others in the world. He reclaims and empowers us to be God's children, not only so we can go to heaven, but also so that we might reflect his glory in this present world.

In this view of the incarnation, God adopts the role of the divine teacher as well as savior, becoming one of us in order to re-educate us about the nature, purpose, and goal of human existence. Though we have turned away from God in our thought and behavior, Jesus confronts us in our rebellion, face to face, prodding us to reconsider the purpose and direction of our lives and rediscover the reason we were created. Jesus is able to challenge us because he is the one and only Son of God, a unique participant in God's very life. Jesus and the Father "are one," and anyone who has seen him "has seen the Father" (John 10:30; 14:9). When we behold Jesus with unveiled faces, we are experiencing God—but we are also meeting the truly human being. As the picture of God, Jesus is the mirror in which we learn to recognize the distortions in the view of our humanity that our sin has taught us, so that we can begin to see our true appearance as God's children instead.

The image we see in Christ is not just an instructional one. It renews and transforms us, because when we enter

25

Christ we become participants with him in the life of God, "participants of the divine nature" (2 Peter 1:4). Jesus not only reveals to us the picture—he puts us right into it. "To all who received him, to those who believed in his name, he gave the right to become children of God" (John 1:12). The best part about this wonderful birthright is that everyone in the family gets the privilege of being conformed to the image of God's Son, "the firstborn within a large family" (Romans 8:29). In Christ, the distance between us and God is removed; the veil is lifted. We behold him face to face and find ourselves being transformed each day into his image (2 Corinthians 3:18). This is the Christian journey. The discipline of following Jesus isn't works-righteousness but an adventure of gradual growth into our new identity. Living like Jesus is not something we do to get salvation—it is our salvation. As participants in the divine life of God, we live out the vision of the new humanity, enjoying the richer and fuller experience of life that our discipleship brings us.

> **A Doctrine of Participation**
>
> "The Incarnation equally is a doctrine of sharing or participation. Christ shares to the full in what we are, and so he makes it possible for us to share in what he is, in his divine life and glory. He became what we are, so as to make us what he is.... Christ enables us to share in the Father's divine glory. He is the bond and meeting-point: because he is man, he is one with us: because he is God, he is one with the Father. So through and in him we are one with God, and the Father's glory becomes our glory...the divine likeness that we are called to attain is the likeness of Christ."
>
> *Kallistos Ware (1979)*

Discipleship: Radical Surrender to the Vision

Just as in Jesus Christ the human and divine coexist, the life of the disciple also holds together certain difficult tensions. For one thing, discipleship built on a mature understanding of Christ encompasses both world-rejection and world-affirmation. Churches tend to gravitate towards one side or the other, but the gospel involves both. On the one hand, the call to discipleship is not a call to something strange and different, but a call to what comes naturally. It is a call to come home. God made us to live here and be radically committed to him as our one source of life and the fulfillment of our purpose. He also built us to enjoy peaceful relationships with each other within his creation. These are some of the hallmarks of life in Christ. To respond to the call of Jesus and enter into him through baptism is to rejoin the ranks of the fully human as a new creation embarking on the voyage of human rediscovery navigated by the Second Adam (1 Corinthians 15:45–49; 2 Corinthians 5:17). Yet the picture of Jesus as *Second* Adam reminds us that something has gone deeply wrong in the world, and a fresh start is in order. The first Adam made huge mistakes, misleading the human race and scarring us deeply. As the prototype of a new humanity, the Second Adam not only showed us the right way to live, but he pioneered the way for us. He took humanity back through its basic first steps, doing it right this time.

Jesus' call to discipleship is a reorientation, but it feels disorienting at first. After all, even though Jesus has our flesh, he does very different things with it than we are accustomed to. He may be inviting people to come home, but he makes it clear that severe shifts in thought and lifestyle will be necessary to get there. Zacchaeus got the point. He declared, "Here and now I give half of my possessions to the poor, and if I have cheated anybody out of anything, I will pay back four times the amount!" Jesus celebrated Zacchaeus' sudden change of direction: "Today salvation has come to this house!" (Luke 19:8–9). The eternal life to which Jesus called people is life indeed—but not exactly life as they had known it.

This is why Jesus' call to discipleship is so radical. When he said, "Come, follow me," and we learn that "at once they left their nets and followed him" (Mark 1:17–18), we may initially be confused. How could this be? How could Peter and Andrew drop everything, seemingly without warning, reorienting the direction of their lives around him so completely? The text insists that people

27

who become disciples of Jesus Christ experience a total life adjustment. When Jesus calls, everything else moves to the margin. Everything. Coming home to share life with God requires transplanting—a traumatic, perhaps even violent, uprooting. The world-rejecting side calls us to disconnect ourselves from the ways of the world, while the world-affirming side sets us back in the world as new people.

> "Make Christ the only goal of your life. Dedicate to him all your enthusiasm, all your effort, your leisure as well as your business."
>
> *Desiderius Erasmus (1504)*

To orient us to his radical vision of new life, Jesus did not call people to become members of an institution. He called people to himself, because within the person of Jesus, the world-affirming and world-rejecting dimensions of God's work exist side by side, in harmony: "Whoever serves me must follow me; and where I am, my servant will also be" (John 12:26). The disciple is immersed into Christ, connecting intimately to Jesus' heart and lifestyle and enjoying communion with God. Jesus called people to become disciples whose allegiance to him—and therefore to God's plan for the world—would be absolute and uncompromising. This is what it means to believe in Jesus, to have faith in Christ. It was Zacchaeus' utter trust in Jesus that guaranteed his standing as a true "son of Abraham" (Luke 19:9; see Romans 4). The responses of people like Peter and Andrew, or Zacchaeus, show us that accepting Jesus' call requires a change so drastic that, by the standards of any other worldview, a disciple's behavior might seem bizarre, even insane. After all, even Jesus' own family was so disturbed by his actions that they concluded he must be crazy (Mark 3:21). His disciples can also expect to feel as if they don't fit the pattern of life that everyone else accepts as normal. Yet they know that the life they live is life eternal; they have living water that is so much more satisfying than the stale beverages on which other people seem content to subsist (John 6:32–51; 4:10–14).

Nevertheless, the disciple's distance from the ways of this world in no way separates him or her from the

28

world. In his prayer, Jesus acknowledged that his disciples "are not of the world," just as he is not of the world. The world will hate them as it hated him. Yet he specifically requested that the Father not remove them from the world, but instead, that he send them into the world as he himself had been sent, a people sanctified by Jesus' own sanctity (John 17:14–19). The incarnation reveals the extent to which Jesus' mission has become our own. In Christ, God is reaffirming our humanity and the part we play in the drama of salvation, calling us to be collaborators with him in the world.

Working with God

In Jesus Christ, the divine and human are not opposites or enemies—they work together in seamless unity. When we look at Jesus' life, it is difficult to determine where his humanity leaves off and his divinity picks up—in fact, it is impossible to do so. We find the same difficulty throughout scripture. The Bible makes it clear that God is active in the world and is just as clear that human beings are active, but rarely does it distinctly mark out some event as strictly a "God-thing." Even in such amazing occurrences as

> "The gospel is not about a God abstracted from historical particularity. It is about the God who becomes human, experiences the vicissitudes of earthly existence, even to the point of death, is resurrected and seeks to work through his body of believers to accomplish his purposes."
>
> *John Sanders (1998)*

Israel's exodus from Egypt or Paul's rescue from shipwreck, divinely orchestrated events still express themselves in the physical world and are shaped by the choices and actions of human beings. God's preferred method of working in the world is an incarnational one.

The best example is Jesus Christ himself. The Son of God not only died as a human; he lived as one, too. He got hungry and tired. He laughed and wept. He knew what it was to sweat and to bleed. Things did not always turn out the way he wanted. Sometimes he could not get away from

29

the crowds, try as he might. There were days when, for every person who accepted him, there seemed to be many others who didn't. He worked hard to maintain intimacy with the Father, learning scripture, taking time for prayer, and joining others for worship. For Jesus, the human journey was filled with struggles and real decisions, just as it is for all of us. When Jesus struggles in Gethsemane, praying for other possible ways of securing salvation, we recognize in him a brother (Matthew 26:36–46). Having been tempted as we are, he is "able to sympathize" with us, and he knows our suffering (Hebrews 2:18; 4:14–16). This is a complex and wonderful mystery of salvation. Jesus shows us that doing God's will means joining the Father in the work of salvation as a full partner, with divine and human working alongside one another to spread his reign throughout the world.

It is all too easy either to overstate the divine aspect of Jesus' life or to narrow the focus to the human dimension of his life, but in the incarnation, it becomes clear that God enters and submits to real life experiences. In Christ, God shows us how he longs to restore dignity to human beings, honoring our nature and our freedom even at the risk of our rejection of him. As Paul reminds us, Jesus did not use his divinity to his own advantage, but he actually stepped into our shoes:

> Though he was in the form of God,
>   he did not regard equality with God
>   as something to be exploited,
> but emptied himself,
>   taking the form of a slave,
>   being born in human likeness.
> And being found in human form,
>   he humbled himself
>   and became obedient to the point of death—
>   even death on a cross.
> Therefore God also highly exalted him
>   and gave him the name that is above every name,
> so that at the name of Jesus
>   every knee should bend,
>   in heaven and on earth and under the earth,
> and every tongue should confess

that Jesus Christ is Lord,
to the glory of God the Father.

Philippians 2:6–11

Though he could have used his divinity for his own advantage, the Son of God became human and experienced the struggles of life as we do. Life confronted Jesus with real choices, and he refused to trump temptation by exploiting divine power. The urge Christians sometimes feel to deny the realities of Jesus' experiences because he was God is a rejection of the mystery of the incarnation. Likewise, the rejection of the divinity of Jesus because he was human denies the mystery of the incarnation. The temptation to underplay either the divine side of the equation or the human side in Christian living is strong, but it finds no support in the person of Jesus. He is the Son of the Most High, yet he also grew in wisdom and stature as a human being, becoming perfect through the things he experienced (Luke 1:32; 2:52; Hebrews 5: 8–10).

> **High or Low Christology?**
>
> A *high christology* focuses on the divinity of Jesus but struggles to explain the extent to which the Son of God experienced life, suffering, and death. It gives us the picture of a powerful Christ, but one far removed from our own experience.
>
> A *low christology* emphasizes the human dimension of Jesus but fails to do justice to his divine nature. It depicts a comfortable, familiar Jesus with whom we can easily identify, but resists confronting his glory and holiness.
>
> The church needs to keep both tendencies as complementary perspectives; they are inextricably woven in the incarnation.

These ideas are important. Not only do they help us understand who God is, but they also show us who we are, because Jesus Christ is the most vivid expression of our new humanity. A mature understanding of his incarnation shapes, nurtures, and moves us toward our created purpose. We have a part to play in God's scheme of things. As followers of Jesus, we learn how to perceive what God is up to and work with him, reflecting his glory in the world and showing others how the human and divine fit together.

31

Accepting the role of God's collaborators impels our beliefs and our actions to match up. One implication of the incarnation is that Christian faith translates into Christian practice—not just in our "religious" observances and ideas or church procedures, but in every area of life. In the Christian walk, boundaries between sacred and secular often seem contrived and unhelpful, since discipleship presupposes full immersion into the image of Jesus, with no segment of life held back or tucked away. Schedules, budgets, career choices, entertainment preferences—all are made to submit to Jesus' lordship in daily habits of worship.

Similarly, the transformation we experience as we behold Jesus touches the tiniest details of daily life, helping us to see and appreciate them as God intended. We surrender our daily tasks to the Master, rejoicing in the rediscovery of our proper vocation as those who share God's image and tend his creation (Genesis 1:26–28). Whether we're gardening or performing surgery, painting or parenting, the one who entered his own creation, the one in whom "we live and move and have our being" (Acts 17:28) gives us a heightened sensitivity to perceive that the labor of our hands is sacred to

> "One of the greatest hindrances to internal peace which the Christian encounters is the common habit of dividing our lives into two areas—the sacred and the secular.... I believe this state of affairs to be wholly unnecessary.... The Lord Jesus Christ Himself is our perfect example, and he knew no divided life."
>
> A. W. Tozer (1949)

him. The simple pleasures of good food and conversation with friends speak to our hearts about the Father's love and provision. We are tutored in the subject of divine beauty and goodness when we take in a marvelous piece of music or quietly study the gentle ripples fluttering across the surface of a lake. As God's collaborators, we discover that he has given us a marvelous place in which to work, and the work suits us. The world-affirming dimension of the incarnation opens up many avenues for enjoying and furthering the peaceful connections between us and creation.

However, the world-rejecting side reminds us that the world as it is does not fully satisfy, and the transformation God has set in motion is not yet complete. Furthermore, not everyone has joined the new creation. Many experience the world as a curse, not a blessing, due to the injustice, abuse, and pain they suffer in it. Others have rejected the invitation to collaborate with God, choosing instead to warp the material of creation into their idol, setting their hands to the work of gratifying only themselves. Our collaboration with God involves joining him in his mission to repair the brokenness that surrounds us. With this in mind, Christians seek to be incarnations of Jesus Christ in a lost world, thereby revealing to others God's desire for people to be like him—which actually means becoming truly human. Each disciple opens up a dimension of Jesus' ministry. As Christ's body, the church as a whole reveals God's heart for the lost by coming alongside them in their need, just as Jesus has done for everyone in the church. The incarnation inducts us into God's own mission.

Conclusion: Embracing the New Humanity

The doctrine of the incarnation is our unique possession as Christians, an unusual belief that sits at the core of the church's identity. Yet it is not just an idea or a mysterious formula. Christians believe that it expresses the nature of God and displays the essence of humankind. The momentum of the world seems to be flinging all the pieces of human existence in every direction, making it hard to see how the scattered fragments could ever fit together. Division and separation thrive. A proper understanding of the incarnation resists this momentum, seeking ways of peace and countering the temptation to keep the pieces separate. Seemingly incompatible elements, such as world-rejection and world-affirmation, divinity and humanity, body and spirit, can merge in the service of the one God when seen through the lens of the incarnation.

33

Although God encourages us to live among the tensions in these "incompatibilities," for us the comfortable appeal of over-simplifying is strong, even though doing so reduces our lives to fragments and gets in the way of a church's growth in maturity. Our resulting fondness for either-or questions is a symptom of the problem: Does God's kingdom exist on earth or in heaven? Is the church human or divine? Is worship something we do for us or for God? Is Christianity about the here and now or about the afterlife? Is salvation our work or God's work? Do we make our own decisions or does God make them for us? Most of the time, questions like these are as unanswerable as the question "Is Jesus human or divine?"

One reason we're tempted to oversimplify our faith has to do with the allure of idolatry. Oversimplifying typically doesn't begin as idolatry, of course. We may focus on one aspect of Jesus or of discipleship because that particular facet offers just what we need at the time, perhaps something we've been lacking. But if that one morsel becomes our whole diet, the result can be unhealthy. When we try to reduce Christ or his calling to one select piece, we're often acting on the hidden desire to make him a little more manageable, more controllable. And we're usually hoping to keep some major part of our lives out of his hands, quietly presuming that he'll be disinterested in anything but what we've chosen to elevate as his prime concerns. What may have started as a natural delight in something good and true becomes an excuse for idolatry.

When we come to recognize that Jesus is the Christ, the Son of God, the veil has been removed. We see him as he truly is. We want to be more like him. By faithfully preserving the mystery of the incarnation, acclimating ourselves to the tensions inherent within that vision, we can begin to discover the truth about unhelpful either-or dichotomies. This in turn fosters a spiritual maturity that enables us to deal honestly and effectively with the many facets of authentic Christian living.

34

In order to experience an ongoing transformation, we need to keep looking at Jesus, wholly God and wholly human, our king and our brother, our shepherd and the lamb of our salvation.

2 Witnessing the Humble Glory
of Jesus' Birth

I saw a stable, low and very bare,
   A little child in a manger.
The safety of the world was lying there,
   And the world's danger.
                    Mary Elizabeth Coleridge (1861–1907)

One summer my family visited the Swiss village of Brienz. Lying alongside a pretty lake at the foot of snow-capped mountains, the village is a quiet gathering of homes ornately decorated in the Swiss alpine style. In fact, Brienz is best known as a community of wood-carvers. It hosts a historic training academy for budding artisans, and finely carved wooden objects of all sorts are the most common products to be found in the shops lining its main street. Especially numerous are the sets of nativity figures, intricately carved tributes to the cast of the Christmas drama.

My family and I were drawn into a particular shop, where we studied the selection of nativity figures for a long time. People, animals, angels—they were of different sizes and styles, their fine detail showcasing the skill and devotion of their makers. Two things about them stood out to us. First, we'd need to get a second mortgage before we could afford a set. Second, in spite of their different styles, the figures all shared a meticulously crafted aura of sanctity. Beginning with Joseph and Mary, every figure managed to strike a saintly pose, and each face was radiant with

35

blissful piety. Even the donkeys and sheep were endowed with uncommonly beatific expressions. They were all aglow in the hallowed presence of the Christ-child.

Then my wife Linda noticed a figure set apart—it was another Mary, with the baby Jesus. But this pair was different. The detail was exquisite, but this Mary did not beam with celestial sanctity, and the baby seemed rather ordinary. Mary was in period costume, but otherwise she seemed a typical young woman, holding her baby in the way young mothers do. The plainness and realism of the figure captivated us. It reminded us that the story of Jesus' birth is the story of a Most Holy God who humbles himself before us and does extraordinary work through ordinary means. Immanuel.

Jeff

In the last chapter, we looked at some of the implications of the incarnation. In this chapter, we will gaze upon Jesus at a pivotal moment of the incarnation, the episode of his birth. It's a familiar story, beloved ever since the early days of Christianity. The ancient church used the hymns of Luke's nativity in its worship, referring to them in the West by their Latin openings: the *Benedictus*, the *Nunc Dimmitis*, and the celebrated *Magnificat*. In this chapter, we not only want to praise the one who visited Bethlehem, but to look at some of the ways Jesus' birth can unveil God's humble glory in our lives.

A Humble Glory

It was about a three-day journey from the village of Nazareth in Lower Galilee to Bethlehem, five miles south of Jerusalem. It was not an especially long or difficult trip, even in those days, but for Joseph and Mary it was a remarkable time. The journey, and even the impending delivery of her first child, might have seemed fairly routine if it weren't for the strong sense that this family was being swept into the flow of great happenings. There was the imperial census, of course—a policy matter affecting people throughout the empire, and the incident that set

36

Mary and Joseph on the road to Bethlehem. It was a major event. Yet in the Gospel narratives, something is happening on a much grander scale than anything Caesar Augustus could instigate.

Divine promises were coming to pass. Matthew's genealogy, chanting name after name, situates Jesus as the culmination of God's constant and faithful work throughout the generations. It helps create an identity for Jesus that roots his life and work in the ongoing story of Israel's salvation. He would be the Messiah, the Lord's own anointed, whose life and rule would express God's faithful commitment to his covenant relationship with his people. Joseph, himself a "son of David," was anticipating the son of David, a child destined to fulfill the hope of Israel: a king from David's line, appointed by God himself to inaugurate an endless rule of peace and justice (Matthew 1:1–17, 20; Luke 1:32–33, 50–55).

Like Matthew's, the very atmosphere of Luke's account is a breath of hopefulness for Israel's consolation: a barren, old couple wondrously favored by God, the temple setting, the prophetic voices of Simeon and Anna, along with hymns proclaiming justice and hope. Luke's nativity also prepares us to embrace the story of Jesus as the fulfillment of Israel's past. Set against the backdrop of these expectations, the advent of God's Messiah was momentous indeed.

Yet the Gospels make claims about Jesus' coming that are more astounding than anything even the most visionary Jews would have been prepared for. The Gospels insist that, in Jesus, God himself was joining his people, more personally and directly than ever before. After all, Mary's pregnancy was anything but ordinary. Still a virgin, she was carrying a miracle child,

> When the time was right, God sent his Son, born of a woman....
>
> *Galatians 4:4*

formed by God himself. The conception was the work of his Spirit, producing within her a fully human child who was also completely divine (Matthew 1:18, 20). He would have a normal family, live in a normal house, and appear to be the normal son of a carpenter, growing naturally into normal adulthood. Yet the demons, with their uncanny insight, would recognize his divine credentials, decrying him as God's Son. The one through whom all things were made actually became flesh and sojourned among us (John 1:1, 14), a human Son who mirrors his Father perfectly, the visible image of the invisible God and the exact representation of his being (John 14:9; Hebrews 1:3; Colossians 1:17). For God to visit the world is extraordinary, but for him to do so as a human is so wondrous as to be nearly impossible to imagine.

The nativity story captures the strangeness of all this. On the one hand, the story repeatedly stresses Jesus' heavenly origins, beaming with the divine glory that attends the event. For example, Mary and Joseph and Zechariah receive visitors from another world, angelic messengers who emanate the fearful wonder of the celestial court, conveying dispatches from God himself. They proclaim that this child will be the Son of the Most High, Immanuel, "God with us." A bright star decorates the skies above his cradle. At his birth, the fabric separating heaven and earth is ripped wide as angelic hosts descend out of the heavens upon dark, earthly plains to intone songs of praise in harmonies never before heard by mortal ears. The recital is fitting. God himself has arrived, in his majesty and awesome splendor. In honor of his royalty, wise men arrive from the East, bowing low before him to offer their precious, kingly gifts. As spectators of the nativity, we behold a radiant glory that draws our gaze upward to the heavens to look for a salvation that comes from beyond this world.

Yet this salvation is also thoroughly grounded in the simple things of the earth. The mother of Jesus is a Jewish peasant girl. She and Joseph are people of no great importance whose lives would otherwise have passed without any notice or mention in history. They're among the world's chattel, subject to the whims of emperors, the sort of people who might find no room at the inn. Mary endures all the discomfort and anxiety of bringing a baby to term, without even the dignity of a proper marriage to make it respectable and tolerable. As for the baby, he is flesh and blood—small, vulnerable, hungry, and crying. His crib is a food trough, his nursery a stable. The sublime tones of angel voices are joined by the lowing of sheep in a concert performed before an unrefined audience of anonymous and notoriously disreputable shepherds. The fine aromas of myrrh and frankincense mingle with the earthy smell of livestock.

The juxtapositions in the nativity—high and low, earthy and spiritual, divine and human—are striking. With its undeniable glory and indisputable coarseness, the story paints a picture so filled with apparent incongruities that it compels us to have a closer look, peering into the profound depths of God's character in order to contemplate the full breadth of his purposes. There's nothing inconsistent about what he does, but his vision for us is so sweeping and grand, revealing his glory in ways that transform our eyesight too, that we begin to perceive reality in light of his

> **The Master Painter**
>
> "Glorious is the Wise One Who allied and joined
> Divinity with humanity,
> One from the height and the other from the depth.
> He mingled the natures like pigments
> And an image came into being: the God-man."
>
> *Ephrem the Syrian (c. 370)*

character. He is a humble God, and his ways are humble ways. The victory that he accomplishes in Christ is won through the practice of humility. This shows up dramatically in the nativity. And the tensions within the nativity create an energy that conforms us to the picture we see there, bringing us back to our true selves. Its humble glory reminds us of our own low estate—and our high potential— inviting us to embrace both by practicing the humility of the nativity in our own lives.

39

Meeting Us Where We Are

Practicing the humility of the nativity begins with an awareness of who we are. As we learn from the mystery of the incarnation, God humbly declines to reject humanity, arrogant and self-willed as we are, committing to complete the work he began long ago. He chooses to join us where we are, gently showing us the truth about ourselves. For all the airs we put on to shore up our insecurities and assert our independence, all the trappings we accumulate—clothes and houses, degrees and titles, bank accounts, rights and privileges, and petty victories—the fact is that each of us starts out naked and bawling. We own nothing on our own; even life itself we have received as a gift. It is within our nature to be needy and totally dependent.

Yet we get in the habit of hiding from the truth. Like Adam and Eve, we tend to reject our dependence, seeing it as a kind of poverty, a deficiency we want to fill up on our own. It is close to the root of our lostness, this habit of trying to find our own life and meaning outside of God. Ironically, by balking at our predicament and trying to become independently wealthy, we render ourselves truly destitute. We struggle to manage our own lives without real success. Enslaved to our anxieties, we fight to get more: more power, more stability, more security—to control everything and everyone that might threaten us, destroying lives in the process, including our own. Whatever self-deceptions we buy into in a desperate bid to avoid facing our vulnerability, deep down we realize how fragile we are. A stock market crash, an unexpected divorce, a sudden illness, the threat of war, a lengthy depression—none of us is ever very far from the helplessness of infancy, and we know it.

It is into this very situation that God entered, showing his profound humility. By settling into the manger, the Son's high glory and infinite power was stepping into the human situation at its lowliest and least pretentious point—affirming not our illusions of independence and personal honor, but instead affirming our neediness, nakedness, and dependence. In the stable at Bethlehem, God shows us that the way to cope with our dependence is not to try to escape it or cover it up with a cluttered accumulation of things and entitlements. Instead, the way to gain life is by losing it and emptying ourselves, laying down power and honor, placing all that we receive back into his hands. We find genuine life by surrendering to the one who is its source. He is our true wealth. His children know that care and comfort are to be found in his arms and nowhere else.

Jesus models faith and surrender in the self-emptying of his birth. He lived his life the same way, always surrendering to his Father, openly relying on him. It was not without risks; it led him to the cross. But even there, "he entrusted himself to him who judges justly" (1 Peter 2:23), confident that the road to God's

> **God is Little**
>
> "'God is great,' the cry of the Moslems, is a truth which needed no supernatural being to teach men. That God is little, that is the truth which Jesus taught men, and we find at once so tender and so perplexing. It is of the nature of love to be infinitely minute, as well as soaring in its imagination, and this nature is shown us by God."
>
> *John Neville Figgis (1909)*

exalted purposes for his life was the pathway of surrender. From cradle to grave, the Lord accepted his place as a human being, dependent on God for life and meaning. His humility tenderly compels us to face our own dependence, opening the way back to our Father, breaking our pride so that we learn to acknowledge our need for him.

If it seems undignified for the King of Heaven to put on our lowliness, the notion of his actually coming into contact with our sin is repulsive. Surely, the Holy One ought to keep his distance from a people whose "righteous" acts amount to no more than filthy rags (Isaiah 64:6). Yet here also, we see apparently conflicting elements coming together in the humble glory of the nativity. The picture we get is of a Father who knows well the sins of his children—but who also knows their potential. With persistent optimism, he stays personally involved in redeeming their mistakes and rescuing them from their own foolishness. The genealogy that opens Matthew's account illustrates God's persistence in such redemption.

41

By generations, it rehearses Israel's long history, a checkered tale in which even the greatest heroes, like Abraham, Judah, and David, are capable of dark and hateful deeds. It is a pedigree that includes Tamar, Rahab, Ruth, and "Uriah's wife," women whose stories included certain unsavory elements—culminating in the story of Mary herself, a peasant girl whose circumstances were so awkward that even her betrothed was prepared to put her away. Yet the list reminds us of the Lord's constant presence with his people, year after year, patiently working among them. The Son of God did not disassociate himself from this dubious heritage, but he stepped right into it.

By coming into our experience, the Son of God could not avoid touching a world spoiled by sin and mired in messy situations, nor did he try. The messiness surrounded him, permeating the atmosphere, affecting the lives of everyone in the story. Perhaps the most poignant element of the entire nativity drama is also the most brutal: the slaughter of innocent children in Bethlehem, a ruthless act of butchery carried out to satisfy the jealous ambitions of a cruel tyrant (Matthew 2:16–18). The tragedy casts a cold shadow over the whole joyous affair of Jesus' birth. And what is its lesson? That our God is one who is present amidst both joy and grief.

The nativity is no sanitized, tidy story. It is true to the complexities of human life. Acts of great faith, such as Mary's surrender to the Lord as a willing handmaiden, happen alongside expressions of uncertainty, such as the priest Zechariah's doubtful questioning. God works through them all. Wise nobles from afar bow before Israel's newborn ruler, delivering princely gifts, while the man who wears the title "King of Israel" plots unjust murder. God uses them both. The Lord came into the world as it is, no prior cleanup necessary. In fact, he seems eager to face the world's ugliness head on—the Gospels present Jesus' wilderness confrontation with the devil as his first order of business after baptism. After all, he is "Jesus," the one who saves people from sin. He does so primarily by being "God with us," showing us a Creator whose strategy for rescuing us out of our pain begins with a gesture of humility: joining us in it.

Beholding the humble glory of the nativity catalyzes a transformation within us as we yield ourselves to practice the same spirit of kinship that God, in his humility, has shown us there. It would mean seeking out people in need, joining them in their woundedness, treating them as equals, coming alongside them, getting our hands dirty. The Lord chose to do this, visiting us in our poverty in order to bring good news and restore justice. Mary's heart overflowed with praise for the Father of her child, for she understood that her pregnancy meant that God would lift up the lowly and feed the hungry, showing mercy and help to people in need (Luke 1:46–55).

> **Transforming the Least of Us**
>
> "The doctrine of the incarnation gives us the principle that the humanity in the least of persons is now transformed. And the Christmas story gives that principle a human face, in the baby born in the stable because there was no room in the inn."
>
> *William C. Placher* (2001)

Yet we often lose sight of the transforming picture of the nativity, becoming self-absorbed in our careers and families and preferred church ministries. We pour all our energies and resources into the things that we enjoy and that benefit us most. The church doors may always be "open," but too often churches send out the silent message that they're really only looking for people who make a good fit socio-economically and racially, people who already have their lives together and won't be an embarrassment or cause too much inconvenience. We avoid the messy situations that come with getting involved in the lives of "sinners." Instead of taking the risks that come with full surrender, we cling to our Christianity as one more way of asserting our independence, as if our religiosity were keeping us safe. We often glory in our churches' accomplishments, taking pride in fine buildings, large congregations, and popular programs; or perhaps we hide behind a smug confidence in having attained the

43

perfect religious system, knowing all the answers and enjoying God's special favor because of our knowledge.

Meanwhile, the Lord himself has taken up residence in a manger, reminding us that we're all part of the same needy human family, and that his heart goes out especially to those who understand their neediness best. He invites us to meet him in the sick, the naked, the prisoner, the hungry (Matthew 25:31–40), hoping that we'll see ourselves in them as well. He strips us of our pretensions of materialistic self-sufficiency and shatters our illusions of religious self-reliance so that we'll learn to depend on him and to embrace one another as valued members of the family. His vulnerability shows us our own.

Yet our lowliness and dependence is only part of the picture. The full glory of God unveiled in the nativity includes the great measure of dignity we enjoy in his eyes, since he respects us enough to want to join with us, rather than to dominate us by force.

"God with Us": A Collaborative Venture

God is fully capable of intimidating the world and bending it to his will, yet he chooses humility and partnership. Not that he isn't involved in shaping human affairs. One of the central lessons of the nativity is that God is its author. Angels show up, spectacularly announcing his involvement. Also, the narrators of the story point out that prophets had foretold the event, helping us see it as the fruition of a divinely ordained and carefully tended plan. Surely the cast of characters assembled for the nativity would testify that God was guiding history towards his purposes. When God intervenes to rescue Jesus, Mary, and Joseph from Herod's wrath by sending them off to Egypt (Matthew 2:13–23), we glimpse the foreknowledge of a sovereign God and his direct involvement in the details of people's lives. And God's visitation to the world in the form of Jesus counts as the most impressive sign of his involvement ever. The events surrounding Jesus' birth confirm what we know from elsewhere in the Bible: God is up to something in the world. We are not alone. God intervenes, making an impact on people's lives.

But is it right to assume that God forces himself on us, determining everything that happens in the world? This would mean that in his foreknowledge, he has predetermined a precise flow of events—or at least that he has composed a detailed script he wants us all to follow. This line of thinking respects God's power and plan but is suspicious of human reasoning, keenly aware that our ways are not the Lord's ways. It is this thinking, for example, that leads people in a ministerial search to say, "We know that God has already selected our preacher; we just have to ask him to show us." Or, in a worship service: "Lord, we know that you have scripted this evening's events. Please give us the right words to say." The key for living, in this approach, is to read the signs in daily life, figure out exactly

> **God's Sovereignty & Human Frailty**
>
> "I will be gracious to whom I will be gracious, and will show mercy on whom I will show mercy."
>
> *Exodus 33:19*
>
> "My thoughts are not your thoughts..., so are my ways higher than your ways."
>
> *Isaiah 55:8–9*
>
> "The foolishness of God is wiser than human wisdom."
>
> *1 Corinthians 1:25*
>
> "In him we were chosen, having been predestined according to the plan of him who works everything out in conformity with the purpose of his will."
>
> *Ephesians 1:11*

what God is up to, and live accordingly, discounting the human factor as an intrusion or a contaminant liable to muck up God's work and interfere with his will.

Yet relegating the human side of things to a low or nonexistent status doesn't square with the divine-human collaboration we see in the incarnation of Christ or here in the nativity. An extreme view of God's involvement has a tendency to sidestep the issue of our responsibility in making decisions and taking action. Also, it struggles to make sense of the tragedies we see every day—child abductions, shootings, natural disasters, wars, unemploy-

45

ment, and church conflicts. Is the death of a child, hit by a drunk driver, the result of faulty human decision-making or an act of God? For all God's intervention to rescue the baby Jesus from Herod, the young boys of an entire village were still slaughtered. This was not providential. Not everything that happens does so according to God's will.

Another approach downplays the divine side of things. In the face of the world's evil and because of the need for people to take responsibility for themselves, it may be tempting to paint God out of the picture. After all, books like Genesis and Proverbs teach us that he designed the world to follow a natural order and that he trusts human beings to make their own choices. Partly due to the historical and cultural reasons explained in *Crux of the Matter*, Churches of Christ have traditionally tended towards this view, acknowledging that God has been directly and dramatically involved in people's lives, but mostly in the past.

Human Responsibility & Potential

"The Lord commanded us to obey...and if we are careful to obey..., that will be our righteousness."

Deuteronomy 6:24–25

"Choose for yourselves this day whom you will serve...."

Joshua 24:15

"You made [humans] a little lower than God."

Psalm 8:5

"You...were called to be free, but do not use your freedom to indulge the flesh."

Galatians 5:13

"Continue to work out your salvation with fear and trembling...."

Philippians 2:12

"His divine power has given us everything..., that you may participate in the divine nature."

1 Peter 1:3–4

These days he's more retiring, a distant deity who stands aloof from daily events. But he has left us the Bible, and now it's up to us to order our lives. This extreme view of God's non-involvement takes a much higher view of human potential—and human responsibility—while relegating the direct activity of God to a lower status. As a result, many in Churches of Christ, hungering for a deeper sense of God's immediate involvement in their lives, recently find themselves gravitating away from the traditions of self-reliance they've known, and moving toward the first extreme. They search for a God who will walk alongside them each day, intervening and guiding directly.

Questions like these about divine providence can be difficult to deal with because the Bible—and our own experience—give us reasons to affirm both views. The tension between them is real, tempting us to go for quick, one-sided answers about God's activity in the world. But watching Jesus helps clarify things. The baby Jesus embodies the union of the divine and the human. It's a story of collaboration, with both elements working together seamlessly—yet so mysteriously that we may never fully understand how. Nevertheless, the example of Jesus gives us a sense of the overall picture: God has a plan for the world, and he is at work in our lives. He is sovereign and may act to control as he chooses. Yet there would be little reason to create us if our lives were scripted, and we brought nothing of our own to the relationship.

Christ's humble advent in a Bethlehem stable amid the lowing of cattle and the high praise of angels reminds us that he prefers not to coerce and control but to come alongside us in partnership. Some, like Mary, choose to cooperate beautifully; others, like Herod, do not; God allows and honors both sets of choices, working in both circumstances.

> "So it is true that God is almighty, but yet his omnipotence is fulfilled in total weakness; he allows others to exist in their freedom, a freedom which can turn towards good as much as towards evil.... God cannot do anything in the world except through hearts that open freely to him; but when hearts do open in this way, he acts like an inrush of light, of peace, of love. He can never act from the outside, like a dictator or like a hurricane."
>
> *Olivier Clément (1997)*

Not only does he allow them the freedom to choose, but for those who decide to partner with him, he welcomes their creative contributions. The beauty of the sinful woman's act of anointing Jesus' feet is not that she chose to go along with a predetermined script, but

47

that she freely devised a creative way to honor the Lord (Luke 7:36–48).

He is "God with us," not "God instead of us." He is love. The fundamental nature of love is a concern for the *other* and a refusal to control the other. Paul reminds us that love doesn't "insist on its own way" (1 Corinthians 13:5). We must accept and be grateful that the Lord may intervene decisively and powerfully, according to his own wisdom, as he did in sending his Son to us. So we pray for healing, help, and guidance. But we must also notice that he tends to use his power to maintain our freedom, choosing not to micromanage everything but to engage each of us in a real relationship with a real person—including the freedom to respond to Jesus as we choose and the creativity to do so according to our own inclinations and design. Like the father who grants the son his inheritance, God knows that this kind of love entails risk (Luke 15:11–32). He came to his own people, knowing full well that they might not accept him (John 1:11). The irony of his move is nowhere more poignant than when the people of his hometown take his mother Mary as proof that he was no prophet (Matthew 13:55–57), when in fact she had been a prophet herself (Luke 1:46–55). God took a risk in creating us, and he took a risk in becoming one of us. Both actions blend the human and the divine, and both actions allow for human freedom, acknowledging the possibilities of acceptance and rejection.

Throughout the rest of his life, Jesus Christ keeps the posture he adopted in his birth. He relinquishes power and control over others, allowing people to make real decisions. He invites them into the kingdom, bidding them to leave their nets and follow him—but he does not coerce them. He is the suffering servant, choosing loving service rather than iron-fisted dominance (Mark 10:45; Philippians 2:6–11; 1 Peter 2:21–24). He celebrates both God's involvement in people's lives (Matthew 16:17; Luke 10:21) and people's free and creative responses (Luke 15:7; 21:1–4), without ever adopting an extreme or one-sided view about where the human part leaves off and the divine picks up.

God in Us

Confronting this picture of divine and human collaboration in the birth of Christ is transformative in several ways. First, it encourages us to imitate our Lord, to be people who pursue God's plans in peaceful and humble ways. At times, we yield to the temptation to bully and brag, using violent means to force people into submission. Critics of Christianity point to the Crusades of the Middle Ages as one notorious example. Preaching that attempts to manipulate people by terrorizing them, or that ridicules those who hold differing views, is another example. Dictatorial elderships following a strict top-down approach, who hand out ultimatums with a take-it-or-leave-it attitude, is another. In contrast, God's way is to come alongside people on level ground, serving their needs and honoring their humanity, trusting them, even to the point of risking loss, since without mutual love and partnership there can be no real gain anyway. Those who practice God's humility are gentle and inviting rather than forceful or presumptuous. In leadership, they concentrate more on relationships than on hierarchies and chains of command. In proclaiming the word, they display the quiet confidence that comes from trusting a Messiah who commenced his gospel message with the unassuming voice of a baby's cry. They may overflow with passion, but it pours out in their commitment to service, not in their drive to control others. They are at least as devoted to the art of listening as to the act of telling.

The humility of Jesus' birth leads to a second transformative feature. The God who trusts us can be trusted. We can lay aside our impulse to control everything and everyone, entrusting ourselves to him with peace in our hearts, since we know that we have an all-powerful God who loves and respects us. He takes an interest in our lives and gets involved. Like Simeon holding the baby Jesus, we embrace the events of our lives with a thankful confidence that in them we're seeing God at work. The impossibility of determining where his

49

humanity leaves off and his divinity picks up gives us a crucial insight: we must not arrogantly draw hard lines between the "God-things" and the "human-things" in our lives, realizing that the occurrences of each day are involved in the unfolding of God's redemptive purposes for the world. This insight liberates us to make sacrifices and take risks.

However, since the human and the divine are so tightly bound together, a third transformative feature is the reminder we get of the impressive role and responsibility we have as God's children. He expects us to do our part and rejoices when we do. We ought to behave as people who realize that God made us to be his partners, co-creators in the world, exercising our creative energies in ways that are consistent with his character and that further his plans—but are not scripted in every detail. Like the great heroes of scripture, at times we wait on him, and at other times we take initiative. At times we receive clear and spectacular signals of guidance, like Paul got in the vision calling him to Macedonia (Acts 16:9). At other times we don't, relying—also like Paul—on the wisdom and character that God forms within us, learning to trust his trust in us. Spiritual maturity calls for a balance between the passive reception of God's activity in the world (and within oneself) and the active pursuit and fulfillment of our identity as his friends, free to shape the outcomes in our lives and in the world.

This involves full investment in the processes of formation that implant God's heart and discernment within us, a fourth transformative feature inherent in the nativity. The baby Jesus developed in Mary's womb normally; after his birth, he grew in stature and wisdom in a normal way, as God originally designed (Luke 2:52). He participated in human processes of growth. And though we see in his life spectacular signs of God's involvement and planning, we also see a Son who makes real decisions. When tempted in the desert, he didn't wait to receive the exact response. Rather, a life of spirituality cultivated over a period of time and rooted deeply in

50

prayer enabled him to offer a response. His reaction was shaped by his education in scripture. Fasting and praying forty days and nights empowered him to see through the weak logic of the devil's position (Matthew 4:1–12). Throughout his life, we see that he spent time alone with God; he spent time in scripture; he spent time in the synagogue; he spent time working among the needy; he spent time instructing his disciples—all of these were formative experiences.

Like him, we're involved in processes of growth. Habits of good Christian living don't come to us by magic. There are no short-cuts. Formative processes of prayer, study, reflection, instruction, and life experience all play a role in the growth of wisdom and the shaping of behavior. Though God may choose to accomplish works of sudden transformation in a person's life, the fact remains that there are natural processes of growth, processes that he designed and is so committed to that he even underwent them himself. Jesus, along with "prayers and supplications," also "learned obedience through what he suffered" (Hebrews 5:8).

God's approach to our salvation doesn't sidestep human responsibility, nor does it short-cut natural processes of gradual spiritual development, but it actually affirms both. Becoming a discerning Christian decision-maker involves collaboration, entailing our investment in the hard work of submitting to the disciplines through which God's Spirit shapes us with a deep and lasting imprint, as Jesus' first disciples submitted to the discipline of being trained by him over time. For their part, churches should collaborate with God in this by taking seriously the need to design and pursue balanced, ongoing programs of spiritual formation for all their members, calling people to go beyond simple conversion and asking them to return to the existence for which they were made: a lifetime of growing in their relationship with God and in their service to one another. These are all ways that the humble and collaborative glory of the Lord that we glimpse in the nativity transforms us into his image.

51

An Inclusive Family Picture

As we have already noticed, at the nativity God shows no favoritism. People of all sorts are involved in the story: old women like Elizabeth and Anna, and a young girl like Mary; priests such as Zechariah and the chief priests of Jerusalem, along with the royal class of Herod. There were Jews alongside non-Jews from the East, wealth and position alongside the peasantry of Joseph and the shepherds. The coming of Christ was a leveling event, instigating "the falling and rising of many in Israel," even reversing roles so as to reduce the proud while exalting the humble (Luke 2:34; 1:52–53). In the humble glory of the nativity, God is showing us that we all belong to the same family; we're all equally impoverished—and equally high-born. By becoming human, God is drawing the entire human family to himself without any distinction, proclaiming the good news that for those baptized into Christ, "there is neither Jew nor Greek, slave nor free, male and female" (Galatians 3:28).

> ### Rearranging the Parade
>
> "Christmas turns things tail-end foremost. The day and the spirit of Christmas rearrange the world parade. As the world arranges it, usually there come first in importance...the Big Shots.... Then at the tail end, as of little importance, trudge the weary, the poor, the lame, the halt, and the blind. But in the Christmas spirit, the procession is turned around. Those at the tail end are put first in the arrangement...."
>
> *Halford E. Luccock (1960)*

The diverse picture of humanity that God gathers to himself in the tiny body of the newborn Jesus should find its expression in the church of our day. As we've said, it has always been tempting to focus on only one dimension of Jesus and try reducing discipleship to a single experience. But we can no more do that than we can paint an accurate portrait of Jesus using a palette having only one color. The eclectic group that assembled for the nativity foreshadowed the diversity that would characterize his band of followers. Jesus attracted soldiers and rabbis, housewives and children, the sick and the wealthy. Even the tight little circle of his closest followers was a seemingly mismatched assortment, including fishermen, a Zealot, and a tax collector. Some criticized him for being too open, too ready to receive the wrong sorts of people. Yet Jesus called them all together to form a community.

Anna and Herod—also Zacchaeus, Martha, the rich young man, Nicodemus, Paul, the woman at the well, and Pontius Pilate—each was challenged by Jesus in different ways. Some met the challenge; others did not. Yet for those who did, their expressions of discipleship were not identical. No single disciple can be or do everything. Jesus Christ is too rich, too diverse and multi-talented for any one person to imitate fully. So the Lord graciously bestows a host of gifts on the members of his body, the church. The church is a community of interlocking pieces, none of which finds its true purpose apart from the whole, but each of which contributes something special to the body so that it will measure up to the Lord's fullness (Ephesians 4:7–16). Prophesying, serving, encouraging, teaching, contributing to the needs of others, leadership, even cheerful mercy—each represents the abilities of particular people within the body, yet all are equal, so long as they begin with the person's self-offering as a living sacrifice to God (Romans 12:1, 4–8). Anna and the wise men responded in different ways at Jesus' birth, but both sets of gifts were equally valuable.

One of the persistent mistakes Christians and churches make is to elevate one expression of discipleship over other legitimate expressions, insisting that every Christian should look and behave in precisely the same way. The problem often begins with attitudes of arrogance, as when Christians who tend to be more intellectual ridicule the faith of others as too naïve and simplistic. Or when people who have naturally emotional dispositions decide that those who are less openly emotional must also be less spiritual. Some are turned on by worship, others by Bible study, yet sometimes members of each group are convinced that the others just don't get it. Experienced Christians often show little patience for those who are less mature. Perhaps charter members of the church accuse newcomers of pushing

53

change agendas, while the newcomers deride the old-timers as inflexible traditionalists. Too often, the person who spends hours each day in prayer and the person who gets practical church jobs done don't respect one another's contributions. These attitudes do not reflect the humble glory of Christ's advent.

A Colorful Garden

"All the flowers He has created are lovely. The splendor of the rose and the whiteness of the lily do not rob the little violet of its scent nor the daisy of its simple charm.... It is just the same in the world of souls— which is the garden of Jesus.... Perfection consists in doing His will, in being that which He wants us to be."

Thérèse of Lisieux (1899)

To be sure, all expressions of discipleship share common ground since they are part of the same overall picture of the one Lord and Christ. True discipleship exists within certain boundaries, but the boundaries are the borders of Jesus' own self and the very nature of God. In Jesus and God there is great depth and breadth and the flexibility to meet changing circumstances. It's true that the church is not primarily a venue for people to express their special talents or find individual fulfillment. Yet it's also true that each disciple depicts a portion of Jesus' image, and no disciple is meant to be a carbon-copy of another. The church needs variety: young and old, professionals and tradespeople, housewives and college students, wealthy and poor. There is a need for the intellectual and the emotional, the reserved and the demonstrative, the practical and the visionary. And always, there is a need for mutual respect and collaboration. In the church, one woman may sing like an angel while another woman who sits three rows back has a voice that sounds more like a braying donkey—yet both angels and donkeys were present at the nativity, celebrating the generous heart of a God who would join his people as one of them, ignoring the value distinctions we typically make.

54

Our heritage has traditionally been committed to the pursuit of unity, yet Churches of Christ have sometimes construed unity as uniformity. These attitudes die hard. Some insist that any deviation from the traditional norm is a corruption of truth. To them, when a church adopts a different worship style or comes to a different conclusion about how to interpret a particular scripture, it has departed from "the faith once for all entrusted to the saints" (Jude 3). Ironically, others, sometimes unconsciously, have turned loose of what they perceived to be the oppressively narrow styles of our past, only to peddle a different flavor of the same intolerance by elevating their preferred styles or agendas as spiritually superior. Even within a single congregation, it can be difficult to find ways to worship and work together, respecting one another. Yet it is precisely the victory of such partnerships that catches and reflects the Lord's humble glory, accomplishing his mission of reconciliation in the world.

Elitist attitudes are damaging, but they're not the only problem in this area. Sometimes segregating into groups is well-intentioned, but it is nonetheless devastating, since it runs counter to the dynamic of inclusion and connectedness that we see in Christ. In today's "marketplace" of church options, the tendency of people to congregate with others who are most like them creates churches that specialize in one facet of discipleship, with all that facet's strengths—and all its deficiencies. Larger churches manufacture their own sub-groups, dividing the body by age and education level and social groups in ways that are partly helpful but also partly corrosive. When we constantly fragment the body into the separate pieces of age-segregated Bible classes, youth ministries, singles ministries, small groups whose members are all basically alike, and so forth, we are able to address certain needs. But we're also liable to worsen the splintering that is already wounding the inhabitants of this world.

The instinct to appeal to certain groups or meet their special needs is a good one, but it should be tempered with a preference for inclusion, such as we see in the nativity and in Christ's ongoing ministry. Giving in to our impulse to avoid uncomfortable people and awkward situations is not Christlike. Creating churches that are extremely lopsided doesn't reflect the glory of God unveiled in Jesus either.

The church should be a place where people are put back together rather than a place that condones and accelerates segmentation. Of course, keeping people together takes hard work; it moves against the prevailing currents of social pressure. But the work pays off—it helps everyone involved become stronger and more mature, since many of the resources that God's Spirit provides us for growth and help come to us only in community. The congregation that consists of many different kinds of people, yet looks and behaves like a healthy family unit, is truly unveiling the image of Christ before the weary eyes of a broken world.

Conclusion

If you were to ask a young child in your church, "How do you feel about the incarnation?" you'd probably get a blank stare. The term *incarnation* is not one we commonly use. On the other hand, if you were to ask the same child, "Can you tell me the story of baby Jesus?" she could probably rattle off all the details with a grin on her face. The nativity story is a beloved tale that delights even many non-Christians in our society.

In the Christian faith, however, the nativity is much more than a charming story. It is a transforming moment in human history. Jesus' baby picture is a master portrait, revealing to us the heart of God and his plan for our renewal. But the picture is also a dangerous one, as Mary Coleridge observed in her poem about the stable, for it threatens to transform us, inviting us to practice the humility of the nativity in our own lives. To welcome the baby Jesus is to be inclusive and appreciative of diversity; it is to acknowledge our dependence and to learn habits of trustful surrender; it is to appreciate God's humble, non-coercive efforts to collaborate with us by pursuing processes of spiritual formation; and it is to imitate him by respecting and honoring each other. As spectators at the nativity, we behold with unveiled faces the glory of a humble Lord, a newborn baby who is also the firstborn of creation, and his glory changes us into people who practice the same humility, which is our glory.

56

3
Picturing Discipleship:
The Meaning of Baptism

Baptism is designed to introduce the subjects of it into the participation of the blessings of the death and resurrection of Christ.

Alexander Campbell (1866)

Many exciting things happened in the little church where I grew up, but nothing captured our attention like an impending baptism. Whether a long-planned event or the spontaneous response to an inspiring sermon, a public baptism was an event of great importance. The preacher would announce the candidate's intent with joyful solemnity. Then he took the confession of faith. We all knew the words by rote, but we felt a comfortable sense of satisfaction hearing them repeated once again. It was part of a well-worn routine—more than routine; the words and actions of the whole event seemed by their familiar ceremony to involve us all in something deeper than the moment, something extraordinary.

As the candidate and the one baptizing him withdrew to get ready, men came forward to remove the pulpit that was blocking our view. Someone would lead a few songs or offer a meditation. He might fill the time with stirring remembrances of the days when baptisms occurred in rivers and ponds, or stock-tanks. Women bustled to check on the facilities, helping female candidates get dressed and ready for the water. While the pre-baptismal arrangements progressed, the air was charged with expectation.

Finally, as the pair went down into the water, children craned their necks to get a better look. They strained to catch every detail—partly in case they might witness a rare but memorable baptismal mishap, maybe even a capsizing. But they stared mostly because they knew instinctively that something special was underway. The very young understood little about what was happening, yet even they could sense the energy of the moment.

Then the person baptizing would lift a hand, invoke the names of Father, Son, and Spirit, and plunge the candidate beneath the water. After that, a transformation occurred. Something changed. We knew it had changed because people kept saying so. They quoted scripture to prove it. But there were other signs. For one, we immediately began singing the most cheerful songs of celebration. But also, once the person was dressed and among us again, he became a star. After the service, we would all press in around him, congratulating him, reveling in his celebrity status. He was special; what had just happened was special—for all of us. But most of all, if the baptism happened on a Sunday, as it often did, the transformation was signaled by his very first participation in the Lord's Supper. We would hold off serving it, delaying the whole service until he was dressed and ready. It was almost a meal prepared especially for him. He was a guest of the Lord's church, entitled to the first portion of his body. And from that time on, we would call him "Christian."

Jeff

Baptism unveils a picture of the Lord. The waters of baptism show us a portrait of the Jesus who calls people to change their lives and become his disciples, accepting a total immersion into him and embarking on a lifelong journey of following in his footsteps.

In our churches, debates about the essentiality of baptism have been common—yet serious discussions of baptism's essence have been rare. Baptism is not just a command to be obeyed, an essential requirement to be checked off the list. Baptism is important because, in its essence, it connects the disciple to Jesus Christ. That is its basic meaning and the key to its significance. Discussing

58

baptism's essentiality reveals little, but looking into its essence can open our eyes to see the power of Jesus to cleanse and renew broken lives, directing them towards a new purpose. To understand Jesus' ministry and to celebrate the intimate connection we share with him as his disciples, we start at the place where the ministry of Jesus and the life of Christian discipleship both begin: the baptism of Jesus.

Viewing Jesus from the Riverbank

The Jordan river may seem an unlikely place for a divine epiphany. Sublime scenes call for extraordinary settings, but if there was anything extraordinary about the place of Jesus' baptism, it was not obvious. The Jordan river was a useful place, but not a grand or extraordinary one—hardly a locale befitting divinity. It was a place to fill buckets and jars, a place to water animals, a place for washing clothes and scrubbing pans. As the Aramean general Naaman had observed long before, the waters of the Jordan were not the most appealing, a far cry from the clear mountain streams and sparkling springs you could find elsewhere. Yet it was onto this plain stage that the Son of God stepped, proceeding down into the muddy current that was the lifeblood of his homeland. The brown water swirled around his knees as the coarse sediment of the river bottom squished up between his toes.

The assortment of humanity gathered on Jordan's banks emphasized the unrefined earthiness of the scene. John the Baptist was there. He had the appearance of a desert rascal, a wild man living on the edge of civilization, whose lifestyle and sermons called into question the social conventions that most decent people took for granted. To many, he would not have seemed fit to entertain royalty—except perhaps as a royal prisoner and victim.

Then there were the people who came to hear John. All kinds of people. Some were despised tax collectors, representing a sort of government-sanctioned banditry.

59

They had plenty, but it would never occur to most of them to share even their spare tunics with the destitute. Soldiers were there too, the habitual extortionists of the poor, who bullied the weak for profit and sport. Even the religious leaders who came out to the river were exposed as hypocrites, proud of their heritage and religious devotion but devoid of genuine good fruit. Then there were the crowds of ordinary people, women and men and children of all sorts, some content, others in deep need, all of them moving within the rhythms of joy and grief that mark the fragile and uncertain days of human life.

At the Jordan, Jesus' humanity is clear to see. The atmosphere of the riverbank setting is saturated with the aroma of everything earthly and human, and to the casual observer, Jesus seemed to fit right in. Yet even within the spectacle of human frailty that we encounter in that Judean desert, we experience the full presence of God. Sinners were assembling at the riverside because they believed the Lord was up to something. These sad specimens of depravity and corruption were ready to practice repentance by confessing their sins, receiving baptism, and changing their lifestyles. By God's power, the muddy waters of Jordan were becoming a symbol of the divine purity that was capable of washing clean even the most filthy hearts. Repentance and transformation were clear signs of God's presence. God had not distanced himself from the world but was as deeply involved in it as ever. John confirmed this with his preaching, insisting that God's ancient promises were on the move. The kingdom of heaven was near. The ragged man clothed in animal skins was a messenger, pointing to the work of God in their midst and preparing for the arrival of the Lord himself (Matthew 3:1–12; Luke 3:1–20).

60   Then he came. As a man, in the water, surrendering himself into the hands of a fellow man, he came to be baptized. Yet for all his humanity, the divine presence in this scene is overwhelming, not only in the riverbank atmosphere, but in the event itself. By the time it was all

over, Jesus was drenched from head to toe, lanky strands of hair pasted to his glistening forehead. In a small and desolate part of the world, far away and long ago, a carpenter's son was baptized. Yet, only moments before, the infinite expanse of heaven had opened and the voice of the Eternal One had spoken over him, confirming that he was the obedient Son who was well pleasing to his heavenly Father, while the Spirit of God passed between them both, conveying divine love and power. A small event—but of cosmic significance.

Matthew, Mark, and Luke each present Jesus' baptism as a pivotal moment in his life and ministry, a key to understanding who he is (Matthew 3:13–17; Mark 1:9–11; Luke 3:21–22). In John's Gospel, the Baptist describes it as a moment of divine testimony to Jesus' identity (John 1:31–34). By his own admission, Jesus was baptized "to fulfill all righteousness." It was the right thing for him to do. Though people have argued about the precise reasons Jesus underwent baptism, the picture we get at the Jordan is unmistakable. At the river is a picture of God's fullness in his activity as divine Father, Son, and Spirit, embracing one another in an unspeakably intimate relationship. We see the full Jesus, human and divine. As in his birth, in his baptism the Messiah is "God with us," unveiling for us a vision of divinity and humanity working together.

Jesus' baptism marks the beginning point of his ministry, but even more, it shows us what he is calling us to. He's inviting us to share with him in the whole life of God—Father, Son, and Spirit, entering an intimate relationship with the Lord by allowing ourselves to be immersed fully into Christ and embarking on an adventure of radical discipleship. Like the incarnation itself, baptism presents a full picture, holding together many diverse pieces that seem nearly incompatible yet are reconciled in Christ. The call to a holiness that makes us distinct from the world is here joined to a call to ministry that irrevocably connects us to it, all under the auspices of Christ's invitation to wade with him into the waters.

61

And in order to understand fully what is involved in this call to discipleship, we need to explore the significance of our own riverbank scene, the moment in which we join Jesus in baptism.

Christian Baptism: Stepping into the Picture

Christian baptism enacts the very meaning of salvation, because it instigates and celebrates a connection with Jesus Christ. When a person is baptized "in the name of Jesus" to receive "the gift of the Spirit" (Acts 2:38), he or she is putting on Jesus, like putting on a different suit of clothes or a new skin (Galatians 3:27). This is why early Christians often decorated their baptistries with the scene of Jesus' baptism in the Jordan, depicting with paint and mosaic tile their belief that the person stepping down into the water for baptism was joining Jesus there. He or she was stepping into the gospel story, merging into the picture of the gospel that is unveiled in Christ.

> **Baptism and the Drama of Salvation**
>
> Early Christians saw connections between the waters of baptism and key moments in history:
>
> • Creation (Genesis 1:2; John 3:5–8; Titus 3:5; 2 Corinthians 5:17)
>
> • Salvation from the Flood (Genesis 6–8; 1 Peter 3:20–21)
>
> • Crossing the Red Sea at the Exodus (Exodus 14:21; 1 Corinthians 10:1–2, 6)
>
> In each instance, water represents life and salvation—yet it is also a dangerous force that can be faced only by faith in the power of God to transform its deadliness into redemption.

Jesus' baptism not only marks the beginning point of his ministry; it also teaches us what discipleship looks like and actually puts us into the picture of God's saving work. In baptism, we're stepping into the gospel landscape at some of its most prominent points:

First, we're reborn by water and the Spirit, experiencing a "washing of rebirth and renewal," as a new creation cleansed of sin (John 3:5–8; Titus 3:5; 2 Corinthians 5:17)—all because God entered the world as a newborn baby when the same Spirit descended on a young girl named Mary. Our baptism connects us to the birth of Jesus. It is as if the Spirit of God were hovering over the waters, ready to bring forth a new creation at God's command (Genesis 1:2). We put on the "new self, which is being renewed in knowledge according to the image of its creator" (Colossians 3:10).

Second, in the water, we're also joining Jesus in the Jordan river. His presence in the water purifies it, transforming it from a muddy stream into the cleansing waters that sanctify us to become his servants. We come up out of the water as disciples, listening to his teaching and following him as he goes about in the world helping people and proclaiming the gospel. Long after we've dried ourselves off, we continue to learn from him, fleshing out our baptismal commitment by remaining loyal to him, going wherever he leads us, growing in faith and maturity, and following his example.

Third, taken under the water, we also join Jesus in the tomb, meeting him in his death and entering into his resurrection (Romans 6:3-4). Baptism is death and life, burial and resurrection—a turning point and a fresh start. Connected intimately with the Lord in baptism, we learn to fulfill our baptism by dying to ourselves and "presenting [our] bodies as a living sacrifice" (Romans 12:2). Rising up out of the waters, we are awakened from a deadly slumber to walk in the fresh daylight of a new morning (Ephesians 5:14).

In short, our baptism paints us into the central portrait of God's salvation—the life, death, and resurrection of Jesus. It lands us squarely in the middle of the gospel action so that the Jesus story becomes our story. This is the essence of baptism and ought to be the gist of our teaching about it. Baptism is a marvelous point of entry for disciples and should not be commandeered by agendas that reduce it to a simple rule or that focus solely on debates about its essentiality. Such agendas distract us from the essence of baptism, weakening our understanding of the discipleship it pictures.

A Picture of Collaboration

Churches of Christ are famous for discussing—and debating—baptism. In sermons, books, pamphlets, magazines, and lectureships, we have taken on a multitude of questions about the nature, function, and mode of baptism. Is it essential to salvation? How should we do it—and does that matter? Who needs it—and at what age or level of understanding? The questions are potentially endless, and it's unlikely that total agreement on every baptismal issue can ever be achieved. Yet often such questions drive a wedge between elements of discipleship that should never be separated.

For example, when we ask, "Is baptism the work of God or a human work?" we are forcing a false distinction that does not fit the full incarnational glory of God being unveiled in Christ. Like salvation and the Christian life, baptism is neither solely God's work nor solely ours. Salvation is a free gift of God, to be sure, yet the manner in which we experience it entails a response of gratitude and the full investment of our own efforts. When we are thrust under the water, we surrender control of our bodies to the one baptizing us, and we surrender control of our lives into the hands of the one who saves us. We confess our inadequacies, accepting the unmerited gift and work of God and recognizing the sufficiency of the incarnation, the cross, and the resurrection (Romans 5:1-2; Ephesians 2:8-9). Yet we stand there in the water because of our own decision, and the words—and sins—that we confess are our own. We rise up out of the water to become God's partners, not his puppets, putting all our efforts into the pursuit of a new lifestyle (Romans 6:1-4, 12-14).

> "No doubt the gospel is quite free, as free as the Victoria Cross, which anyone can have who is prepared to face the risks; but it means time, and pains, and concentrating all one's energies upon a mighty project. You will not stroll into Christlikeness with your hands in your pockets, shoving the door open with a careless shoulder. This is no hobby for one's leisure moments...."
>
> *A. J. Gossip (1924)*

Baptism recognizes and conveys the picture of collaboration that has been a part of God's design for his creation from the beginning. It invites us to trust God, each day falling back into the arms of the only one who can support and save us. Yet it also invites us to reverse the evasive, finger-pointing tendencies that we learned from Adam and Eve by taking full responsibility for ourselves and recognizing that the effectiveness of Christian living depends a great deal on the strength of our commitments and our own hard work as God's new creatures. Is baptism a human work or a divine one? The question itself pits humanity against God, physical against spiritual, and external against internal. It breaks the mystical union of divine and human that we see in Jesus. Salvation in Christ and discipleship combine these things, however, just like baptism does.

Church leaders need to liberate discussions about baptism from such false dichotomies. The way we talk about and practice baptism ought to remind us that there is a real connection between the work of Christ and the Christian life. The Christian life reflects an ongoing transformation into the likeness of God through the Spirit, and it is by our identification with Christ that the image is renewed. Baptism initiates us into the new humanity by connecting us with the Second Adam. It is not primarily an act of obedience that qualifies us for salvation. It is not like a lever we throw to receive the membership card that will gain us entry at the pearly gates. Nor is it

> "Baptism is no human trifle, but instituted by God Himself.... It is of the greatest importance that we esteem Baptism excellent, glorious, and exalted, for which we contend and fight chiefly, because the world is now so full of sects clamoring that Baptism is an external thing, and that external things are of no benefit."
>
> *Martin Luther (1530)*

> *"All the means of salvation are means of enjoyment, not of procurement.... No one is to be put under the water of regeneration for the purpose of procuring life, but for the purpose of enjoying the life of which he is possessed."*
>
> *Alexander Campbell (1866)*

65

a mere external human work, to be downplayed due to an emphasis on God's grace or to be superseded by an emphasis on a person's internal conversion experience. The picture we get at the baptistry should match the one we get at the Jordan, where the fragments of our humanity are being put back together under God, not broken further apart.

A Picture of Growth

Baptism also reminds us that discipleship is both a one-time commitment to Christ and an ongoing journey with him. Churches of Christ have tended to look at salvation through the window of conversion, emphasizing salvation as an object we come to possess or a situation we enjoy—it is forgiveness of sins, a legal status of guiltlessness before God, or a blanket transfer of membership from "world" to "church." Salvation is all these things, but it is also so much more. Unfortunately, by focusing on the legal and static dimensions of salvation, we've handicapped our ability to appreciate baptism's power to shape all of life.

It's true that baptism pictures discipleship as a moment of decision, a one-time act of obedience and dedication to Christ, perhaps the culmination of a long process of thinking and studying. Once immersed, we have "crossed over from death to life" (1 John 3:14); we belong to Christ and become one of the saved, all the way, all at once. It is a crucial moment, worth all the attention and fanfare we can give it, a bright day that we mark forever on our calendars and look back on fondly. When parents and church leaders strive to find the most effective ways of bringing people to the point of decision, their energies are not misdirected. In fact, most congregations should work even harder to explore creative ways of investing their church's practice of baptism with its full meaning and of amplifying the excitement surrounding this wonderful rite of passage. Baptism is a unique celebration crowning a person's final commitment to Christ.

66

Yet baptism also pictures that once-for-all moment as a starting point, the induction into a continuous process of "being saved" (1 Corinthians 1:18). We're accepting the call to follow Jesus every day. By being united with him in his resurrection, we start a journey towards a final destination that is a lifetime away—being conformed to the image of Christ. As a symbol of new birth, baptism directs the church to emphasize the importance of Christian growth. It's therefore not enough to get our children and converts baptized. We bring them to the riverbank, but we also wait for them on the other side, ready to walk alongside them, telling them stories of the kingdom, challenging them to grow, and providing the resources they need to mature and to serve their Lord. Being preoccupied only with baptism as the culmination of salvation can cause us to neglect the importance of providing for Christian growth. Pre-baptismal instruction should take its cue from Jesus' teaching, focusing more on the demands of discipleship,

---

The Meaning of Baptism

Some ways churches today are exploring the depths of baptism:

- Planning sermon and class series on: the different meanings of baptism; biblical images connected with baptism; connections between baptism and different phases or experiences of life

- Encouraging public baptisms and emphasizing baptism's communal witness and celebration

- Planning the structure of Sunday worship around baptismal events; involving the person baptized in the planning

- Having a church-wide feast following a baptism

- Reading and discussing some of the many fine spiritual meditations written about baptism over the centuries

- Composing special songs for baptismal events

- Recovering balanced curriculum aimed specifically at preparing youth for baptism and discipleship

- Encouraging family celebrations of baptismal birthdays

- Having the church gather around after a baptism to offer specific blessings or personal services

- Clothing the person baptized in a new outfit picked out for the occasion

the meaning of baptism for a person's lifestyle, than on the singular goal of getting him or her into the baptistry. The education of new disciples needs to include training in the habits that will cultivate the continuing formation of their knowledge, character, and abilities to serve. Baptized into Christ, disciples ought to find themselves in a body that helps them grow, one devoted to the practices of gazing on Jesus so fixedly that transformation happens naturally.

However, if we treat salvation only as a tidy, wrapped package delivered at baptism, we won't know what to make of growth when it occurs. At baptism, the disciple may "know enough," but it won't be enough for long. Over time, disciples learn more, and they change in remarkable ways, sometimes gradually, sometimes in great leaps. Throughout our lives, there will be times when we come to see our Lord and our discipleship in such fundamentally different ways as to make our earlier understandings seem obsolete and childish. This is all natural. Jesus' first disciples revised their understandings of him as they went along. This did not invalidate their original faith, though, nor did it prompt them to seek rebaptism. Reaching new levels of understanding and commitment was a normal part of the discipleship experience. Paul saw his life as an adventure of constant progress towards the goal of fully knowing Jesus (Philippians 3:10–14).

New disciples should be taught to expect and welcome seasons of growth. For their part, older disciples show their maturity when they recognize that they also are works in progress. They know their limitations. They listen to others humbly because they've learned that there is always more to learn. They know that not all change is growth, yet they also realize that there is no growth without change. The thought of adjusting their beliefs, accepting new practices, or correcting their understanding of some passage of scripture does not frighten them. They have learned to walk each day in the freshness of their baptism, living at the horizons of their own experience as they are being transformed daily into the image of the Lord. They're mature enough to be

68

at peace in their relationship with Jesus, wise enough to know that he is always calling them forward.

To sum up, the multi-faceted picture we see in Jesus' baptism is reflected in our own baptisms and in the Christian life: salvation is a possession, but it is also a process; baptism is a destination, but it is also a point of departure; it is God's divine work, but it also involves our human efforts. The Christian life, just like the life and work of Jesus, has various aspects. The danger is in allowing ourselves to be so mesmerized by one of these facets that we neglect, or even reject, others that are equally indispensable. Guarding against this trap is one of the principal reasons for coming back to the full picture of Jesus over and over again. The total image of Christ that is being unveiled to us cannot be reduced to any one fragment. The claim that he lays on us as his disciples is just as absolute. Baptism presents us with a picture of what it means to live within these tensions, and we thereby mirror his image in discipleship, for discipleship swallows up a person's whole life into Jesus as surely as the waters of baptism swallow up her whole body.

A Deadly Vision

"Can you be baptized with the baptism I am baptized with?" Jesus asked his disciples, referring to his death. "You will be," he insisted (Mark 10:38–39). The Jesus pictured in children's Bibles is a safe and welcoming figure, the sort of person who smiles a lot and tousles kids' hair. They sit on his lap as he tells them he loves them, as if to say that following him will be a warm and cozy experience, making for a happy life on earth. This picture isn't fake—so long as it's not the only picture one has. Jesus is also the terrifying Lord of judgment pictured in Revelation 1 and the stern critic of the Gospel texts, who accuses even his closest followers of being people of little faith who are stubbornly hard-hearted. The full picture of Christ reminds us that his call to join him in baptism has a hard edge. Jesus desires to have a close

69

personal relationship with each of us, but he insists that the intimacy can be genuine only after we've made some hard decisions and major sacrifices.

With a marvelous upside-down flair, Jesus captures the essence of this new life by depicting it as death: "if anyone would come after me, he must deny himself and take up his cross and follow me" (Matthew 16:24). Following Jesus means shouldering a cross and treading a grim path to a certain death (Luke 14:25–35). The path of discipleship is like the journey of a death-row victim walking the long mile to his or her own execution. That walk has a way of putting things into perspective. What used to be so captivating—getting more money, building a larger home, settling petty grievances, impressing people, advancing career status—hardly seems important any more, because disciples carry their own deaths around with them, and the ordeal gives them a drastically different vision of reality. As Dietrich Bonhoeffer said, "When Christ calls a man, he bids him come and die."

> "He will be the Truth that will offend them one and all,
> a stone that makes men stumble and a rock that makes them fall.
> Many will be broken so that He can make them whole;
> many will be crushed and lose their own soul."
>
> *Michael Card* (1985)

There is no legitimate way to domesticate Christ's call. In order to find your life, you must lose it (Mark 8:35). Despite the tenets of some popular versions of Christianity, discipleship is not simply another item you can build into your portfolio of activities, like Little League, school programs, and camping trips. It allows no competition. Some people hope to find in Jesus that "little something special" they need in order to round out their lives, but Jesus is not just another product that people can drop into their shopping carts. Jesus said, "if anyone comes to me and does not hate his father and mother, his wife and children...yes, even his own life—he cannot be my disciple" (Luke 14:26). Entering the kingdom is an all-or-nothing venture. It's not like joining a club or watching a football game from the stands. Nor is it a simple matter of adopting a body of teachings or quaint religious practices—what many think of as "joining a church." To become a disciple is to move from one world to another—to emigrate from a false world of shadows and lies to the world of God's original intent.

After his baptism, Jesus started his ministry, inviting people to step into that picture of fellowship with God that we're privileged to see from the banks of the Jordan. Even after his resurrection, Jesus' apostles continued to welcome others into the picture by making disciples all over the world, "baptizing them in the name of the Father and of the Son and of the Holy Spirit" (Matthew 28:19). Like Jesus and his apostles, we should be excited about inviting people to join us as Jesus' followers. However, also like them, we need to be up front about the cost of discipleship. Church leaders should resist the temptation to pull punches for the sake of attracting more customers or to emphasize free grace.

Churches that focus on God's grace in salvation and on Jesus' open reception of sinners sometimes get into the habit of glossing over the high standards and rigorous demands of discipleship. The fact is, following Jesus isn't for everyone. It is only for those willing to give up everything. Against the instincts of our consumer-oriented society, a fair presentation of the gospel message doesn't just try to entice people with all the things Jesus will do for them; it illuminates what

Grace & Discipleship

"Cheap grace is the preaching of forgiveness without requiring repentance, baptism without church discipline, Communion without confession, absolution without personal confession. Cheap grace is grace without discipleship, grace without the cross, grace without Jesus Christ, living and incarnate.

Costly grace is the treasure hidden in the field; for the sake of it a person will gladly go and sell all they have.... It is the kingly rule of Christ, for whose sake a person will pluck out the eye which causes him to stumble.... It is costly because it costs a person his life and it is grace because it gives a person the only true life.... What has cost God so much cannot be cheap for us."

Dietrich Bonhoeffer (1937)

71

Jesus is calling them to be. Jesus holds a winnowing fork in his hands. The hard edge of his message is like sharp tines, shaking out the chaff from the good grain (Luke 3:17). Jesus does not invite people to accept the gospel because they will find it fulfilling or enjoyable, nor even just because it will be good for them and their families—though it may turn out to be all these things. Jesus invites them to lose their lives for him, to join a fellowship where they will be expected "to serve, not to be served" (Matthew 20:28). Our evangelistic efforts should make these costs clear.

The Jesus who draws all people to himself is a man who has been lifted up on the cross, and it is in the display of this image that the world glimpses the antidote to the poison that is killing it (John 3:14–15; 12:32). "Whoever wants to save his life will lose it, but whoever loses his life for me will save it" (Luke 9:24). Discipleship that begins with baptism and holds the image of Jesus as its inspiration is driven by the dynamic to surrender, to find life in death, to serve and to sacrifice—not to be served. When we draw people into our fellowship under the pretense that Christianity is all about being served and feeling satisfied, we create a momentum in the wrong direction, one that can be very difficult to redirect and that leads people away from the true picture of a Jesus who wades humbly into the water. Such false images create communities enslaved to self-serving motives.

But we who are seeking Christ in his fullness are continuously reminded that we are buried with Jesus in baptism. Putting faith in Christ requires accepting the full implications of that death. It is not a matter of placing Jesus' name at the top of an old list, but of throwing away the list altogether and receiving a new one, where Jesus is the only item and where his kingdom is the only agenda, the only reality:

"No one can serve two masters" (Matthew 6:24).

"No one who puts his hand to the plow and looks back is fit for service in the kingdom of God" (Luke 9:62).

"Any of you who does not give up everything she has cannot be my disciple" (Luke 14:33).

These are hard sayings. Before the Master Builder constructs a new luxury home on the property of our lives, the site must be cleared and leveled, the ruins of the dilapidated and condemned old building removed and thrown away. The opportunity is a marvelous one; the kingdom of heaven is like a hidden treasure, easily worth the investment of everything we possess. But it does cost everything. Just as Jesus' own baptism holds together many tensions, Christian baptism simultaneously plunges the disciple into the termination of one life and the creation of a new one. These rhythms of death-and-life draw us into Jesus' own practices and cause us to share in his miraculous identity.

> **The Shape of Christian Spirituality**
>
> "When we enter into the waters of baptism, we enter into a divine connection with the suffering of Jesus and with his resurrection. We are brought into a pattern of life that is an actual identification with Jesus. Baptism is therefore not only an identification with Christ but a calling to live the baptized life. The calling which baptism symbolizes gives concrete form to our spirituality...."
>
> *Robert E. Webber (1999)*

Practicing the Death & Life of Baptism

The death that comes with discipleship is difficult, but it is also liberating. It rejects one world for the sake of affirming a better one, a world where we enjoy freedoms that the old world can never know. For example, the death we experience in discipleship liberates us to be more generous with our possessions. Like the stingy person who demonstrates uncharacteristically charitable attitudes when preparing his final will, Christians who have died so that their "life is now hidden with Christ in God" (Colossians 3:3) will not hesitate to dig deep into their pockets to help others. They feel only a loose attachment to the cars they drive, the houses they use, and the bank accounts they manage. Losing them would be no real loss; giving them up is a comparatively trivial matter. Viewing their possessions from within the tomb of baptism, they find it easier to

73

take the risks that come with sharing sacrificially. Out of their sacrifice comes new hope for those in need.

The dead in Christ can also be more lavish with their forgiveness. They can relinquish their grudges against each other and lay aside their differences. By focusing on their common life in Christ, they learn not to be distracted by the peripheral matters that are usually at the root of interpersonal conflicts and church division. Keeping unveiled eyes locked on Jesus, the glory they behold transforms their vision so that most of what people argue about appears uninteresting. By accepting Jesus' call, they've signed on to an agenda more grand than anything church fights offer, an agenda so rewarding that they're willing to make personal sacrifices in order to stay on track. Wherever Christians are in the habit of fighting with one another, they show that they have lost sight of their true calling and have forgotten whose servants they are (Romans 14:4). They have not learned to keep practicing the self-denial of their baptism, having forgotten the principle that death to self is usually just the thing needed to breathe new life into a relationship.

The disciple's passage to death in baptism also becomes the doorway to vibrant congregational ministry. When people surrender fully to the Lord, they exhibit new levels of commitment and become more willing, like Jesus, to brave risks for the sake of the kingdom. We value what we've invested in. Having committed everything to the Lord's kingdom vision, we discover that other activities don't matter

> "A community is only a community when the majority of its members is making the transition from 'the community for myself' to 'myself for the community,' when each person's heart is opening to all the others.... This is the movement from egoism to love, from death to resurrection...."
>
> *Jean Vanier (1979)*

so much. We find life and significance in our involvement in the church's mission. And rather than griping that the church doesn't meet some need of ours, we follow the path of Christ by expending our energies serving and helping others. Rather than focusing on what we get out of the church, we're preoccupied with discovering what we can put into it.

These are all ways in which the death we experience in baptism is really life. The water of baptism conveys this message. Water is precious to us because we need it to live, but it also frightens us, because a person can drown in it. In the same way, baptism presents us with a difficult picture. The deep joy and full life to which Jesus calls us seem to be in tension with the grim chore of carrying a cross. It's tempting to turn loose of the challenging side in order to embrace something warm and comfortable. But to do so is to corrupt the very meaning of baptism, muddying its beauty and power.

Over the centuries, many people—and even churches—have tried to re-mold Jesus into a shape easier to manage and more compatible with their own programs, hoping to pass off a poorly forged portrait of Jesus as the real thing. Wherever the teaching of Jesus becomes uncomfortable, they learn to ignore it, devising ways to sidestep his plain demands or substituting their own hobbies for the items he was truly passionate about. Not everyone claiming to follow Jesus really does so (Matthew 7:21–23). Yet when enough people agree together on a counterfeit definition of discipleship, the image they present can be deceptively compelling. A whole church can buy into a forgery.

We need to remain aware that a tendency lurks within us to soften his claim on our lives. As he did with his first disciples, Jesus calls us to be completely attentive to him. And, like them, we must learn that what he often speaks to us are stinging rebukes and demanding instructions. Yet he has the heart of his Father, and even his harshest challenges are meant to be redemptive, rescuing us from our own self-destructive ways. Discipleship may be as severe as death, but for Jesus' followers, it is the only way to live.

75

Conclusion: The Benefits of Mutual Commitment

Baptism is not the sort of thing that comes naturally. It's an unusual spectacle. We all take baths, but this is different.

Baptism involves rituals and words and a background story that only make sense within the Christian worldview and nowhere else. The ceremony, like the life it pictures, is nonsense to outsiders. What is life to us seems to them like death. Undergoing baptism implies that we are changing cultures. It reminds us of the seriousness of our decision to wear the name of Christ, to be his disciples. It celebrates the union of divine and human, not only in our Lord and savior, but in ever-increasing ways in our own lives as we serve the God who met us at the river's edge.

> **Buried with Christ in Baptism**
>
> "Christ's burial is more clearly represented by immersion: wherefore this manner of baptizing is more frequently in use and more commendable."
>
> *Thomas Aquinas (c. 1265)*

Discipleship is an experience of following Jesus with an extreme level of commitment, being immersed into him, living within him as if he were the very environment of our lives, whatever the cost or stigma. This utter commitment to him is the foundation of much that disciples must be and do in order to reflect the Lord's glory. Yet the wonderful thing about discipleship is that the radical commitment works both ways. The Lord is just as devoted to us as he wants us to be towards him—even more so. God loved us enough to send his Son, who faced rejection and death, yet he came anyway. Even Jesus' most dedicated followers repeatedly misunderstood him, willfully disobeyed him, and ultimately abandoned him to the cross. Yet Jesus was merciful and faithful, keeping up his end of the relationship. Some of them followed him only because they hoped he would defeat the Romans. Others sought personal glory by requesting privileged status in the kingdom. Peter was so off-base at one point that Jesus identified him with Satan. Even in his darkest hour, Jesus' closest friends drifted off to sleep rather than keeping a supportive vigil at Gethsemane. Yet Jesus remained devoted to them.

Utter commitment to Jesus is not easy. It involves sacrifice. Like his first disciples, we fail and we fall down.

We misunderstand and we get it wrong sometimes. We try to be like clean reflective lenses, showing the Lord's glory in our efforts to gaze only upon him, yet we often behave in ways that chip and scratch the surface of our lives so that the image we present is flawed and blurred. Sometimes we turn away to focus on something else altogether, losing the picture completely for awhile. The great comfort of radical discipleship is that it happens in an atmosphere of extreme love. Discipleship is not one-sided. It does not begin with us. Discipleship begins with the Lord. It is a response to the commitment God has already made to us, founded on a relationship and a covenant established in a muddy river in a tiny country where one who is both God and man humbled himself in the waters of baptism.

4
Glimpsing the Kingdom
in Jesus' Ministry

> Without our suffering, our work would just be social
> work, very good and helpful, but not the work of Jesus
> Christ, not part of the Redemption. Jesus wanted to help
> by sharing our life, our loneliness, our agony, our death.
> Only by being one with us has he redeemed us. We are
> asked to do the same.
>
> *Mother Theresa (1975)*

*"Are You Sowing the Seeds of the King, Dumb Brother?"
Even as a kid I knew that wasn't really the song title, but
the song's cadence made it fun to joke about. Growing up
in Churches of Christ, with weekly worship and weekly
sermons, I heard a lot of religious jargon and insider
language. Our songs were full of it—pious phrases in the
King James style and plenty of flowery religious images
drawn from the farm or seafaring life, all delightfully
old-fashioned. It was a kind of dialect that I picked up
early in life.*

*I knew the song's real words, though: "sowing the seeds
of the kingdom, brother." That song used a term that
showed up in many of our songs. It seemed old-fashioned
too, but it was one of our most important words: kingdom.
Though not commonly used in American English vernacu-
lar, "kingdom" was a word I heard all the time in church.
We were "citizens of the kingdom of God"; we were doing
"the work of the kingdom"; we were "putting the kingdom
first." Kingdom business was our business. Sometimes we*

even put things off until "kingdom come." We used the word
as a way to talk about things Christian, as opposed to things
of the world. But most especially, we used it to talk about
church. From the way we used the word, I got the notion
that "kingdom" and "church" were interchangeable, and
that both had been established on Pentecost.

Jeff

Jesus grieved over the menacing spectacle of a universe overthrown by evil: "Woe to the world because of the things that cause people to sin!" (Matthew 18:7). Yet he believed that God's redemptive work of restoring his creation was underway and being fulfilled in him and his ministry. His was a life committed to the process of mending a shattered world and repairing its fractured relationships. As we saw in Chapters 1 and 2, Jesus' purposes of reconciliation are partly realized within his very self. The incarnation brings together the divine and human, providing an environment in which the spiritual life can flourish once again as people are brought into Christ. Jesus' teaching also furthers his program of restoration, and so in the next chapter we will focus more on Jesus' role as our teacher and trace the contours of his kingdom ethics.

But a third aspect of Jesus' work of reconciliation concerns us here—his ministry of service to the world. Jesus loved the world and the people in it, but he believed that the world was about to undergo some major changes. Perhaps no other statement Jesus made lets us glimpse the world through his eyes like the one he preached at the beginning of his ministry: "The kingdom of God is near. Repent and believe the good news!" (Mark 1:15). Throughout his ministry, Jesus built

---

The Picture of Health

Christ's three antidotes for brokenness:

• Incarnation—reconciliation through his person

• Ministry—reconciliation through his healing and service

• Teaching—reconciliation through his principles and instructions

---

80

expectations about the impending arrival of God's kingdom, trying to persuade people that his life and work were intertwined with its restoration. Matthew's recurring formula, "This happened to fulfill what the Lord had said through the prophet...," expresses the conviction that God's promises of old were coming to pass in Jesus, a conviction confirmed throughout the New Testament (Matthew 1:22; 2:15, 17, 23; 4:14; 8:17; 12:17; 21:4; 26:54, 56; 27:9).

Centuries of institutional development make it easy for Christians to equate God's kingdom with the institutional church, but Jesus' teaching fits the Old Testament ideal that God's kingdom is equivalent to God's own reign. Though the Lord formed Israel as a kingdom of priests in the world (Exodus 19:6), he wanted them to understand that he is active throughout the whole world and cannot be confined to Israel's land, politics, or race (see Jonah 4:11). He is their true king (1 Samuel 8:6–22; 1 Chronicles 29:11), and the deeper proofs of his rule in people's lives were not to be found in the trappings of their religious institutions so much as in their collaboration with him in the work of taking care of aliens, widows, and orphans (Jeremiah 7:4–8).

> "What does the Lord require of you? To act justly and to love mercy and to walk humbly with your God."
>
> *Micah 6:8*

Faced with the repeated failures of Israel to retain God's vision for his kingdom, the prophets envisioned a new day, one dominated by "an everlasting kingdom," in which the Lord would extend his reign "from sea to sea" (Daniel 7:27; Zechariah 9:9–10). The anointed king himself would visit Zion, proclaiming "peace to the nations." The reign of God would be complete, a kingdom transcending geography, politics, and even religion.

The New Testament presents Jesus as the fulfillment of these hopes. He is the son of David, the Messiah, the one appointed by God to be Lord and Christ (Matthew 1:1–16; Mark 8:29; Acts 2:36). By his work, the reign of God in the world was being restored (Acts 1:6–8; 2:14–36). Since Jesus is the best expression of God's rule, he shows us what it means to live in the kingdom, exercising his kingly office by proclaiming good news—freedom from imprisonment, recovery of sight, release from oppression (Luke 4:18–19). These are the genuine signs of the expanding kingdom, the increasingly manifest power of God in people's lives. Talking about Jesus' kingdom mainly in terms of institution and boundaries and rules runs the risk of losing sight of the thing that makes kingdom what it is: God's rule. When John the Baptist sent word to find out whether Jesus was truly God's chosen one, Jesus' answer shows us what to look for in the kingdom—signs of God's revitalizing reign in the lives of needy people: "the blind receive sight, the lame walk, those who have leprosy are cured, the deaf hear, the dead are raised, and the good news is preached to the poor" (Matthew 11:4–5).

Similarly, in a verbal showdown between Jesus and some critics who were saying that his power came from Beelzebub, Jesus did not point to any institutional proof of the kingdom. Instead, he insisted that the presence of God's kingdom is proven by the evidence of the Lord's benevolent rule in people's lives. He said to the crowd, "if I drive out demons by the finger of God, the kingdom of God has come to you" (Luke 11:20). If you see people being delivered from evil, you're seeing the kingdom. In this sense, "the kingdom of God does not come with your careful observation, nor will people say, 'Here it is,' or 'There it is,'" because it has an elusive, dynamic, spiritual nature, confined to no institution. Instead, it is identified with the person and activity of the Lord (Luke 17:20–21).

Looking at Jesus, we see the kingdom and are called to be transformed into people who live under his lordship, sharing his values. But, like Jesus' first disciples, we often find it hard to get a clear look at his agenda because our own preconceptions get in the way. The institutional church is God's instrument in the world, called into existence by Jesus Christ and sustained by the indwelling presence of the Spirit. But religious institutions have a tendency to focus on their institutional features. The challenge for the institutional church is to ensure that its identifying characteristics genuinely correspond to those of the kingdom Jesus was proclaiming. Maintaining the institutional *status quo* is not necessarily the same as being faithful to Jesus' call, nor is being a "member in good standing" necessarily the same as living under the rule of God.

The true marks of the kingdom are grounded in Jesus' foundational principles, the "weightier matters" of justice, mercy, and faithfulness (Matthew 23:23). These express the heart of God and are hallmarks of his reign; wherever they prevail, it may be said that the kingdom has come. These values form the core of Jesus' lifestyle. They run counter to the world's usual values. Sometimes, they even run counter to values enshrined in the institutional church. For example, when interviewing candidates for a ministry job, some church leaders grill them over a list of controversial hot button issues to see where they stand in relation to certain earmarks of the institution. Or they focus primarily on the candidates' skills in successfully managing and promoting busy, exciting organizations. Yet Jesus' kingdom values suggest that we ought to pay more attention to the candidates' track records of service and their abilities to be agents of God's healing rule in people's lives. The King came into the world in order to serve and save it, and that is the business of his subjects as well.

Jesus—In the World but Not of It

Traditionally, Churches of Christ have tended to present Jesus as a person concerned primarily about heavenly existence. As we saw in Chapter 1, Jesus' example was double-edged. On the one hand, he strongly affirmed his Father's world, investing himself in the daily lives of regular people in the here and now and teaching his disciples to do the same. Yet Jesus also called people to deny the world and take up a cross in imitation of

83

him. The vision of discipleship Jesus gives us involves both world-rejection and world-affirmation. The world-rejecting posture is more familiar to us in Churches of Christ. Much of the preaching of our past emphasized the rewards of heaven more than an experience of discipleship in the here and now. Songs like "This World is not My Home," "I'll Fly Away," and "I've Got a Mansion" have been long-time favorites. We have typically had a strong streak of independence and more than a trace of nonconformity. We have not hesitated to adopt distinctive religious forms, use different vocabulary, and embrace different social customs as expressions of discipleship. Our ministers do not wear vestments, and we have tended to shy away from terms that others commonly use, such as "pastor," "clergy," "liturgy," and "eucharist," preferring instead to "call Bible things by Bible names." We have shown a lasting ambivalence towards religious holidays like Easter and Christmas and a reluctance to display political flags in our church buildings. Indeed, a significant proportion of members of Churches of Christ felt so strongly about their other-worldly alignment that they chose the path of pacifism and conscientious objection during the World Wars of the twentieth century. By our customs and habits, we have displayed a traditional conviction that the "narrow way" that Jesus

---

World-rejecting or world-affirming?

Our traditional hymnody reflects an awareness of both:

"This is my Father's world, the birds their carols raise,

The morning light, the lily white declare their Maker's praise.

This is my Father's world, he shines in all that's fair;

in the rustling grass I hear him pass, he speaks to me everywhere."

Maltbie D. Babcock (1901)

"Earth holds no treasures but perish with using,

However precious they be;

Yet there's a country to which I am going:

Heaven holds all to me."

Tillet S. Teddlie (1932)

---

blazed before us must be quite different from that of the cultural mainstream.

However, it is not enough just to be a peculiar people. Jesus calls us to be peculiar in particular ways for particular reasons. Jesus' call is challenging not so much because it is counter-cultural, but because it runs counter to the impulses of the selfish and sinful human heart in every age and place. Jesus' solution to our sinfulness involves world-affirmation as well as world-rejection. For example, Jesus warns that "a person's life does not consist in the abundance of possessions," reminding us that treasures on earth are not worth our investment, since moth and rust destroy them. What good is it to gain the world and lose your soul (Luke 12:15; Matthew 6:19; 16:26)? Yet when Jesus offers these insights, he is also trying to enrich life in this world. In the first passage, he wants to reconcile two brothers alienated by greed. The other passages instruct disciples to hold their wealth loosely so that they may be free from unhealthy obsessions—and free to share what they have with those who need it.

In recent years, more among us have emphasized the ways in which Christian discipleship and church involvement are for the here and now. Singing fewer songs about heaven, we are showing a preference for teaching and ministries that enrich daily life. Some critics argue that these changes are occurring mainly because many of us are more affluent and better educated than our ancestors. We are finding ourselves more at home in this world, they say, and have decided to ride the cultural mainstream, so that our spending patterns, career paths, and entertainment choices are less likely to set us apart. As for religion, critics proclaim that many in Churches of Christ seem more prone to imitate other religious groups than to maintain a distinctive identity. Such admonitions warn us to stay on guard against the wayward leanings of the world and to renew our commitment to radical discipleship. They remind us that, although it is good to make the same investments in this world that Jesus did, we must also maintain the same distance from its corruption that he kept.

85

We need to get clear on just what it is that distinguishes the rest of the world from Jesus' disciples as they live under the reign of God proclaimed by Jesus. Being a disciple means learning a new language and participating in new practices. Discipleship is a topsy-turvy lifestyle, in which the first will be last and the last first, where people turn the other cheek, sacrifice themselves for the sake of others, and give generously without expecting anything in return. They do not leave the world, but in imitation of Christ, they enter it

> In the second century, the *Epistle to Diognetus* captured one early Christian perspective on what it meant to be "in the world but not of the world":
>
> Christians cannot be distinguished from other people by country, language or the customs they observe.... They dwell in other countries, but only as aliens. As citizens, they share in all things with others, and yet endure all things as foreigners. Every foreign land is to them as their native land, and every land of their birth is as a foreign land to them.... They beget children, but they do not cast away their offspring. They have a common table, but not a common bed. They are "in the flesh," but they do not "live according to the flesh."
>
> To sum it up.... What the soul is in the body, that Christians are in the world.

as God's servants. After all, Jesus loved even those who did not love him. He often clashed with the ways of "this wicked generation," the strict purity of his life mirroring God's own holiness.

As we focus our attentions on Jesus, our hearts and minds become attuned to the melody of his foolish wisdom, wisdom that only the spiritual may discern: the wisdom of the cross whose foolishness is wiser than any human wisdom (1 Corinthians 1:21–25; 2:14). This wisdom, baffling to the non-Christian onlooker, leads the Christian to make equally baffling choices in lifestyle, relationships, careers, spending, and entertainment. In short, Jesus' claim on us cuts across the grain of human culture. It challenges us to adopt his worldview by leaving home and family and fields to unearth the treasures of the gospel—and with them persecutions (Mark 10:30).

Standing apart is not easy. But we must keep our gaze fixed on Jesus if we want to be imbued with genuine kingdom values and be set apart in the right ways for the right reasons.

One way Jesus helps us to acquire the right kind of distinctiveness is by calling us to himself. He insists that our allegiance must be to him, not to an institution. Only then will his body remain faithful to its purpose. Also, he calls people to himself because the world-affirming and world-rejecting dimensions of God's work harmonize within the person of Christ. Jesus invites us to reject the world, not just so we may escape it for the sake of heaven, nor so we may become members of a self-serving or isolated institution, but so we will be, like him, agents of the world's healing. Wherever Jesus stretched forth his hands in compassion, the reign of God made headway in a broken world.

Picturing Jesus' Ministry

Jesus used his hands to apply the salve of peace and good news to wounded lives. In Jesus' ministry, we learn of God's deep mercy and love for people. He is a God of compassion, who knows the hurts of his people and grieves alongside them. He is moved by the desperation of a hemorrhaging woman, the sympathy of a paralytic's friends, the emptiness of a tax collector's life, the plight of a prostitute trapped in webs of her own spinning. On facing the grief of two beloved sisters who have lost their brother, "Jesus wept" (John 17:35). Amid the cries of pain and in an atmosphere of mourning, he acts in order to comfort, he teaches in order to liberate, he dies in order to connect with those who die and also to furnish healing. Jesus' ministry shows us that, in our God, we have one who not only cares deeply about us, but one who is willing to make sacrifices and work hard so that we can recover wholeness and peace.

The outstanding features of Jesus' ministry of care are his healing ministry and miracles. Jesus' miracles were not

87

publicity stunts, nor were they random displays of power tossed out to convince the crowds of his identity. At times, Jesus' signs and wonders do inspire faith, but at other times they do not. His critics suggested that his miracles were the work of demonic powers, and his healing ministry could even be derailed by unbelief (Mark 3:30; 6:5). According to John, Jesus' miracles attest to his connection to the Father, but for the person who has not made the investment of faith by becoming one of Jesus' flock and listening to his voice, the miracles supply no convicting proof (John 10:25–26). These passages show us that more is at work in Jesus' miraculous ministry than simply the certification of his authority, important as that is.

Jesus' miracles show us that the Son of Man is Lord over creation and that he is in the business of restoring the world as God intended it to be. By calming the storm, Jesus asserts the divine prerogative over the seemingly chaotic natural elements, renewing the harmony that should exist between humanity and the world that it was created to rule over (Mark 4:35–41; Genesis 1:26; 2:15). His feeding of five thousand hungry people is a sign of the kingdom, not only because it proves Jesus' divine power but also because it expresses anew the divine intent within creation. The Creator did not mean for people to go hungry. He wanted them to experience the world as a hospitable home, learning to rely on the gracious provision of their welcoming host and to share alike. Like God's provision of manna in the wilderness for Israel, Jesus' miraculous feeding recaptures that dream (Mark 6:30–44).

In the same way, Jesus' healings and exorcisms are repair jobs. They are acts of compassion conveying God's mercy to suffering people, to be sure, but that is not all. By healing and exorcizing, Jesus is taking hold of something broken in the world, some part of creation that is cracked, and fixing it. God did not intend for people to experience blindness or lameness or leprosy. In the face of so much brokenness, he had made a promise, through the Old Testament prophets, to repair what had gone wrong with the world. Jesus fulfills that promise. His healing miracles are signs that God is establishing his kingdom. By casting out demons, Jesus reiterates God's vow to fight for his people, liberating them from the forces of evil. To a race of people whose hopes have long been dimmed by hard bondage, Jesus' ministry reveals God's original intent, reminding them that their Creator's ambition for them is one of freedom from the evil that weakens and disables them. He is the rescuer, stepping up to defend us from powers that are too strong for us to overcome on our own.

Jesus' healing ministry shows us that he is Lord, with power over disease, nature, death, the forces of evil— even sin. Because of this, we may rely on him, confident that no other power in the world trumps his. Yet again—he is Lord; he cannot be manipulated through magic or prayer to exercise this power in ways that conform to the whims of our desires. He does what he chooses to do; not every leper of the first century was cleansed.

Jesus' ministry of healing has always been a favorite subject in song:

"The great Physician now is near, the sympathizing Jesus...."

"Grant that all may seek and find Thee a God supremely kind; Heal the sick, the captive free; Let us all rejoice in Thee."

"Bring Christ your broken life, so marred by sin, He will create anew, make whole again...."

"Hear Him, ye deaf; His praise, ye dumb, your loosened tongues employ; Ye blind, behold your Savior come; and leap, ye lame, for joy!"

Basking in the triumphant glory of Jesus' miracles, we are prone to forget that, during his ministry, Jesus did not make himself available to heal everyone on earth who suffered from illness. Nor did he solve world hunger. Peter's feverish mother-in-law undoubtedly appreciated Jesus' care, but she just as certainly became sick again later in her life. Jesus' healing of her was not a thorough, permanent resolution of all her problems. People such as Lazarus had the dubious distinction of dying twice. Even Paul, himself a confirmed healer, was allowed to go on suffering with some infirmity, though we do not know just what it was. In fact, Paul understands this tormenting circumstance to be a more convincing and meaningful demonstration of Christ's power than any straightforward deliverance, since it conveyed the upside-down message typical of the Lord: "my power is made perfect in weakness" (2 Corinthians 12:7–10).

Factors such as these should alert us that, in Jesus' ministry, a larger program is at stake than could be accomplished by waving the magic wand of Jesus' miracles over the world's hurts. God is so committed to his creation that, rather than demolishing its original nature by canceling and rewriting its basic traits, he chooses to work mainly within the processes native to it. Rather than violating the basic principle of human freedom and forcing his people into the blessings of his reign, he invites them. In fact, he hopes that they will join him as his collaborators in the work, in a relationship of participatory love, as it was meant to be from the beginning. In light of these considerations, full-scale, immediate, and magical solutions to the world's problems would be no solutions at all.

> **Holistic Healing**
>
> Commenting on Jesus' healing ministry at about the turn of the second century, Clement of Alexandria remarks:
>
> "The physician's art, according to Democritus, heals the diseases of the body; wisdom frees the soul from its obsessions. But the good Instructor, Wisdom, who is the Word of the Father who assumed flesh, cares for the whole nature of his creature. The all-sufficient Physician of humanity, the Savior, heals both body and soul conjointly."

The intricacies of Jesus' program also have something to do with the nature of our brokenness. The work of restoration is involved and lengthy because our fundamental problems run much deeper than physical illness and hunger. Jesus raised the paralytic from his mat so that he could walk again, but Mark directs his readers to understand Jesus' deeper intent: Jesus wanted people to "know that the Son of Man has authority on earth to forgive sins" (Mark 2:11). Jesus may not have healed every sick person, but he was totally committed to resolving the deepest human problem of all: the plague of sin and the tragedy of our alienation from God. This resolution is what drove his ministry, and no one is excluded from the benefits of his healing work in this tricky area. All the other pieces of his ministry, miraculous or otherwise, served this over-riding agenda, since it is at the root of all the other brokenness. "The Son of Man came to seek and save what was lost," he explains (Luke 19:10). As the Pharisees reluctantly discovered in a little social gathering at Matthew's home, Jesus is primarily a doctor of sick souls, a physician who hangs out his shingle to alert the sick—the "sinners"—that a gifted specialist has come to town, able to prescribe the cure for what ails them (Matthew 9:12–13).

More than bread and fishes, or manna, we need the Lord. He is the true bread coming down from heaven. A lifetime of feeding on him provides the cure for our deepest weaknesses (John 6:25–59). He came "to give his life as a ransom for many," sent by the Father so that "whoever believes in him might have eternal life" (Mark 10:45; John 3:16). Sin is deep-seated among us, its corrosive effects on individuals and human society long-lasting. Our spiritual rehabilitation requires long-term attention, entailing processes of growth and transformation.

Rather than pronouncing a magic fix-it formula over the world's hurts, the Father deals with the problem of evil by entering our situation and sharing it with us as a king who serves and suffers, one who takes up the infirmities of his people, even to the point of offering himself for death on a cross. He triumphs over pain and evil by experiencing them fully and by supplying us with help through his presence.

A Picture of the Gracious Host 91

In his ministry, Jesus displayed a welcoming attitude. He invited people into relationship with him, attracting the sort that many others pulled away from—sinners, lepers, tax collectors, Gentiles. He had his Father's heart, ready to run out and embrace the prodigal child who returns to him, no matter what the offense may have been. In a manner of speaking, his door was always open and his table always spread to receive guests. He was the sort of shepherd who would leave the ninety-nine to recover one lost lamb, the sort of housekeeper who would sweep under every piece of furniture until she found her one lost coin (Luke 15). He acted as if it were more blessed to give than receive, even sacrificing his personal down-time for the sake of people who needed him (Matthew 14:13–14). In Jesus we see the graciousness of our God, forgiving and compassionate. He is a generous host who welcomes any who will come to him. Tired and burdened high-maintenance people are all the more welcome: "Come, to me," Jesus said, "all you who are weary and burdened, and I will give you rest" (Matthew 11:28). In a sense, the ministry of Jesus is one of hospitality.

Having provided so lavishly for his children, the Father expects them to exercise the same hospitality, to be as welcoming and forgiving and compassionate as he has been. "Freely you have received," Jesus points out. "Freely give" (Matthew 10:8). The picture of ministry that we see in Jesus leaps onto the canvas of our own lives as we adopt the practices of service and healing. Jesus is not a one-man show. His counter-attack against evil involves the strategy of gathering a community

> "Hospitality means receiving the other, from the heart, into my own dwelling place. It entails providing for the need, comfort, and delight of the other with all the openness, respect, freedom, tenderness, and joy that love itself embodies.... Hospitality begins with God.... [W]e have a supremely hospitable God."
>
> *Marjorie J. Thompson (1995)*

of people, themselves broken and wounded, who will follow him and together form a hospital for the sick of soul and defeated in spirit. He commissioned the twelve to "heal the sick, raise the dead, drive out demons," and especially to proclaim the gospel message, "the kingdom of heaven is near" (Matthew 10:7–8). It is a message disciples proclaim, but it is also one they embody as they become instruments of bringing about God's healing rule in the lives of people who have been long battered by the enemy.

Like Jesus, true disciples invite others into the kingdom, baptizing and training them to join as partners with Jesus in his ministry. Church work is a ministry of hospitality. Jesus' disciples take pity on the sick and hungry. They work to alleviate the suffering of people ensnared by sin. They utilize every resource God provides for the relief of needy people. Whether those resources include what we normally call the miraculous is up to God—when, where, and how to perform wonders is entirely in his hands. We pray for wonders in the sterile halls of hospitals or by dark bedsides in our homes, and we welcome them when they come. But it is clear that God intends for his people to exert every effort in compassionate ministry towards others. It is also certain that God, who is able to make all grace abound to us, will ensure that we have all we need, in all things and at all times, to abound in every good work (2 Corinthians 9:8).

Unfortunately, we do not always capture the picture of Jesus' hospitality as well as we should. Our selfishness often drives us to look inward instead, though we appeal to distorted views of Jesus in defense of our self-indulgence. For example, the preaching of our heritage has traditionally taken seriously the commission to carry on God's most profound healing work, the cure of people's souls and the moral transformation of their lives. We embraced the task of proclamation, inviting people to repent, be baptized, and receive the remedy of forgiveness. However, this emphasis has caused many to minimize the importance of ministries of compassion—particularly if they are unlikely to result in baptisms. After all, the thinking goes, if "the elements will be destroyed by fire" (2 Peter 3:10), we should devote our resources to the task of alerting people to the certainty of final judgment. Rather than recognizing in Jesus the connection between the earthly and the heavenly, we have tended to separate

93

them, supposing that, for all practical purposes, God is mainly concerned with the hereafter.

Another distortion of Jesus' image downplays his role as our example in ministry. In this thinking, he is the founder of the church and the doorway into eternal life, not so much a model for our current behavior. Instead, the institutional features of the church take the lead, so that discipleship is defined in terms of meeting the conditions for membership and faithfully upholding the traditions of the institution. In direct defiance of Jesus' teaching and example, matters such as adherence to specific worship forms become more important measures of faithfulness than whether or not one is showing mercy to those in need. The church's vast resources are pledged to support and defend its traditions in such matters. Straining out the gnat of procedural details, we fall into the danger of swallowing the camel of apathy towards the sick and wounded (Matthew 25:23–25).

Ironically, strong currents of reaction against traditional preoccupation with the institution can produce a similar distortion of Jesus' ministry. Some among us

---

Ministries of Compassion—Dissonant Voices within Our Own Heritage:

"Man has never invented any system or scheme to ameliorate the condition of human society that was ever a success.... Let Christians, therefore, give their time and energies to the propagation of Christianity, if they would benefit men."

E. G. Sewell (1909)

"Let us realize that every helpless, needy one of our brethren is the personification of Christ to us appealing for help. He is our Christ, to be kindly welcomed and generously treated."

David Lipscomb (1870)

"Without timely aid, the masses, unable to raise crops the coming year, will be in as bad condition another winter as they have been.... We must sacrifice our luxuries, our comforts, our wealth and pride, to relieve our brother's distresses, just as Christ sacrificed his honors, glories, joys, and possessions in heaven, to help poor helpless, fallen man on earth. This was the fellowship of God to man."

David Lipscomb (1867)

have felt the need to reject what they see as a religion of maintaining rules and regulations about procedural matters. They refuse to carry a Pharisaical yoke of legalism that burdens people unnecessarily and distracts them from pursuing a personal relationship with the Lord and cultivating matters of the heart. They yearn to experience the liberty of the gospel. However, at times this impulse becomes so all-engrossing that it leads us to suppose that the freedom Jesus brings is an escape from our own traditions, from obedience, and from duty. Rather than understanding the good news to be about deliverance from sin and the opportunity to serve others as slaves of God, we see it as delivering us from the bondage of our religious ancestors and from the oppressive burden of religious obligation. People start to judge the spiritual vitality of churches based on how non-traditional they are in certain areas and how well they avoid creating uncomfortable feelings of guilt or obligation, rather than using the rigorous standards of servant spirituality that Jesus shows us. Taking up the anthem that "it is for freedom that Christ has set us free," we run the risk of using our freedom "to indulge the flesh" rather than serving one another in love (Galatians 5:1, 13), so that the world's homeless and despondent languish while we celebrate our freedom.

Distorting Jesus' world-affirming side can block compassion as well. The growing interest in the benefits of discipleship for this life is good, but it threatens to delude us into believing that Christ has called us to him just for our own earthly comfort and satisfaction. So much Christian teaching and writing these days appeals to our desires to indulge ourselves, encouraging us to define the essence of the Christian life as an experience that meets our own needs so that our lives will be rich and enjoyable. God has so much to give, and we want it all! When that impulse takes hold, it can cause churches to look inward, designing ministries primarily to serve those who are already inside, shying away from taking on any work that might be messy or difficult—like ministries of compassion to people in desperate situations. We give self-indulgence a new face by calling it merely a desire to claim God's blessings for our lives, learning to camouflage greed and materialism under the guise of appreciating God's creation. "It is easier for a camel to go through the eye of a needle than for a rich person to enter the kingdom," Jesus warned (Matthew 19:24). Jesus' disciples were stunned at this admonition. So should we be. Those who enjoy both material wealth and the rich blessings of a life in Jesus must be on special guard against hoarding either of these treasures.

These distortions of Jesus' image make it hard for us to portray his ministry in our lives. Along with God's people over the centuries, many Christians today find that some of the features of Jesus' ministry do not come naturally: feeding the hungry, tending the sick, championing the oppressed, and equipping people for the daily struggle with sin and evil. Yet we do not want to soften Jesus' indictment against those who won't follow him into the trenches. Scripture echoes with sharp and relentless condemnation of any religious doctrines or practices that, for whatever seemingly admirable reasons, excuse us from doing Jesus' work:

> "Stop bringing meaningless offerings!... Seek justice, encourage the oppressed. Defend the cause of the fatherless, plead the case of the widow" (Isaiah 1:13, 17).

> "If anyone has material possessions and sees his brother in need but has no pity on him, how can the love of God be in him?" (1 John 3:17).

> "Religion that God our Father accepts as pure and faultless is this: to look after orphans and widows in their distress." "Faith without deeds is dead" (James 1:27; 2:26).

> "Give to everyone who asks you" (Luke 6:30).

96   According to Jesus, what will separate sheep from goats at the time of judgment hinges on a person's behavior towards the hungry, the naked, the prisoner, and the stranger—not institutional affiliation or procedural details or one's sense of freedom or one's level of personal

satisfaction. This is as sobering today as it was in his day. Rejecting opportunities to minister to the needy is a rejection of Jesus, both because we are neglecting his command and example and because he is personally present in the needy, as he himself explains (Matthew 25:31–46). For this reason, we rejoice in the increase of compassionate ministries in our churches. Large-scale efforts involving feeding the poor, urban missions, ministries of marital counseling, prison ministries, families who are devoting considerable resources to bless those in want—these and other expressions of God's heart are taking their places alongside our continuing proclamation of the gospel. Indeed, they also express the gospel.

Still, too many struggling people have not yet seen Christ clearly portrayed before their eyes as crucified, too many have not experienced the relief that should come to them as we sacrifice ourselves to serve. And, as always, we remain vulnerable to the temptation to serve ourselves instead. May we keep exploring creative ways to carry out Jesus' ministry of compassion among the world's needy, for this is Christ's mission.

Conclusion

When early Christians used to gather for a meal together, sometimes they used the occasion as an opportunity to feed the poor. The Lord's Supper, which in the early days often occurred within the context of a fellowship meal, provided such an opportunity. In the Supper, Christians were joining together as guests at Christ's table to partake of the cup of thanksgiving. They were the recipients of his gracious hospitality. By sharing the Supper, they were proclaiming his death "until he come," joyfully anticipating the time when they would share it with him again in the final fulfillment of his kingdom (1 Corinthians 11:26; Matthew 26:29). In a sense, it was an other-worldly moment, a foretaste of heaven and the marriage supper of the Lamb (Revelation 19). Yet the celebration of future abundance spilled over into the here and now, so that the heavenly feast welcomed the needy and comforted the poor here on earth.

It was precisely the breakdown of fellowship during communion that bothered Paul so much in 1 Corinthians 10:20–21: "When you come together, it is not the Lord's Supper you eat, for as you eat, each of you goes ahead without waiting for anybody else. One remains hungry, another gets drunk." The Corinthians had lost sight of what it means to gather as family at the Lord's table. The Lord's Supper captures a picture of full spiritual salvation in Jesus, a salvation of body, soul, mind, and strength, all together,

> "Eating together expresses mutuality, recognition, acceptance, and equal regard. Shared meals are central to every community of hospitality—central to sustaining the life of the community and to expressing welcome to strangers."
>
> *Christine D. Pohl* (1999)

individually and as a people. It stands as a regular reminder that the church must extend Jesus' invitation, finding ways to convince people that they are genuinely welcome at the feast, whatever their background or mistakes or social condition.

We celebrate the Lord's Supper not just to commemorate Jesus' death. We do it to stay connected with his heart. Those who know Jesus well know that they will find him most often in the places where people are hurting and suffering. Since the disciples' highest ambition is to imitate the Lord, they meet him in these places to join him in what he is doing. Disciples who are being transformed into the image of Christ reach out to the lost and needy. Like Jesus, they address people's problems by entering into and sharing them. In so doing, the body of Christ discovers that it is actually serving Christ, because "whatever you did for one of the least of these, you did for me" (Matthew 25:40). Christ really is all in all. As the Father sweeps the broken fragments of our world under Jesus' feet, his reign expands, and the body of Christ further realizes its stature as "the fullness of him who fills everything in every way" (Ephesians 1:22–23).

By their proclamation of the kingdom and by their ministries of compassion, Christians are removing the veil from before the world's eyes so that it too may see Jesus and find deliverance. Even though we were poor, crippled, blind, and lame, Jesus came out into the cold darkness to invite us to his table. There is still room. Though the hour is late, we have been commanded to go out into the roads and country lanes with great urgency, bringing the outsider in until the Father's house is full (Luke 14:15–24).

5
Fixing Our Eyes on the Master

> Christian faith in its original version…is centered on a
> person who said, "I am…the truth." Jesus did not say "I
> will speak true words to you" or "I will tell you about
> the truth"; he claimed to embody truth in his person.
> To those who wished to know truth, Jesus did not offer
> propositions to be tested by logic or data to be tested in
> the laboratory. He offered himself and his life. Those who
> sought truth were invited into relationship with him, and
> through him with the whole community of the human
> and nonhuman world.
>
> *Parker J. Palmer (1993)*

Jesus was a remarkable teacher. Ask any of those who
came into contact with him, and they'd tell you. In fact,
he was so well-known for his teaching that not only his
disciples, but many others also called him "rabbi," or
"teacher." Even those who did not believe in Jesus as Messiah often acknowledged his role as a teacher (Matthew
22:16). But what kind of teacher was he? What lessons
was he teaching those who knew him so long ago as he
walked the dusty roads with them, and what lessons is
he teaching us as he walks the roads of our lives?

In many ways, Jesus was just what you'd expect from
a rabbinic teacher. He used the same teaching methods:
interpreting scripture in the synagogues and elsewhere
for learners who came to him privately for questions; frequently illustrating his lessons with stories or examples
drawn from everyday life that resonated with his hearers; tutoring a group of hand-picked pupils whom he

expected eventually to "graduate" and become teachers themselves. Matthew paints a robust portrait of Jesus as this kind of teacher, the first strokes of which are laid down in the Sermon on the Mount (Matthew 5–7). The Sermon begins with brief, provocative statements, one of the rabbis' favorite methods of piquing students' interest. In the Sermon, Jesus reflects on various teachings of *Torah*, applying them to daily life in God's kingdom and using them to instruct his hearers about God's purposes and practices. None of this would have seemed out of the ordinary to his first-century audience. He met many of their expectations for teachers and acknowledged the worth of the world's teaching paradigm, often affirming what his hearers thought they needed to hear.

However, just as often, Jesus' teaching challenged people's expectations, threatening their comfort as students, bending and even breaking the rules for what a good teacher was expected to do. In the Beatitudes, Jesus not only grabs our attention, in rabbinic style, but he radically disorients us. His description of mourners and the persecuted as among the specially blessed is still deeply unsettling. His call not just to meet, but to exceed, the righteousness of the religious leaders of his time is no less than spiritually revolutionary, and his call for radical inward purity forces all who hear him to reassess their lives. Throughout the Sermon, Jesus' teaching challenges and subverts his audience's expectations, calling people to extreme levels of kingdom commitment. His lesson—on the one hand, so simple, and on the other, so challenging and difficult—makes clear that Jesus is no ordinary teacher. He is not merely out to instruct people about a topic or a few principles; he asks his pupils for radical change.

And it is not just the content of his lessons that people find disconcerting. His teaching strategies are also disorienting. For example, instead of smoothing the way for hearers, he frequently makes the lessons harder for them to understand. Many of his parables illustrate this. Jesus admits freely that he speaks in parables so that "seeing, they may not see" (Luke 8:10). It seems clear that he is intentionally hindering his own communication—an unusual teaching strategy. Clearly, he sometimes does so to protect himself, evading open conflict with those who oppose him until the time is right. But this can't be the only reason for him to veil his lessons. Even his own disciples frequently wrestle with the meanings of his teachings and have to guess at the interpretations. For example, when Jesus warned them to "beware of the yeast of the Pharisees" (Matthew 16:6), he spoke in a riddle that the disciples couldn't decode. They thought he was upset that they'd forgotten to buy bread. Jesus never did interpret the riddle for them, but after a hint or two, they figured it out. Still, what was his purpose in creating a roadblock to decoding his meaning? In this case, he was alone on a boat with his followers. He could have spoken openly without any risk, but instead he spoke in a parable. Why?

Jesus created barriers to his teaching in other ways as well. Most Christians have struggled with the story of the Syrophoenician woman (Matthew 15:21–8). How could the Jesus who had such compassion on others sit in silence as this grieving mother cried to him for help? How could he say to her, "It is not right to take the children's bread and toss it to their dogs"? It seems so uncharacteristic. Perhaps he was testing her or offering some lesson for his disciples. Some might contend that he was only joking. We try to explain it away, but still it's there, an anomaly—an obstacle for us as well as for that woman who faced Christ determinedly and argued back two thousand years ago. What was Jesus trying to teach her? What was he trying to teach his disciples? What is he trying to teach us?

Learning from the Master

You can tell a lot about a teacher's expectations from how he or she teaches. If a teacher spends most of her time lecturing behind a podium and interacting formally with her students, it's likely that she expects them to sit quietly in their seats, taking notes and raising their hands if they have questions. On the other hand, if an instructor sits on his desk, gesticulating broadly and frequently getting up to pace around the room, emphasizing more give-and-take in the class, he is sending the students a signal that he is comfortable with a less formal class structure. If a teacher wants students to do a lot of thinking, talking, and even arguing with her, she will organize her class and her teaching to send that message.

> "Community, or connectedness, is the principle behind good teaching, but different teachers with different gifts create community in surprisingly diverse ways, using widely divergent methods."
>
> *Parker J. Palmer (1998)*

In other words, teachers aren't simply concerned about presenting the material they teach; they also shape their students through the methods they use.

Based on his teaching techniques, we can tell a lot about Jesus and what he expected from a learner, and this continues to have broad implications for us today. Of course, all kinds of people came to learn from Jesus—poor and rich, powerful and powerless, male and female, Jew and gentile. His teaching broke across all the barriers and divisions that humans recognize. And this in itself is an important part of Christ's lesson. Those who come for instruction must be ready to sacrifice their preconceived notions and biases. After all, like the incarnation itself, the goal of Christ's teaching is to reunite the human and the divine, restoring the relationship that once characterized creation. For this reason, other lines of division will also have to fall. This, in part, is why Jesus' teaching is so challenging and subversive. He isn't interested in just fulfilling his students' expectations; he wants to renew their vision and change their hearts. To do so, he has to break down the barriers they've erected. Jesus' students have to be willing to let him free them from their own perceptions and expectations; they have to be willing to subject themselves to a new teaching. In short, they must be extraordinary people to learn from the master.

104

Jesus' disciples certainly weren't extraordinary in the usual sense, though. In fact, although there were certainly some important exceptions, Jesus didn't typically attract scholars and experts in the law. It was mostly common, uneducated folk who became his closest pupils. They were "unschooled, ordinary men," yet something was special about them (Acts 4:13). When the disciples asked Jesus why he obfuscated his teaching by speaking to the crowds in parables, he told them: "The knowledge of the secrets of the kingdom of heaven has been given to you, but not to them" (Matthew 13:11). This is a mystifying statement. What was special about the disciples that the crowd lacked? Why were they given a privileged understanding when others weren't? What did Jesus see in them as students that made them teachable? Jesus often concluded his parables with the injunction, "the one who has ears to hear, let that one hear…." How does one acquire "the ears to hear?" These are crucial questions, for if we are to be students of Christ, we need to understand what his teaching expects of us—how it's transforming us into those who can hear and learn from his message.

> "The word 'education' is derived from the Latin *educere*, which means 'to lead, to draw out, to bring forth' and, by extension, 'to rear, nurture, and foster growth.' It is in this original sense, of one who draws young people out into encounters with what they do not yet know, while honoring what they do know that I define myself as a teacher. For me, to be a teacher means to help students move toward a larger and continually expanding encounter with knowledge and experience…."
>
> *Herbert Kohl (1998)*

Of course, the Gospels are also full of stories of people who experienced unsuccessful learning encounters with Jesus. Not everyone who asked to be taught really wanted to learn from him. Matthew 22 records a series of questions put to Jesus, interrogations designed to trap him. In the first, the Pharisees sent their disciples and the Herodians to ask Jesus whether it was right to pay taxes to Caesar or not. Although they prefaced their request for instruction by saying, "We know you are a man of integrity and that you teach the way of God," they clearly didn't want the instruction (Matthew 22:15ff). Then the Sadducees tried to lure him into their own crafty web with a tricky question about the marital status of a woman who had seven husbands before the resurrection (Matthew 22:23–32), but they were not genuinely seeking help with a troublesome problem. On another occasion, the Pharisees asked Jesus by what authority he performed his miracles, but they were clearly trying to force him to say something that would allow them to accuse him of blasphemy. Jesus responded by giving them a taste of their own medicine rather than answering their question (Luke 20:1ff). Obviously, in these encounters the "students" learned nothing of real value from Jesus. They did not have "ears to hear." As far as we can tell, their hearts were neither touched nor changed.

Not all unsuccessful students were malicious, though. There were some who seemed to want to learn, but couldn't. When the rich young man asked Jesus what he must do to gain eternal life, it appears that he was asking the question honestly, with a genuine desire to learn. He certainly wasn't trying to trick Jesus or harm him, and Jesus was overwhelmed with love for the young man. But something went wrong. When Jesus told him, "One thing you still lack. Go, sell everything you have and give to the poor," the teaching ended. The man walked away. Mark tells us that the man left "because he had great wealth," but this explanation is puzzling (Mark 10:17–22). After all, Zacchaeus was also wealthy (Luke 19:2), yet somehow his riches didn't get in the way of his ability to learn from Jesus. The quality of an ideal student must lie elsewhere than in socioeconomic status or in some other external characteristic; the characteristics Jesus seeks must lie deeper.

The Heart of the Learner

The Pharisees; the rich young ruler; the man who wanted to follow Jesus after first burying his father (Matthew 8:22); those who continually asked for a sign from Jesus, although they'd seen him feed the five thousand and do many other miracles (Matthew 16:11); the followers who turned away from Jesus after being told they'd have to eat his body and drink his blood (John 6:66)—how were these potential students different from the disciples? Why were the secrets of the kingdom so hard for these people to perceive and learn?

Perhaps the most obvious characteristic present in the disciples, but lacking in these others, is humility. Most people who encountered Jesus had their own agendas. They were trying to use him for their own purposes or expected him to rubber stamp policies they endorsed. The kind of student Jesus insists on, though, is one who has an open heart and a willingness to listen—the kind of student who allows Christ's teaching to reshape his or her priorities and perceptions. Sometimes the disciples didn't

"What it seems to amount to is this, that both as to matter and method the teaching of Jesus is conditioned by the nature of the audience. The blank opposition of the religious authorities is met…with destructive criticism…. [The crowd's] interest is apt to be focused on wonderful cures of bodily ailments rather than on the things of the spirit…. The disciples form the third class…in some way they must have commended themselves to him as worthy of receiving the secret of the Kingdom."

T. W. Manson (1935)

like what Jesus said, but they were humble. They didn't walk away. Their defenses were down. Even when they were perplexed by his teaching, they realized that it was special and that Christ was a special kind of teacher. This is why, even though they didn't understand all that he was teaching them, they could still confess "Lord, to whom shall we go? You have the words of eternal life" (John 6:68). These pupils were simple, humble, honest. Sometimes they were stupid, sometimes bumbling and weak, but they were always invested, always committed. Of all the people we see experiencing the teaching of Jesus, they are the ones still there after the parables, asking what they mean, wanting to know. Others pose hard questions to Jesus to trick or trap him, but the disciples ask questions because they

107

truly want to know the answers and follow the teachings. There's a humility and an honesty in their attitude that's an essential part of the learner's makeup. Where do they learn these traits? From the master himself, who said, "Take my yoke upon you and learn from me, for I am gentle and humble in heart" (Matthew 11:29). In the "classroom" of Christ's life, humility is one of the foundational principles. After all, this teacher came not "to be served, but to serve" (Matthew 20:28), and those who truly want to learn from him must do likewise. They have to be willing to see with his eyes and hear with his ears.

Another key characteristic of the disciples was their capacity to trust. Jesus was a remarkable person, to be sure, but he didn't inspire unquestioning awe and faith in everyone. Not everyone followed him. Not everyone believed him. It takes a trusting heart to be moved by the master teacher. Matthew left his tax collection booth immediately to follow Jesus (Matthew 9:9). Peter, Andrew, James, and John walked away from their nets. When Jesus set out on his last trip to Jerusalem, the disciples willingly followed, although they knew trouble lay ahead. And although Thomas is often seen as the antithesis of trust because of his demand to touch Jesus' hands and side to verify the resurrection, the truly remarkable part of the story is that he trusted Jesus even with his uncertainty. While the others seemed willing to take the resurrection on faith, Thomas once again turned to the master to teach him. Some are troubled by Thomas' apparent weakness, but he had learned to trust from the one who would later say, "My grace is sufficient for you, for my power is made perfect in weakness" (2 Corinthians 12:9) and who entrusted us with the treasure of the gospel even though we are merely "jars of clay" (2 Corinthians 4:7).

> "Faith in the learner leads some teachers to find strengths where others see nothing but weakness and failure."
>
> *Herbert Kohl (1988)*

A third trait Jesus expected in his learners was a confessional attitude. Good students recognize that they need instruction. They recognize that they must apply Jesus' lessons, however harsh, to themselves first of all. The disciples certainly weren't perfect students. Jesus was sometimes angry with them, sometimes frustrated, sometimes sick of them. They were all too ready to call down fire on an unrepentant village, or to put restraining orders on some people outside their group who were teaching in Jesus' name (Luke 9:51–6; Mark 9:38–41). When the disciples failed to cast a demon out of a sick boy, Jesus said to them, "How long shall I put up with you?" (Matthew 17:17). Another time, he rebuked Peter by calling him "Satan" (Matthew 16:23). And yet the disciples continued to repent and resubmit themselves to the lordship of Jesus. At one point, we see them arguing over who will be the greatest, yet later they submit to a lesson on foot washing. Peter denied Jesus three times, yet he repented and accepted forgiveness. Others who came in contact with Christ weren't able to be confessional in this way: rather than accepting his guilt and allowing the teacher to instruct him, Pontius Pilate washed his hands in a futile attempt to absolve himself of blame, thus proving himself to be an unfit learner (Matthew 27:24). Judas Iscariot, unlike Peter, was unable to confess and accept forgiveness for his betrayal of his master, but instead assigned and carried out his own punishment, refusing to learn and grow (Matthew 27:5).

Humility, trust, and a confessional spirit. These aren't the characteristics for which students are tested on the SATs, but without them, people simply cannot understand Jesus. They are absolutely essential qualities if you want to learn from the great Teacher; they are the traits that give a person the ears

> "It is not mere application, however exemplary, which introduces the mind to truth, nor the reading many books, nor the getting up many subjects, nor the witnessing many experiments, nor the attending many lectures. All this is short of enough.... Such a power...is an acquired faculty of judgment, of clearsightedness, of sagacity, of wisdom...qualities which do not come of mere acquirement."
>
> *John Henry Cardinal Newman (1852)*

109

to hear what he's saying. But why? It's not that Jesus is trying to keep out those "bad learners" in an elitist way. It's simply that he's the kind of teacher that not everyone "gets." By clothing his lessons in parables and presenting other obstacles, he ensured that his students' level of understanding couldn't surpass their depth of personal investment. Or, to put it differently, provoking personal investment was a major part of his lesson. Jesus' teaching doesn't only require students to excavate and regurgitate ideas; it demands a change of heart. Without the right kind of heart, people simply couldn't understand what Jesus was talking about. Take Nicodemus for example. Although he seemed to have been sincere in his desire to learn from Jesus, he obviously also had much invested in his position as a Pharisee—he came to Jesus at night (John 3:2ff) and was unwilling to approach Jesus in entire humility and trust, with a fully confessional spirit. As a result, when Jesus tried to teach him about spiritual rebirth, Nicodemus responded almost comically, with "How can a man be born when he is old?" Of course, the disciples had also asked foolish questions, but Nicodemus' lack of comprehension showed a flaw that was keeping him from learning. Jesus finally cried in frustration, "You are Israel's teacher?" How could a man who was supposed to be a teacher reveal such a poor level of understanding? Surely, as a Pharisee, Nicodemus would have known the Law and the Prophets very well, so his level of knowledge was not the problem here. What did Nicodemus lack? At least at that point, he did not have the heart for instruction.

> "The one without the Spirit does not accept the things that come from the Spirit of God, for they are foolishness to him, and he cannot understand them, because they are spiritually discerned."
>
> *1 Corinthians 2:14*

Humility, trust, and a confessional heart have always been necessary for those who truly want to understand the word of the Lord. These inner traits of the spirit sustain a certain kind of logic, enabling the student fully to comprehend Jesus' teaching, for his lessons are

110

never merely informational—they are transformational. Christ's teaching starts in the heart. No matter how scientific or clever the methods of interpretation may be, without the right heart, good learning cannot happen.

Lord of the Sabbath

Not everything about Jesus' teaching has to do with the learners, though. Jesus' teaching also reveals truths about himself and his Father. He called people to a high moral standard, consistently reminding them of what is truly important in life. But all great teachers do that, to some extent. Many of the Old Testament prophets, as well as many recent teachers like Ghandi and Martin Luther King, Jr., have followed similar teaching paths. If we stop at simply calling Jesus a powerful teacher, we do him a great injustice. Many people today honor Jesus as a great teacher but don't acknowledge him as Lord. Jesus himself never left room for that kind of comfortable compromise. When he sat in a house in Capernaum and a crippled man was lowered by his friends through the ceiling (Mark 2:1ff),

> "Jesus belongs to the world. Yet in the midst of it he is of unmistakable otherness. This is the secret of his influence and his rejection.... We become aware of the fact when we try to fit this figure into any of the descriptions and categories then prevalent in Judaism.... This rabbi differs considerably.... The reality of God and the authority of his will are always directly present [in Jesus' teaching], and are fulfilled in him."
>
> *Günther Bornkamm (1956)*

Jesus didn't allow the onlookers the easy choice of viewing him as just a good teacher; they had to decide whether he could forgive sins or not. When he allowed his disciples to break the Sabbath by gathering and eating heads of grain (Mark 2:23ff), he forced those who confronted him to make a tough choice: is Jesus merely a rabbi authorized to teach, or is he truly the Lord of the Sabbath he claimed to be?

The key difference between Jesus and all other teachers is that, while most master the particular subject they teach, Jesus is himself the subject he is teaching. He not only instructs, but he also embodies—he is—the truth that is being revealed. All rabbis taught the word of God to their followers, as even Jesus indicated when he said to his disciples, "the teachers of the law sit in Moses' seat. So you must obey them and do everything they tell you to do" (Matthew 23:2–3). But teachers can make mistakes; they can let their own agendas or perceptions get in the way of their teaching. According to Jesus, the teachers of the law had abused their role by emphasizing the less important and ignoring the essentials, like justice, mercy, and faithfulness (Matthew 23:23). Because of this, he tells his disciples not to call anyone else "teacher, for you have one Teacher, the Christ" (Matthew 23: 10). Why is he the one and only Teacher? How is he essentially different from the others? Is it only because his teaching priorities are better—because he teaches the weightier matters of the law rather than becoming sidetracked by non-essentials? Or is it just because he's an authentic teacher, one who lives by his own teaching? Neither, though both of these are true. He is different because he doesn't just teach us *about* the word of God; he is the Word of God. He is Immanuel—"God with us"—and we must not only learn from him, we must become like him. His teaching is yet another avenue by which the truth of the incarnation is revealed: he is uniting all things in himself so that he can radically restore our relationship with God.

Jesus himself makes this point clear. Though he teaches with authority, he does not speak on his own initiative, instead tracing his teaching to the one who sent him. In speaking to the Pharisees, he insists that "I do nothing on my own but speak just what the Father has taught me" (John 8:28). Here he clearly identifies himself as a teacher who has also spent time as a learner—one who is in sub-jection to the Father. However, a short time later, Jesus also claims that "the Father and I are one" (John 10:30). Jesus is a teacher—true. But he is also *the* Teacher; he is in profound relationship with God and is therefore the center of the teaching itself, its very core content.

Perhaps John captures this idea best in the opening of his Gospel when he says that "in the beginning was the Word, and the Word was with God, and the Word was God" (John 1:1). "I am the way and the truth and the life," Jesus declares, requiring us to accept that the *truth* is not so much an idea or a statement, but a person (John 14:6). It's a mysterious and even confounding element of his lessons that we nevertheless can't ignore. Instead of equating knowledge of God with facts to be observed and memorized, Jesus embodies a relational message. It's one of the most striking and fundamental truths about him. The Teacher draws people, not simply by rhetorical mastery or brilliant ideas, but rather by his perfect fusion of thought and practice, the way he couples instruction and character. The knowledge we acquire is not abstract, distant information; it is real and vital, and it must not just change our minds, but must transform our hearts and lives.

> "It is widely understood that people learn by example."
>
> *Alfie Kohn (2000)*

The implications of this principle are profound. While most teachers must resist the temptation to become the center of attention and strive to keep their students' focus on the subject matter, this is not true with Jesus. He is the lesson we must learn. His students aren't attracted to a set of facts or rules or a body of literature; they're drawn to the person of Christ. Attitudes of trust and heartfelt investment in Jesus are pre-requisites for understanding the Lord's teaching. Jesus' students are not sitting at his feet simply to learn a bunch of techniques and strategies that they can use to benefit themselves; they're drawn to the transforming power of Christ. They confess personal faith in Jesus, abandoning their old knowledge to become lifelong learners who are steadily shaped by the teaching the Teacher provides. Like him, they come to embody the teaching. Their love for the Bible and for knowledge of all kinds, if it doesn't grow out of a love of Jesus, is worthless.

113

The Lord's Supper: The Lesson & the Lesson-Giver

Since Jesus is the Teacher—since it is not merely his words, but also his life itself that instructs us—we must be open to his teaching on a number of levels. Some facets of his teaching are comfortable for us; others will challenge us to learn in unaccustomed ways. But one thing is certain: for Jesus' students, receiving instruction is more a matter of accepting transformation than of merely getting information. And to be transformed, we must learn the lesson of his life and become like him. Nowhere are the transformative implications of Christ's dual nature as teacher and lesson more evident than in the Passover meal he shared with his disciples just before his death.

Although John's Gospel doesn't tell about the institution of the Lord's Supper, it narrates one of the most remarkable events occurring that night—Jesus' washing of the disciples' feet (John 13:1–17). Here Jesus teaches by example, by visual aid, which is a common teaching practice even today. But what he does goes beyond that. This was not merely a case of a good teacher using a dramatic device to aid retention. The fact that a teacher, or master, would stoop to wash his subordinates' feet shocked them so much that Peter cried out in protest. It would be as if one of us were entertaining our mayor or senator in our home and found the distinguished guest cleaning up crumbs on the floor or scrubbing the toilets. We would admire the humility while at the same time feeling embarrassed and horrified. Why? Because we have an innate sense that some people are too important, too big, to stoop into our ordinary lives. Some are meant to serve, others to be served. While teachers are "servants" in the sense that they serve knowledge to others, they are respected for that knowledge, and we are used to giving them respect. The organization of most classrooms sends this hierarchical message: the teacher stands at the front, often on a raised dais, and the students sit below. When we are small, if we act disrespectfully, the teacher sends us to the principal. Often,

114

notes are sent home to our parents informing them of the degree of respect we've shown our teachers. This message that teachers are above us and are worthy of our honor is communicated to us at an early age, and the disciples clearly felt the same way when Jesus knelt down to wash their feet.

But Jesus didn't undo the message that teachers should be respected; instead, as the master teacher, he rewrote it, just as he rewrote all the rules. He wanted the disciples to be true followers of his teaching, true learners. He didn't want them to crave position and respect. To be sure, they offered him respect, and it is reasonable to assume that they would want to follow in his footsteps by one day becoming teachers with disciples of their own who respected them. That is the way of the world and its teaching. But Jesus challenged them to break free from the old order, to learn the subject matter in a completely new and transformative way. So instead of sitting at a table and telling them to wash each other's feet, he "got up from the meal, took off his outer clothing, and wrapped a towel around his waist. After that, he poured water into a basin and began to wash his disciples' feet, drying them with the towel…" (John 13: 4ff). By relinquishing his own position, he allowed his learners to relinquish their claim to position, as well. In other words, he didn't just want them to learn what he said—he wanted them to become what he did. Through foot washing, Jesus not only showed them the depths of God's love, but modeled for them a way that they could become the love of God to one another.

As we learn from the other Gospels, the eating of the Last Supper also illustrates Jesus' remarkable qualities as teacher and subject. He was gathered with his disciples to eat not just any food, but the Passover, a highly ritualistic meal filled with traditional foods and ceremonies, a meal instituted by God himself. For the Jews, the Passover was a critical teaching moment—indeed, that was the main point of the whole affair, as Moses explained in Exodus 12:26-7: "When your children ask you, 'What does this ceremony mean to you?' then tell them, 'It is the Passover sacrifice to the Lord....'" The meal was dominated by the re-telling of the exodus story, a lesson constructed to teach the children by all the means that divine Wisdom uses to teach: using words, story, worship, the elements of God's creation, and relationships. In a traditional Jewish home, the father takes the lead in the Passover ceremonies, but in this case, it would have been Jesus, as the teacher, who would have led the ceremony, and the disciples would have played the more subservient roles at the meal.

Perhaps because his disciples were so used to this tradition, and perhaps because Christ seemed to be doing exactly what they expected, the supper seems to have started off without incident. Jesus and his followers were "reclining at table" (Matthew 26:20) and eating, dipping their hands into communal food bowls (Matthew 26:23). Jesus was troubled and hinting about his approaching betrayal, but while this mystified the disciples, it doesn't seem to have stopped the meal.

However, suddenly, everything changed. In the middle of the traditional scripted Passover ceremonies, Jesus did something different. The Lord of the Sabbath began to connect elements of the meal and the story with himself, revealing to his disciples a fuller interpretation of *Torah* than they had previously known. He took the bread and broke it, but instead of talking about how the bread symbolized sudden flight from Egypt and God's provision in the wilderness, he said, "Take and eat; this is my body" (Matthew 26:26). Then he lifted the cup, recalling not only the cup of redemption from the slavery of Egypt, but instructing them, "Drink from it, all of you. This is my blood of the covenant, which is poured out for many for the forgiveness of sins" (Matthew 26:27).

116   In his instruction on the Passover, Jesus does much, much more than simply teach an abstract moral lesson. Once again, we see him fulfill the dual function of teacher and subject matter. Yes, he is instructing his disciples in a new way of viewing the bread and the wine, redefin-

ing these elements and reshaping how they are received. But at the same time, he becomes the elements—Jesus himself becomes the bread and wine. It is his body; it is his blood. He is, in a very real way, both the curriculum and the teacher. And this is a radical departure from the teaching practices of his time—and ours.

Once again, we see the world-rejecting and world-affirming elements of Christ here in this story. Jesus chooses a very old, very established custom of his culture—Passover. It is a tradition that his disciples, and others, will accept without question. This very world-affirming gesture enjoys the elements of God's creation within a warm atmosphere of home and family. It celebrates the ongoing story of God's gracious provision of salvation and help in this world. And yet Christ modifies the custom, using terms guaranteed to be offensive—the taboo against drinking blood runs deep in Jewish culture, and cannibalism is an equally abhorrent practice. While seeming to embrace a common cultural practice, Jesus simultaneously rejects the world, demanding that his followers trust him and trust his teaching, even to the point of overcoming deep misgivings based on cultural norms. This issue of eating his body and drinking his blood caused many to turn away (John 6: 66), yet Jesus calls his true students to transcend what they do not understand and trust him, whatever the issue might be; only in doing so will they be able to surrender themselves to the transformative power of the Lord's Supper and learn the new table manners of its host.

Teaching Because of the Teacher

What issues do the elements of Christ's teaching raise for Christians today? What are the implications for us as we struggle to reflect the Lord's glory in our own lives and to unveil that glory for others? One implication has to do with seeing ourselves as part of a learning community. We're Jesus' disciples, his students, part of a family defined by adherence to Jesus' teachings (Mark 3:34–35). The journey with Jesus on which we embark in baptism involves a lifetime of learning and growing. For the disciple, school never lets out. We have only one lesson to learn—Jesus Christ—but that lesson is as big as God's heart and as deep as a fully transformed life. No matter how old a Christian is, how learned or credentialed, he can never afford to imagine that he knows it all, especially since the real lessons of Christianity are not so much about ideas and facts as about changing character. This is one of the things that makes the Christian life exciting—there's always so much more to learn, so many frontiers yet to cross.

Many of Jesus' lessons are to be found in the places we've come to expect: Bible study, good preaching, sincere worship, conversations with knowledgeable friends, helpful books. Yet Jesus' students quickly discover that many lessons in discipleship come from unexpected places. Some of the Gospels' most poignant lessons occur in unlikely circumstances: the trusting touch of a hemorrhaging woman, the declaration of faith on the part of a Gentile centurion, the indicting example of little children. The disciple ought to be ready at all times to receive instruction humbly, whether it be in the form of a rebuke from another disciple, the stinging accusation of a non-Christian that the church is a bunch of hypocrites, or the naïve voice of a child, speaking in wonder about the stars or a butterfly.

> "The Christian community is a teaching community. In each generation it faces a new challenge: teaching emerging young minds as well as adult believers about the saving acts of God. Christianity is not only doctrine, but also a life, an ethic, a mode of behavior that must be taught and transmitted, from generation to generation...."
>
> *Thomas C. Oden (1983)*

For those who have ears to hear, the lessons come at many different times and in many ways. In school, teachers' lesson plans vary, based on the subject. In part, the content dictates the manner of teaching. Effective methods for learning math can be completely different from good methods for learning literature, and a setting suited for teaching sculpture will not be the same as one suited for teaching car repair. But these divisions don't pertain to

118

learning from the master. God spoke the world into existence by his Word, and that Word is everywhere (John 1:1–3). Because of this, Jesus' lessons are not just for the head, but encompass all of life. Learning them requires many different methods and a host of different settings. It involves learning Bible facts and basic doctrines, but it also involves learning behaviors and attitudes. Part of the learning takes place when we read or when we listen to our teachers and preachers, but part of it happens only in relationship, when we are fellowshipping with each other, praying together and being accountable to each other; or in a hands-on environment, where we're working alongside one another in service. Churches that are dedicated to the Lord's curriculum will not fall into the trap of favoring head-knowledge over heart-knowledge—or vice-versa. They'll acknowledge that both are important. Nor will they treat doctrine as something separate from practice and lifestyle. Instead, like Christ, they'll be deliberate about pursuing full-bodied programs of spiritual formation, ensuring that every member experiences constant growth in all the areas of life.

Another implication involves our role as teachers. Obviously, we are still Jesus' disciples today; we are still his followers, his students. But as members of Christ's body, we are also teachers. Communion provides a basic teaching opportunity. In the Lord's Supper, we "proclaim the Lord's death until he comes" (1 Corinthians 11:26). In other words, we have taken Jesus' place on earth as the ones who enflesh his word and teach it to others. One way we might respond to this calling is by reexamining our communion practices. What kind of teaching occurs when we participate in the Lord's Supper? In our churches, communion is generally a solitary event, presided over by a leader but partaken of in silence and introspection. While we have come to cherish this quiet time for meditation and memorial, our celebration sends certain messages to those participating and observing. We are telling those who come to our churches that perhaps privacy is the most important element of this activity whose very name evokes the notion of community.

In order to proclaim to others the Lord's death by our celebration of the Supper, we need to deepen our own understanding of just what kind of instruction takes place in it. At the Lord's Supper, the family dines together. Too often, we have viewed the Lord's Supper only as a commandment to keep or a set of facts to get right. Commands and facts are part of the story, perhaps a feature of our elementary education, but the unveiling of God's salvation is deeper and richer. As we have seen, in the early church, the Lord's Supper was an opportunity for ministry, a time of welcome to the bounty of God's salvation and a time when Christians celebrated both the kingdom's ultimate realization and its increasing presence in the here and now.

> "Teaching a Christian how to live depends less on words than on daily example."
>
> *Basil of Caesarea (373)*

In the Supper, we also gather with the Teacher to learn new table manners—manners that include graciousness and hospitality. Christ epitomizes the behavior expected of those who sit and dine at his table. By washing feet, distributing the bread of his body as nourishment, and blessing the cup of his blood as an offering poured out for many, Jesus makes it clear that his whole life is essentially about serving others. Through our participation in the meal, we enact his sacrificial example, stepping into the story of Jesus' death. We take our fill of Jesus by learning how to empty ourselves. We share food in common fellowship, recalling that all are invited to receive the blessings of God due to the generosity and example of our great Host. In our lives, we often find it difficult to welcome those who look strange to us, and we shy away from people who act "differently." If the truth were told, most of us would have to admit that there are some people we simply can't stand—perhaps for good reasons according to the world's standards. But as we feast together, we take our nourishment from the Bread of Life himself, rejecting the spoiled food of this world, with its toxic ingredients of hate, discrimination, rivalry, and suspicion. As an antidote to that poisonous diet, we extend the presence of Christ to one another, recommitting ourselves to practices of peace and hospitality and acceptance.

Perhaps there are ways in which our participation in this sacred ceremony of the Lord's Supper could also help deepen others' understanding of who we are and of who we are becoming—not through words, but through lived action, just as Jesus did. In one congregation, that might look like a love feast to which outsiders are invited; in another, it might involve having each person turn and speak to someone while taking communion; in another, it might involve rearranging the chairs in an effort to reclaim the familial atmosphere that characterized the Passover celebrations and house-church gatherings of the first century. The methods will vary with location and culture and ultimately aren't the features on which we must focus. What's important is the spirit of instruction: the awareness that, to teach, we must take on the person of Christ. Like the Passover, the Lord's Supper could be one of our best teaching and learning opportunities, where anyone present—not only the baptized who partake, but also our children and even non-Christians who are present—can experience the very presence of Christ and learn more of him. Especially in the intimate moment of communion, we must remember the heart of the master, who welcomed the outsider, the downcast, and the needy one to come learn from him. The Lord's Supper is a training ground, a chance to practice the habits of hospitality that come to characterize the daily lives of Jesus' students.

Life in the Classroom

A further implication of Jesus' example as teacher involves the place of specially designated teachers among us. Though in a sense all disciples are on the same level before Christ, we shouldn't let our cultural biases about equality and our love of personal freedom lead us to forget that God always shapes some of his people to become our leaders and teachers. Over time, by God's

121

grace, some disciples acquire special measures of wisdom and are gifted by God to be teachers (Romans 12:7; Ephesians 4:11). The responsibility is a serious one (James 3:1), and the best teachers are those who remain humble learners all their lives. They're people who demonstrate not only factual knowledge about scripture and doctrine, but also a strong dedication to Christ, their lives taking on the shape of his curriculum in impressive ways. Like Paul, they become people to learn from and imitate (1 Corinthians 11:1), not because they're infallible or all-knowing, but as guides who point the way, they're instruments of Christ's teaching program in the church. Churches should invest deeply in the business of equipping and empowering their preachers and teachers, respecting the authority of their wisdom—and keeping them accountable to the example of the Master Teacher.

However, in our emphasis on teaching, we must acknowledge that facts and arguments, while valuable, cannot save us. From fill-in-the blank Bible school curriculum to Bible Bowl activities for children, our focus has often been on facts. Our tradition in the Churches of Christ has tended towards an emphasis on argument and rhetorical strategies, as well. Our church lobbies may be filled with tracts on how to win arguments with members of other faiths. Many of us grew up learning proof texts for various doctrines, and we have always considered sound doctrine to be vitally important. Is baptism essential for salvation? Does faith save, or do works play a role? Some issues such as these are clearly essential, yet if we argue them with an angry and divisive spirit, or if we treat them as mere facts to be appropriated and learned, we can lose sight of the "weightier matters" like justice and mercy. Doctrinal conclusions become objects that we master and manipulate, losing any connection to that which shows us their proper use and purpose—the full context of Jesus' life and teaching. Jesus as teacher continually rejected the myth that facts and arguments were the path to truth, even though he was well-versed in scripture and certainly could hold up his end of an argument. Over and over, Jesus taught that finding the path to truth begins with a seeking heart which longs for relationship with him. He taught that those who wanted to learn from him must be humble, trusting, and confessional.

Therefore, as we encounter others, we must be careful about how we try to teach them. One of Christ's most important lessons is that our methods for teaching are as important as our message. To gain a disciple through coercive arguments by which we overwhelm that person's reason but leave his or her heart untouched is both short-sighted and wrong. It shows that we have strayed from the Master's model. Jesus never forces himself on others; he respects his students, allowing them to make their own decisions about him and his teachings. Our goal should be like Jesus'—to allow the person of Jesus Christ himself to become the subject which we teach others. Rather than just convincing potential converts to accept certain facts, we need to lead them humbly to the point where they are willing to engage with the person of Jesus, to introduce them into a relationship and to model for them how to walk in that relationship with Christ. Rather than presenting ourselves as masters who have all the answers and are never wrong, we come alongside others as life-long learners, eager to invite them to join us as we hear the words of the Teacher. We have to show people our own transformation—our own living out of God's Wisdom. The desire to learn truth and doctrine will follow, based on a love of the person of Jesus.

Conclusion

When Mary went to the tomb that Sunday morning to anoint Jesus' body with spices, she was dismayed to find the tomb empty and the teacher gone. Seeing the "gardener," she begged him to show her where he'd taken her lord's body; but Jesus only had to call her name and she knew his voice immediately. "Rabboni!" she cried (John 20: 16). The word is a form of "rabbi," but stronger.

It means "my teacher." In the intensity of the moment, she used the term she most associated with him.

What did that word mean to Mary? It was surely an emotional term for her. The possessive emphasis shows the remarkable connection she felt with this man whose life had been guiding her. She was up at the break of day carrying spices, not even sure how she would get past the guards and the stone covering, yet she had come anyway. Why would she undertake such a seemingly futile and potentially dangerous action?

Her heart was there in that tomb. The one who had challenged her to see with renewed vision because of his own renewing vision was there in that tomb. The one who had taught her, not only through his words but through his very being, was there in that tomb. And now, suddenly, he had emerged from what seemed a horrible violation of everything he had said and been and was standing triumphantly before her. He was a teacher she wanted to hold on to. When she clutched at him, Jesus gently rebuked her. But he was back—back forever, in a way she hadn't even begun to understand. Finally, after seeing Jesus, Mary ran to the disciples to tell them what she'd seen. She wanted to share "her teacher" with others.

When we fully understand Jesus' role as the Teacher, as our Teacher—as "rabboni"—our responses will be much the same as Mary's. Like her, our hearts as well as our minds are drawn to the one who not only teaches us but is himself the lesson being taught; like her, we desire to hold onto him, and although we can't cling to most earthly teachers, Jesus has promised, "surely I am with you always, to the very end of the age" (Matthew 28:20). Not only this, but as we hold onto Jesus, we become transformed more and more into his likeness—which is the ultimate intimacy. Finally, like Mary, when we are transformed by the teacher, we will be inspired to bring others to him because his instruction has been so valuable to us. We become teachers as well, guiding others to the classroom door—starting them on the great journey of discovery with the one great Teacher who will change their lives forever.

6

Seeking the Fullness of Salvation:
Experiences of the Atonement

> How can I pay my debt to Him who redeemed me...?
> In the first creation He gave me myself; but in His new
> creation He gave me Himself, and by that gift restored
> to me the self that I had lost.
> *Bernard of Clairvaux (12th century)*

*I read the Gospels for the first time in the winter of 1983,
while in the United States Air Force. The image that struck
a chord in my heart, as I sat reading in a fire truck on a
cold wintry day, was of a Jesus who heals broken people.
I had come to the Gospels as a restless and confused
young man, expecting condemnation. Instead, I felt them
inviting me to consider a new strategy for living. This
intrigued and led me to a focused search for the meaning
of life. In my search, I met wonderful people like Bruce
Cutshall, a fellow firefighter, who nurtured within me a
longing for God. Along the way, he instructed me on the
finer points of Jesus' teachings.*

*There was also a preacher I knew at the time. He
was very concerned about whether I understood all
of the key verses and essential doctrines. Though his
instruction helped, it didn't resolve a lingering question:
would I accept the call to discipleship, give up my current
lifestyle, and live a radically different way? It wasn't an
easy choice. I sensed that accepting Christ meant giving
up my self-absorption and following his example of sacrificial love. Moreover, I feared that it might turn me*

into something I despised—one of those self-righteous Christians. In high school, I used to think that Christians were nothing more than uppity moralists who checked out of society and hibernated in their churches. Now, I faced the dilemma of entering the Jesus-world, a world that both intrigued and frightened me. Eventually, I made the choice to enter that story, not knowing exactly what it might mean or where it might finally lead.

But I had become convinced that this new life meant wholeness instead of fragmentation, peace instead of anger, and connectedness instead of brokenness—though I would not have been able to name these benefits so clearly at the time. What I knew was that my life had been radically changed. I found myself right in the middle of God's story of salvation. Yet this created tensions, especially since I had inherited a way of talking about faith that tried to capture the whole story in isolated propositions. The more the church instructed me, the more the story seemed to change the image of Jesus as a healer of broken people into the image of Jesus as the revealer of facts, the one who resolved cosmic legal issues. That sort of teaching promised to guarantee my comfortable and settled status as one of the saved whose debt was paid, but the more I listened, the more I found myself being swept back towards the very fragmentation from which I had sought healing.

Fortunately, mature disciples like Aaron Holloway, an elder in a small African-American church in Homestead, Florida, showed me that faith has as much to do with relationship as it does with propositions. He patiently led me from quick assumptions to a healthy and sustainable diet, and he helped me realize that God's story of salvation amounts to more than a legal payoff or a life of holding onto a body of facts. Salvation unveils a new lifestyle, a rich process in which people experience healing and growth. Thanks to him, the gospel took on new meaning—which was really its old meaning for me, going back to that wintry day in the fire truck. Aaron helped me experience salvation as a matter of relationship and an ongoing process, not simply a legal affair.

126

Frederick

Experiencing the transformative power of Jesus opens up a radically new world to inhabit. Forgiveness implies a fresh start and an invitation to see the world anew through the eyes of a crucified and resurrected Lord. In time, we learn a new language and a new set of practices. We also realize the complexity of growing into this new way of life, inquiring about the nature and scope of salvation. As the freshness of the baptismal experience wears off, we seek to clarify the meaning and direction of our Christian lives. Yet sometimes conflicting voices abound, disorienting us. What is life after baptism supposed to be like? What is the nature of salvation, and how does it work?

We talk about salvation in different ways: forgiveness of sin, eternal life, divine healing, rescue from demons, adoption as children, movement from darkness to light, spiritual journey, establishment of kingdom—all these phrases highlight different biblical aspects of salvation. Of course, in some ways, the event of salvation eludes comprehensive understanding. Even scripture contains different ways of describing the work of Christ. But since the very beginning, in the Apostles' first proclamations of the Good News on Pentecost and in the earliest written accounts of Jesus' life that we have, one element has dominated the picture: the cross of Christ.

The Gospels have been described as passion narratives with long introductions. "Passion" means "suffering," and the subject of Jesus' suffering seems to be of paramount importance to the Gospel writers. Though they relate the story of a man who lived for over 30 years, each of them gives a seemingly disproportionate amount of space to the last week of his life, leading up to his suffering and death. Nearly half of John's Gospel focuses on this period (John 12–21), and though Mark is famous for moving from one scene to the next at breakneck speed, when it comes to the episodes of Jesus' suffering, the action slows down to meditate on the details of each moment (Mark 14–16). And it isn't just the Gospel writers who do this. The missionary Paul saw himself as a painter whose basic job was to portray Jesus Christ as crucified (Galatians 3:1). From

127

Acts to Revelation, references to Jesus' suffering and death abound, as if the cross provided early Christians with a key for understanding how Jesus' experience plays into our own salvation.

When the New Testament writers reflected on their own scriptures—the Old Testament—in order to understand God's work of salvation, they showed a preference for texts and images that would help them capture the meaning of Jesus' sufferings in God's plan. They saw in Christ the faithful servant of Isaiah 52:13–53:12, a broken and suffering one whose wounds would accomplish the healing of us all (1 Peter 2:24). But Jesus' early disciples didn't arrive at these conclusions on their own; Jesus held the cross before them. As we saw in Chapter 3, throughout his ministry, Jesus proclaimed that the way to true health leads through suffering and that new life comes only to those ready to die each day. His unjust and inhumane death drove that message home, providing his disciples with a pattern to imitate. Repeatedly, he forecasted the outcome of his ministry, predicting that "he must go to Jerusalem and suffer many things...and that he must be killed" (Matthew 16:21). The Gospel narratives reflect this understanding, building the climax of their stories around the pivotal moment of Jesus' death.

When Jesus finally arrived at Golgotha, the sick horrors accompanying a world reveling in sin were depicted in the wounds upon his body, in the scorn and abuse of his persecutors, and in the lonely anguish of his cry, "My God, my God, why have you forsaken me?" As the sky darkened and the earth rumbled, the image of Jesus of Nazareth, dying upon a cross, struck different people in different ways. To most of the Romans, a petty but potentially dangerous renegade was being dealt with. To many of the Jewish leaders, a troublesome religious reformer and blasphemer was being put out of the way. For most of the disciples, scattered and hiding, their own dreams of a vibrant and just kingdom upon the earth were vanishing like early morning mist in the harsh light of day. As for Mary, the sharp sword that had been suspended over her soul since Jesus' infancy had finally fallen, cutting deep. One condemned criminal, sharing Jesus' fate, spoke cruel taunts out of his bitter despair and rage—yet another saw in the dying Jesus a companion and a symbol of God's hope and mercy. And one centurion, alone of all other human beings in the narrative of Mark's Gospel, declared at the foot of the cross, "Surely this man was the Son of God!"

People have reacted in different ways to the image of the cross, but it is that image, more than any other, with which those who hear the gospel story have to reckon. The Christian faith insists that Jesus' death accomplished something significant. It comes as no surprise that Christians have used the symbol of the cross to draw people (John 12:32–33). The cross has become the defining symbol of Christianity, showing up in our art and architecture, in popular and in very personal iconography.

But in order to glimpse the full picture of salvation, we must see the cross as part of a much bigger landscape. It is not just the death of a human being, however tragic or painful, that delivers our salvation, but it is the death of Jesus Christ—the participation of God himself in human suffering and death—that reconciles us to our creator. This realization draws us to see the broader picture of salvation that this book has been attempting to portray, one focused not just on the cross, but involving the incarnation and Jesus' life, his ministry and teaching, and his resurrection and expanding Lordship. In other words, like each of these others, the cross reveals the full gospel (1 Timothy 3:16; 1 Corinthians 15:1–8). One way to expand our vision so that we can see the whole picture is to peer through some of the different windows from which people have glimpsed the atonement, seeing the implications of these vantages for our perspectives on this central Christian truth.

129

Images of Salvation

The history of Christian thought is the story of how people at different times developed very different—but biblical—images and metaphors of salvation. As we will see, biblical images of salvation address particular experiences. Over the years, people have caught glimpses of various images of salvation in scripture, interpreting and developing them in different social, political, and historical settings. What we learn is that the glory of salvation is broad and mysterious, eluding our attempt to capture it in any one image. Thus, the church has never sanctioned only one view of salvation, even while it has always affirmed the basic truth that God was decisively reconciling the world to himself through Jesus Christ (2 Corinthians 5:19).

Scripture's diverse images of salvation connect it to our varied human experience. Salvation is usually described as *atonement*, telling how the work of Christ repairs or reconciles the broken relationship between God and us. However, such language easily slips into an excessive focus on an event—such as the death of Christ—without any real connection to his way of life. As Chapter 3 showed, discipleship involves us in the whole story of salvation. The sacrificial life of Jesus does not merely refer to a single event but includes the entire character of his life, including his death, burial, and resurrection.

Though scripture contains multiple images of salvation, the foundation of them all is God's love, a love that clarifies the unveiling of this amazing reality, grounding the teaching and ministry of Jesus Christ (John 3:14–17). We love because God first loved us (1 John 4:9–10). His love compels him to seek a renewed relationship with us. None of the images we are about to explore can be fully appreciated without recognizing God's love as the basis of Christ's work.

God's plan for salvation was a "mystery," a wonderful arrangement hidden from humanity but revealed in Christ. It involved the unveiling of this "mysterious design which for ages was hidden in God," gathering and reconciling "all things in the heavens and on earth into one under Christ's headship" (Ephesians 3:10; 1:10; Colossians 1:20). As we saw in Chapter 1, the end result of God's work of salvation in the incarnation of Christ is the fashioning of a new humanity. This work can be described in many different ways, but most of them fit under four key images that run through scripture and also feature prominently in history. These images have captured the imaginations of different ages, as particular generations of Christians discover that one portrait or another speaks to their needs in especially meaningful ways. However, an exploration of other biblical portraits can challenge and correct the distorted vision we get from relying solely on one depiction. With this in mind, this chapter turns to study four basic ways of understanding salvation, attempting to find in the last one an image that captures all the rest in a fuller reflection of the unveiling of God's glory.

Salvation as Satisfaction

The image of salvation as *satisfaction* describes the work of Christ as changing God's attitude toward our sin. Paul often construes salvation in this way. Anselm of Canterbury, an eleventh-century theologian, drew on some of Paul's language to articulate one of the most famous and enduring expressions of salvation as satisfaction. For Anselm, the image of satisfaction reflected the historical setting of feudal lords. God relates to humans like a medieval nobleman does to serfs; if we violate the honor and dignity of God, then reparations must be made. Justice demands satisfaction! God created us to honor him through loving obedience, but the inception of sin in the world dishonored God. Since we are incapable of repairing the situation ourselves, God becomes human in order to pay our debt of obedience and death. Jesus' perfect obedience restores God's honor and paves a path of forgiveness for us, opening the way for a renewed relationship of faithful service to the Lord who protects and blesses us.

131

A related understanding sees salvation primarily as a legal transaction. The basic idea is that sin is a transgression against God's law. Because of our sinfulness and God's perfect justice, we are subject to God's wrath and judgment. In this regard, Jesus Christ dies on our behalf, taking upon himself the penalty for our sin. The death of Jesus changes God's attitude toward us rather than changing something in us. Jesus, in essence, appeases the wrath of God and sets forth a favorable verdict for us. He is "the lamb of God who takes away the sin of the world" (John 1:29). As the Passover lamb, Jesus' sacrificial offering enables us to enter into covenant with God (Luke 22:20).

Is salvation essentially about changing God's mind and averting his wrath? Or does it reflect the activity of a loving God who seeks to change us? Obviously, such questions remind us of the tensions inherent in our attempt to grasp the nature of God's salvation. Scripture clearly emphasizes the image of Jesus as sacrificial offering, but the sacrifice does not manipulate and change God's mind (Romans 3:23–25). The antidote to our disease (sin)

Salvation as Satisfaction

"[Aaron] shall then slaughter the goat for the sin offering for the people....In this way he will make atonement...because of the uncleanness and rebellion of the Israelites, whatever their sins have been."

Leviticus 16:15–16

"God presented him as a sacrifice of atonement, through faith in his blood. He did this to demonstrate his justice, because in his forbearance he had left the sins committed beforehand unpunished."

Romans 3:25

"Every one who sins must repay to God that he has taken away, and this is the satisfaction that every sinner owes to God.... If then...no one save God *can* make it and no one save humanity *ought to* make it, it is necessary for a God-Man to make it....What more proper than that, when he beholds so many of them weighed down by so heavy a debt...he should remit the debt incurred by their sins...."

Anselm of Canterbury (c. 1098)

"Man by himself cannot deal with his own guilt. He must have help from the outside. In order to forgive himself, he must have forgiveness from the one he has offended.... That, then, is the whole reason for the cross."

Max Lucado (1986)

springs from the initiative of God's love: "But God proves his love for us in that while we still were sinners Christ died for us" (Romans 5:8). Moreover, scripture connects sacrifice with moral transformation. More than being just the beneficiaries of a legal maneuver happening in God's mind, we are now free to walk in newness of life and to pursue righteousness through the sacrifice of Christ. In other words, the purpose of sacrifice was to make us holy—really holy, not just by proxy. Jesus "himself bore our sins in his body on the cross, so that, free from sins, we might live for righteousness" (1 Peter 2:24). In offering a final and definitive sacrifice, Jesus "has made perfect forever those who are being made holy" (Hebrews 10:14). The tendency to make salvation largely about God's attitude and his need for appeasement downplays the moral transformation within us that is an outgrowth of God's loving activity in Christ.

The image of salvation as satisfaction rightly stresses God's goal of addressing the cosmic effects of sin and restoring the divine order. Justice and salvation are tied together. However, the image can also create a chasm between the Father and the Son. In essence, satisfaction equates restoring the honor of God the Father with placating his wrath. The picture of an angry God who needs to be pacified by the Son tends to reduce salvation to a transaction rather than a loving act that cements an ongoing relationship with God. Though salvation has a dimension of justice, it is undergirded by love and has more to do with relationship than with keeping legal accounts in the divine ledger.

The notion of salvation as satisfaction has powerfully impacted our churches. Since Anselm's time, Christians in the western world have been prone to define the gospel in legal terms, seeing salvation as a case played out in the "divine courtroom." Martin Luther and other Protestant reformers adapted this image for the modern church, focusing especially on the role that free grace plays in the transaction. As heirs of this western Christian heritage, we vacillate between seeing religion as a matter of

133

keeping God's rules and ordinances and as a release from any obligation to suffer the consequences for our failure to keep them due to Christ's liberating death.

In this image, God's grace is seen almost exclusively as the device that nullifies the law's claim against us, narrowing down the Bible's rich presentation of God's grace until it amounts to little more than an exemption from religious obligation or an antidote to legalism.

> **The Language of Satisfaction**
>
> Some of the most common words associated with the idea of salvation as satisfaction: *justice, righteousness, law, justification, remission, debt, grace, forgiveness, substitution, propitiation, freedom.*

Ironically, despite their bitter wrangling, so-called "legalists" and "grace-based" factions in our churches today tend to share the same assumptions. Both have fixed their attention on the one image: salvation as satisfaction.

Although it may not be a complete picture, the image of salvation as satisfaction is a legitimate one. To be sure, Paul addresses the gospel from within a legal framework at times in order to deal with particular kinds of problems showing up among the Jews with whom he worked. This was due partly to their abuses of God's law and partly to their understandable concerns about justice. But in no way can we boil Paul's doctrine of salvation down until it is solely—or even mainly—about a legal transaction. The deficiencies of this image as a suitable foundation account for much of the antagonism between some groups in our churches. Whether the emphasis is on grace or on law, it is misplaced until it finds Paul's true emphasis: transformation. That is, the tension here between law and grace should be viewed under the lens of God's ongoing desire to transform us into his image and likeness—the new humanity.

Salvation as Victory

Everybody admires a hero, a champion who takes on impossible odds and somehow comes out on top. Salvation as *victory* develops the military metaphors in scripture, depicting Jesus as a cosmic Lord who defeats powerful forces of evil and liberates us from the power of sin. It is through the cross and resurrection that God disarmed "the powers and authorities" and "made a spectacle of them and, leading them off captive, triumphed in the person of Christ" (Colossians 2:15). We no longer fear death, since the devil, who formerly held over us the "power" and "fear of death," has been defeated (Hebrews 2:14–15). Jesus' repeated thrashing of demonic powers during his ministry illustrates his role as the delivering warrior, an image the Gospels make plain with statements like "Now the judgment of this world is done; now the ruler of this world will be driven out" (John 12:31).

The story of victory includes a depiction of Jesus as "redeemer," one who gave his life as a "ransom for many" (Matthew 20:28; Mark 10:45). As a part of the plan of salvation, God offers Jesus' life as a ransom for us, a price for captives who had been under the grip of the devil's power. The idea is that God had to deal with the devil under these conditions, as if the two of them were engaged in a discussion over the future of humanity. God's strategic move was to send his own Son, who hid his divinity under the veil of his humanity and lured the devil into a trap. As Gregory of Nyssa, a fourth-century theologian, describes it, Jesus' humanity is the bait that concealed the fishhook of his divinity:

> [T]he opposing power [the devil] could not, by its nature, come into immediate contact with God's presence and endure the unveiled sight of him. Hence it was God, in order to make himself easily accessible to him who sought the ransom for us, veiled himself in our nature. In that way, as it is with greedy fish, he might swallow the Godhead along with the flesh, which was the bait.

135

The miracles of Jesus persuaded the devil of Jesus' significance and so he desired to take him captive in exchange for us. Not realizing that Jesus was God incarnate, the devil took the bait, swallowing him up in death only to discover that he had ingested something poisonous to his system—the Author of life itself. In the process, he was incapacitated and dethroned.

Scripture's presentation of Christ as a cosmic victor has many practical implications. The work of Christ enables us to live without fear of death and so endows us with freedom to serve God (Romans 8:2). Liberation from cosmic forces of evil implies newness of perspective, a vision of Christ victorious and enthroned who frees us to live a godly life under his rule. The death of Christ exposes the falsehood of life without God. By following the logic of the old order (the fallen world), we seek purpose and meaning in the powers of this world, but these powers cripple and deceive us, facilitating opposition to God's thinking (Romans 8:5–8; Galatians 5:19–21). As Paul says, God has through the work of Christ "rescued us from the power of darkness and transferred us into the kingdom of his beloved Son" (Colossians 1:13).

The work of Christ also impacts the cosmic order. At the most desperate hour, the slain Lamb rallies the beleaguered army of Zion and leads them to defeat the hostile powers oppressing God's people (Revelation 14:1–5; 19:11–16). As participants in this new reality, we join in Jesus' victory over rulers, authorities, and "cosmic

---

Salvation as Victory

"The Lord your God is the one who goes with you to fight for you against your enemies to give you victory."

Deuteronomy 20:4

"In this world you will have trouble. But take heart! I have overcome the world."

John 16:33

"'I am the one who destroyed death, and triumphed over the enemy, and trampled Hades underfoot, and bound the strong one, and carried humanity off to the heights of heaven; I am the one,' says the Christ."

Melito of Sardis (c. 195)

"In heavenly armor we'll enter the land,
The battle belongs to the Lord.
No weapon that's fashioned against us will stand,
The battle belongs to the Lord."

Jamie Owens-Collins (1985)

powers of this present darkness, against the spiritual forces of evil in the heavenly places" (Ephesians 6:12). Our identification with Christ through baptism endows us with a new identity. We are now "seated with Christ in heavenly places" (Ephesians. 2:6). As a result, each day we engage the struggle afresh, but we do so with a correct understanding of just what is at stake, and we cherish our sure confidence that our Lord has achieved success. By claiming that success as our own, we are empowered to rebuke the Enemy boldly.

"Victory in Jesus" also has social implications. Jesus' healing miracles, his feeding the multitude, and his calming of storms clearly show his power and victory over the devil's domain. Jesus employs the power God gives him to snatch victory from the jaws of defeat in ways that rescue the weak and needy. The proclamation of the nearness of the kingdom, followed by concrete acts of ministry, confirms the ever-growing reality of God's reign (Mark 1:15, 24, 39). As victor, Jesus liberates people from oppressive social and religious regimes, as well (Luke 4:18–19).

The image of victory is important. It

> **The Language of Victory**
>
> Some of the most common words associated with the idea of salvation as victory: *redemption, redeemer, triumph, ransom, fight, victory, struggle, powers and authorities, liberation.*

emphasizes the reality of cosmic forces and evil powers at work in our world. It faces honestly the plight of a world enslaved to evil, a world incapable of saving itself. It also captures the spirit of Christian struggle, the sense we often have that the Christian life is a battleground. Traditional hymns like "Faith is the Victory," the children's song "I'm in the Lord's Army," and the contemporary anthem "The Battle Belongs to the Lord" demonstrate the ongoing power of this image for the church.

Yet the image of Christ-as-Victor is not fully adequate to put us in touch with everything that is happening in salvation. If taken literally, it raises questions about the devil's power—is there a real risk that God might lose a

137

fight against the devil? Also, the ransom idea raises questions about God's means of achieving salvation. If we see God as playing a trick on the devil, is deception part of his plan? Does the devil really control the conversation, dictating the conditions under which our freedom should be purchased? It seems illogical to argue that God hid Jesus' divine identity from Satan by veiling it in flesh, since in scripture the forces of evil seem to know Jesus' identity all along. For example, Jesus forbids "the demons to speak, because they knew him" (Mark 1:34). Furthermore, at times a preoccupation with military imagery has led Christians to misread the gospel as a call to become hostile towards others, perhaps even extending the kingdom by force and violence. Instead, victory in Christ must be tempered with the awareness that our combat strategy involves loving our enemies, and that "we do not wage war as the world does," but we use unearthly weapons of divine power (Matthew 5:44; 2 Corinthians 10:3–4).

For all these reasons, it is possible to push the image of salvation as victory too far. In spite of its benefits, it cannot stand alone as the foundation for comprehending salvation.

Salvation as Moral Example

A third image, when combined with the previous two, helps create a clearer picture of Christ's role in reconciling God and humans. Salvation as *moral example* proposes that the work of Jesus Christ is more about us than about satisfying God's honor. For example, the basis of the covenant relationship with Israel is God's loving initiative and holiness: "I am the Lord who brought you up out of Egypt to be your God; therefore be holy because I am holy" (Leviticus 11:45). The command to "be holy" stems from God's prior and gracious activity of bringing Israel out of captivity. We are called to be holy because the one who brings us out of captivity is holy. Moreover, salvation and holiness form a seamless whole, reminding us that following God is connected to all aspects of life. We do

138

not sever thought from practice or religion from daily living. Neither is salvation an exemption from proper behavior. Instead, we connect the story of salvation and life. In principle, the story of redemption forms identity, enables people to experience meaningfully the varied situations of life by providing an overall context, and highlights the celebratory moments of life. Israel's guiding story, after all, is the one about their salvation. The Lord's hope is that Israel will be people after his heart, emulating the God they have encountered in their own story.

According to salvation as moral example, the primary reasons for the life, death, and resurrection of Jesus are to provide a model for us and to elicit from us a response of love and holiness. "This is how God showed his love among us: He sent his one and only Son into the world that we might live through him" (1 John 4:8). As we saw in Chapter 1, the call to be truly human is also a call to be like God, and we see this vividly illustrated in the life of Jesus, who "has set an example" for us so that we "should do" as he has done for us (John 13:14). This is why scripture calls us to be "imitators of God" or, more specifically, imitators of Jesus Christ (Ephesians 5:1;

> **Salvation as Moral Example**
>
> "I am the Lord your God who brought you up out of Egypt to be your God; therefore be holy, because I am holy."
>
> *Leviticus 11:45*
>
> "This is how we know what love is: Jesus Christ laid down his life for us, and we ought to lay down our lives for our brothers."
>
> *1 John 3:16*
>
> "So great a pledge of love having been given us we too are moved and kindled to love God who did such great things for us; and by this we are justified, that is, being loosened from our sins we are made just. The death of Christ therefore justifies us, inasmuch as through it charity is stirred up in our hearts."
>
> *Peter Lombard (c. 1150)*
>
> "The whole life of Christ…excites the love of man, moves his gratitude, shows him what Christ alone was perfectly, and so makes atonement, restores between God and man the union which sin has destroyed."
>
> *Hastings Rashdall (1892)*

139

1 Peter 1:16). The point here is that salvation involves more than a sacrifice for our sins; it illustrates a wonderfully rich way we can live in the here and now.

For instance, the example of Jesus Christ is the basis for forming and sustaining healthy relationships. Paul's injunction to "be subject to one another out of reverence for Christ" (Ephesians 5:21) functions as a general principle for human relationships. It calls for mutual submission rather than an authoritarian and domineering approach, and the motivation for that is found in Jesus, because he was the one who submitted willingly to God and lovingly gave himself up for others. The end result is a community that walks worthily of the calling of holiness (5:25–26), one in which people forgive "one another as God in Christ has forgiven [them]" (4:32).

The sacrificial life and death of Jesus have saving power partly because of the moral picture they give us. Throughout his ministry, Jesus repeatedly tried to get his disciples to see his commitment to habits of humility before God and patterns of service to others (Mark 10:45). Within the Gospels, the image of Jesus carrying his cross becomes the picture of Christian discipleship, a picture of sacrifice and humility. Anyone who follows Jesus must "deny himself and take up his cross daily" (Luke 9:23). The key, then, is to keep the mind of Christ in our relationships with others: love, commitment, honesty, purity, compassion, and patience—all traits of Jesus' mind. The basic Christian model of willing submission is aptly illustrated in the life of Jesus, who voluntarily gave up his divine prerogatives, humbly submitted himself to God, and ministered to others in loving service.

One of the strengths of this view is the importance it places on living out the Christian story of salvation. Jesus is not simply a cosmic Lord who grants a legal pardon or a victorious conqueror, but rather a living example of the life to which we are called; he is not simply a liberator but also our model. Being saved implies changing the way we think and conforming to a new way of life. Our relationship with God involves daily conformity to the example

140

of Jesus. This image also reminds us that God's salvation is for the here and now, not just for some far-off experience in heaven. It entails moral instruction and gradual transformation. Wherever people are behaving like Jesus, salvation is breaking out in redemptive ways. Focusing one's love totally on God gives our lives renewed wholeness and purpose, freeing us from harmful habits that wreck our lives and hurt others. Acts of sacrificial love

> **The Language of Moral Example**
>
> Some of the most common expressions associated with the idea of salvation as moral example: *imitation, example, following Jesus, obedience, instruction, discipleship, Christlikeness.*

and service do much towards healing the hurts of our world and restoring God's peace.

The image also has problems, however, when taken to an extreme. For one thing, it focuses on the individual and doesn't easily translate into a social and communal setting. No one individual can fully realize the ideal of imitating Christ, nor is any Christian person capable of attaining his or her full potential for Christlikeness outside the dynamic context of the church. The writers of the New Testament understood that the example of Jesus must be realized by and within the body of believers. God has called the church as a community to the principle of loving obedience and willing submission in every dimension of life. The negative potential of community can be seen in the many social evils of our world, in which the effects of sin are clear. Yet isolating the cause of the evil is not a simple matter of identifying some individual who made a mistake—the social problems of racism, for example, are not due to the mistakes of only one person. Sin wreaks havoc on communities, distorting God's desire for *shalom*, "peace." The moral example model, in de-emphasizing the role of community, also limits its power to realize the full implications of atonement.

Another problem is that this image tends to reduce sin to a matter of attitude or even to mere ignorance, making light of sin's power and the deep damage it

141

inflicts on human character. The more modern version of this view essentially takes the cosmic nature of sin out of the equation altogether. The presumption is that, with proper training and education, we can learn our way out of a bind. This image tends to place a great deal of confidence in human ability and the strength of human reason. In the extreme, salvation can become little other than a person's willingness to receive instruction and change his or her mind. There is some truth here, of course. Sin is certainly connected to a rebellious disposition in our heart, but it also has larger cosmic and social dimensions that the moral example paradigm, when taken alone, does not address.

Nonetheless, the image of salvation as moral example does correct our tendency to reduce salvation to a legal transaction without tracing out its transformative dimension. Its imagery provides a framework that allows us to appreciate religious observances, not as matters of law, but as participations in Christ that propel lifestyles in imitation of him. As we have seen, if we reduce baptism and the Lord's Supper to tokens of salvation or boundary markers, we will be blinded from seeing them as means of grace that enable us to walk in newness of life.

Salvation as New Creation

One of scripture's images of salvation provides a holistic frame of reference for understanding salvation: the image of *new creation*. This image, like the others explored in this chapter, crops up as a major theme in scripture, and, also like them, it opens up one dimension of our salvation experience. Yet this image also offers us a chance to see a bigger picture, one that includes the other images but places each of them on the larger landscape of salvation. It not only respects the value of satisfaction, victory, and moral example, but it also provides a suitable way of holding them together so that they correct and complement one another. They take their particular places within the grander and more sweeping picture of

142

what God is up to in salvation: the business of creating and forming a new creation —a new humanity.

Salvation as new creation depicts redemption as participation. Jesus enters into and partakes fully in the human situation so that we can share in his life—the glory of God. "You know the grace of our Lord Jesus Christ: he was rich, yet for your sake he became poor, so that through his poverty you might become rich" (2 Corinthians 8:9; see also John 17:22–23). However, sin's distortion of the glorious creation of God—our unwillingness to live out the charge to be like God—precipitated the Creator's quest to restore what he had made and demonstrate for us what it means to be created in his image and likeness. The renewal of humanity was God's special dream, realized in Christ, who is the prime example of the new humanity.

The creation of the new humanity, then, comes through Jesus, the Second Adam (Romans 5; 1 Corinthians 15). As the First Adam's sin brought "condemnation for all," so the Second Adam offers the "free gift" of grace for all (Romans 5:15, 17). As Paul declares, those who participate in salvation as new creation realize that "the old has gone" and "the new has come!" (2 Corinthians 5:17). As we have seen, Jesus embodies a perfect humanity in constant communion with both God and human beings, and thus he

---

Salvation as New Creation

"I will give you a new heart and put a new spirit in you...."

Ezekiel 36:26

"Neither circumcision nor uncircumcision means anything; what counts is a new creation."

Galatians 6:15

"He became human that we might become like God."

Athanasius of Alexandria (c. 318)

"Christianity is very far from being a mere redemption from sin, or salvation from punishment, or selfish rewards for obedience. It designs not only to bestow remission of sins but to effect a renovation—a regeneration of the soul. Indeed, it is not too much to affirm that it can be a means of salvation only as it is a means of renovation...."

Robert Richardson (c. 1847)

provides a new model for us. From this perspective, salvation involves learning what it truly means to be human. Yet the model is not merely an example for us to follow, nor is our education just a matter of memorizing facts. By joining Christ and becoming involved in him and his body, a much closer connection occurs, a deeply personal relationship. We are not simply people who follow him; in Jesus Christ we are swept up and integrated into God's mighty work of forming a new creation.

The incarnation introduces the new creation, the cross paves the way for it, and the resurrection ensures our participation in the life of God. Unpacking the meaning of salvation through the image of new creation leads us to interpret the life, death, and resurrection of Jesus as chapters in the story of salvation, each of them equally important to the story. The climax of the story is still underway, the "summing up of all things" in Christ (Ephesians 1:10), restoring to us the image and likeness of God, which was altered through our identity with the First Adam. From this perspective, salvation is a matter of relationship, not merely a legal pardon, a cosmic victory, or a moral example. Our tendency to reduce salvation to gospel facts, victorious moments, or isolated acts of kindness divorces the divine from the human; salvation is the unfolding of "the glory of the Lord," in which we experience an ongoing transformation into the new humanity. Christ gives us the freedom to participate in this transformation. As a result of this gift, we aim for "the full stature of Christ," shedding our childish ways and growing "up in every way into him who is the head, into Christ" (Ephesians 4:13, 15). Christlikeness is now the new clothing we wear, and we continually help others try it on for size through our sharing in God's transforming work.

144   A major consequence of our participation in the First Adam's rebellion was a radical move away from the call to be like God. Consequently, salvation equals the re-creation of a world that had been distorted and a fresh start offered to a new humanity. Jesus succeeded where Adam failed,

modeling our true nature and restoring the likeness of God. We become children of God by being incorporated into his Son (Galatians 3:26–29). The point of salvation was not solely to satisfy some legal requirement, therefore, but to free us to participate again in the life of God.

This view challenges the polarizing notion of salvation as either a past or a present event, showing that salvation is more about relationship than it is about a moment in time, more about our nature and character than it is about our legal status. Seeing salvation as new creation connects the work of Christ—past, present, and future—and our experience in the here and now, so that we come to view all of life through this picture of God creating us in Jesus "for good works" (Ephesians 2:10). However, good works are the result, not the basis, of salvation (Ephesians 2:8). In other words, salvation as new creation involves discovering how participating in God's life hones our daily experiences and transforms us. We are defined by relationship, not by our performance, and our conduct is an outgrowth of that relationship with God.

Understanding the Experience of Salvation

We have become experts at segmenting life into saved and non-saved moments, religious and non-religious parts, or sacred and secular settings. We also have a tendency to over-simplify salvation by boxing it in through the use of either-or questions that don't fit the glory of God unveiled in Christ. When we segment our lives in this way, we make our fragmentation and brokenness even worse, missing the point that our participation in the life of God is made possible through relationship. Yet God calls us to a new wholeness in his Son. As "participants in the divine nature" (2 Peter 1:4), we see and share in the unveiling of "the glory of the Lord" and "are being transformed into the same image from one degree of glory to another" (2 Corinthians 3:18).

In our heritage, we have often tended to see salvation as static, frequently defining it as an accurate awareness

145

of facts and a correct observation of rituals and forms, or as the upkeep of faithful church membership, with the hopeful result of qualifying ourselves for entry into heaven some day. While we are beginning to correct this lopsided focus by stressing the experiential nature of salvation, overstating the experiential at the expense of the cognitive creates the same problem. The notion of salvation as the creation of the new humanity challenges our attempt to restrict the scope of salvation. It inducts us into a journey that captures every dimension of life. As participants in God's nature, we realize and experience a richer notion of humanity in which we worship God with all of our heart, mind, and being. Compartmentalizing faith and our experiences reflects the age of the first Adam, not the era of the new humanity in which we are participants.

Salvation delivers us from our distorted state and moves us toward our final transformation. Through the ministry of Jesus, God convicts us of sin, justifies us, and initiates us into a rich experience of and participation in the unveiling of his glory. In other words, justification (God's declaration of forgiveness) and sanctification (the process of God's transformative work in our lives), though distinct, are richly woven into the larger scheme of God's life. As participants in that life, we are now capable of fulfilling the call to be like God. The work of Christ eliminates obstacles from us, empowering us

The Language of New Creation

Some of the most common expressions associated with the idea of salvation as new creation: *renewal, transformation, new birth, spiritual formation, newness of life, sanctification, relationship, spiritual growth.*

to be "children of God," to share in his life, and to live abundantly (John 1:12; 10:10). Grace is not a "Get-Out-of-Jail-Free" card that rescues us from condemnation and ignores the need for transformation. Rather, grace frees and empowers us to flesh out our new walk with God, echoing the fusion of the divine and the human in Jesus, the Second Adam.

Salvation entails the whole mystery of God's plan, including the birth, life, death, and resurrection of Jesus Christ. Seen from this perspective, we quickly realize that our experience of the new humanity should follow the same narrative, the claims of which compel us to enact the story daily in our lives.

Conclusion: Is a Glimpse Enough?

In his classic exposition, *The Scheme of Redemption* (1869), the Restoration Movement leader Robert Milligan discussed all these images (although he treated them as ideas instead): Atonement, Destruction of Satan's Works, Christ our Exemplar, and Reconciliation— by which the hearts of people are transformed. Though Milligan leaned heavily on the idea of salvation as satisfaction, he also perceived that all these images occur in scripture and are major ways of understanding how God saves us in Christ. All are good for us. Each deserves our attention. As living pictures, they unlock dimensions of the spiritual life, enriching us personally and in our common life together. Each image empowers us to live authentically and effectively in the world, connecting our experiences with the moral, social, and cosmic dimensions of life. They help us to know God, and knowing God enables us to find ourselves and develop healthy relationships with others in the world.

However, these images are best understood as particular, rather than comprehensive, reflections of our salvation experience. They are slices of a much larger pie or facets of a rich jewel. We do not reject any biblical explanation of salvation, but we want to remain open to the text's full witness about salvation. The Bible appears to support the point that no single image captures everything that salvation is and does. Yet the picture of salvation as new creation is comprehensive enough to gather up the others, a vision that appreciates the manifold diversity of salvation's meaning, welcoming us into renewing and transformative contact with the living Lord.

147

7 Visualizing the Finished Picture: The Resurrection of Jesus Christ

> The first Christians staked everything on the Resurrection....
>
> *Philip Yancy (1995)*

A campfire without marshmallows. A bouquet with no scent. Chocolate chip cookies without the chips. Holidays without family and friends. Some things are just not the same when key ingredients are missing. No matter how rich and wonderful they may be, without that special touch, they just aren't right. They are incomplete. The Christian faith has many special qualities, key ingredients that give it its distinctive flavor. One element is so essential that Christians base their tradition of Lord's Day worship on it. It is a foundation stone, bedrock for the church. More than an item of faith, it is a pivotal event in human history. Without it, Christianity is nothing.

The empty tomb.

For early Christians, belief in the resurrection of Jesus Christ was integral to the Christian life. As Paul declares, "If Christ has not been raised, our preaching is useless and so is your faith.... Your faith is futile; you are still in your sins" (1 Corinthians 15:14, 17). The apostles' earliest preaching repeatedly refers to the resurrection: "God raised him from the dead, freeing him from the agony of death, because it was impossible for death to

149

keep its hold on him" (Acts 2:24). They performed acts of healing "by the name of Jesus Christ of Nazareth, whom you crucified but whom God has raised from the dead" (Acts 4:10). It was as if they could scarcely mention Jesus' name without saying something about the resurrection. The content of the Apostles' sermons varied somewhat from place to place, but this one element keeps showing up. Whether before the Sanhedrin in Jerusalem, in Jewish synagogues throughout the empire, or even in the pagan Areopagus of Athens, they preached the resurrection. The crucified one was still alive.

Traditionally, resurrection has been one of our favorite topics, also. Within our own heritage, the language of resurrection once saturated revival sermons and has enriched our hymnody. Songs like "I'll Fly Away," "Christ, the Lord, is Risen Today," and "Beyond the Sunset" tugged at hearts worn down by the woes of this old world. Victory over death and the hope of an eternity in heaven have inspired many to put their trust in Jesus and provided consolation for grieving souls in times of loss. Yet it might be observed that these days, many of our churches do not sing as many songs about heaven as they once did. In many places, preaching that passionately depicts heaven's bliss in exquisite detail is no longer as common, either.

Perhaps we've come to see heavenly themes as otherworldly and unhelpful. After all, the challenges and pressing affairs of daily life in this world are too acute to spend much time dwelling on the afterlife. This may help explain the shift from old-fashioned revivalistic enthusiasm about heaven towards contemporary worship and preaching crafted to address daily concerns in this world. People want to talk about the present benefits of discipleship. It is understandable that the recent focus of much of our preaching and teaching is on the relevance of Christian belief for life in the here and now. Yet the place of the resurrection in the Apostles' preaching presses us to reconsider. Since they refer to it so often, the resurrection must have been relevant to basic Christian living.

Or did they preach resurrection simply as an incentive, a carrot to entice people into faithful obedience—or even a stick with which to threaten them?

Perhaps we sense a disconnect between the topic of resurrection and the needs of daily life because we have neglected to notice that the cornerstone of apostolic preaching was not the topic of our own resurrection, but *the resurrection of Jesus Christ.* Revival preaching has tended to blend together the subjects of the resurrection and heaven. Yet biblical teaching about the resurrection, while it includes the hope of heaven, does not begin there. Instead, the apostolic message about resurrection finds its center of gravity in the event of the one, definitive resurrection of Jesus. To discover the relevance of resurrection for Christian living, we also must begin there. In so doing, we learn that the power of this miraculous event cannot be confined to the afterlife, since in Jesus' own resurrection we glimpse again the captivating picture that transforms us into the image of Christ in the here and now.

The End—A New Beginning

Jesus foretold his resurrection on several occasions. "Destroy this temple, and I will raise it again in three days," he claimed (John 2:19). When, at another time, his critics insisted that he prove himself by granting a sign, Jesus spoke cryptically of the "sign of Jonah" (Matthew 12:39–41). Apparently, resurrection would be sign enough. Like Jonah, Jesus would suffer a three-day sojourn in darkness as an indicted prophet, awaiting a dramatic deliverance and vindication as God's servant. When discussing the fate that awaited him in Jerusalem, Jesus predicted resurrection from the dead as the final consequence of the religious leaders' lethal persecution (Matthew 16:21).

151

The promise of resurrection runs like a fine but strong thread through the Gospel narratives until the story climaxes in the marvelous event itself, finally resolving the tense conflict of the plot. The growing conflict between

Jesus and his enemies, leading up to his death, had raised many questions: Whose message was true? Who would prove to be the genuine servant(s) of God? The humiliating and evidently powerless end of Jesus' life cast his claims in a very dark light. But by the gleam of Sunday's sunrise, all was set right. Jesus' resurrection vindicated him as one truly sent by God, for only God has the power to overthrow even cosmic enemies and raise the dead.

The apostles got the point. They fill the empty tomb with claims of divine vindication. They stress that Jesus' resurrection proves and establishes something vital about Jesus' identity—"Let all Israel be assured of this: God has made this Jesus, whom you crucified, both Lord and Christ" (Acts 2:36). After all, Jesus had spoken and acted as if he shared some special intimacy with God, as if he were on the inside of a very exclusive group—only divinity allowed. He even claimed the authority to forgive sins, something only God can do. Though for a time he seemed abandoned by God to an accursed death and the shame of the grave, in light of the resurrection, Jesus' claims are shown to be conclusively true. Raising him from the dead, God came down on Jesus' side. Through the Spirit, Jesus "was declared with power to be the Son of God by his resurrection from the dead" (Romans 1:4). In the resurrection of Christ, we see yet another picture of Father, Son, and Spirit collaborating together, finishing their work of salvation.

> "The Resurrection is the central theme in every Christian sermon reported in the Acts. The Resurrection, and its consequences, were the 'gospel'.... The miracle of the Resurrection, and the theology of that miracle, come first: the biography comes later as a comment on it.... The first fact in the history of Christendom is a number of people who say they have seen the Resurrection."
>
> C. S. Lewis (1947)

152   Yet each Gospel depicts the resurrection, not as a final conclusion, but as a new beginning, a transitional move in the story that opens the way for a new course of action. Rather than letting the resurrection serve as the final bow on the tidy package of a finished book, the

Gospels present the empty tomb as a doorway into some new adventure. Far from drawing the curtain closed on the final act of the gospel story, the resurrection enables the story of Jesus to continue, unimpeded, beyond the days of his ministry on earth. In Matthew and Luke-Acts, the disciples receive a great commission to serve as witnesses in an expanding mission to the rest of the world. Mark's Gospel sustains the tension of the story to the very end—will they join Jesus "in Galilee" for a life of ministry and discipleship? Mark invites readers to resolve the tension by their own responses to Jesus. In John, the resurrected Jesus breathes the Holy Spirit upon the gathered community of disciples, equipping them for an inspired ministry of gospel testimony, forgiveness, and shepherding. In each case, the resurrection represents the dawn of a new day in the story of God's relationship with his people.

In this sense, Jesus' disciples were incomplete before the resurrection. His resurrection empowered them, transforming them from frightened and confused people lurking in shadows, away from danger, into the bold and imposing witnesses that stirred the world. Their excitement is easy to understand. Their Lord had emerged from the tomb vindicated. His resurrection meant that Jesus was to play a special role in the fulfillment of God's plans for the world. Paul proclaimed to the Athenians, "He has set a day when he will judge the world with justice by the man he has appointed. He has given proof of this to all men by raising him from the dead" (Acts 17:31). Jesus himself promised, "The Son of Man is going to come in his Father's glory with his angels, and then he will reward each person according to what he has done" (Matthew 16:27). Jesus' resurrection established him as master of the final judgment.

Furthermore, Jesus certified the hope of resurrection for all the faithful. Whereas Adam brought death to everyone, Jesus by his resurrection reintroduces the promise of life: "Christ has indeed been raised from the dead," Paul rejoices, "the first-fruits of those who have fallen asleep"

153

(1 Corinthians 15:20). Jesus was a pioneer discovering the way back to life, conquering the most intimidating frontier on every person's horizon, the tomb. Christ's resurrection had great implications. It meant that he would be a major player in the final judgment, and it stood as a foretaste of what awaited God's people at the end of time.

Yet the resurrection also signaled that the transition from "this age" to the "age to come" was actually underway. A new era was at hand. The apostles treated the life and work of Christ as an end-times event: "He was chosen before the creation of the world, but was revealed in these last times..." (1 Peter 1:20). As they watched his revived body ascending into the heavens, they knew that truly all power had been given to him (Matthew 28:18). Their master had become the Lord, a celestial king reigning in majesty over the universe at the right hand of God himself. Behold, the day of salvation has come, and we are living in the last days! Now that Christ was raised and exalted, it was inevitable that his vision for the world would bear fruit, filling all the world. The signs of its fulfillment were already at hand. God had shattered death. In fact, it seemed as if, in Christ's resurrection, all of God's most extravagant promises were coming to pass in Jerusalem:

> On this mountain he will destroy the shroud that
>   enfolds all peoples,
> the sheet that covers all nations; he will swallow up
>   death forever.
> The Sovereign Lord will wipe away the tears from all
>   faces....
> In that day they will say, 'Surely this is our God; we
>   trusted in him and he saved us.'
>
> *Psalm 25:7–9*

Jesus' resurrection and ascension marked the transition, ushering the world into a new phase of existence by showing that his promises of a new order were coming true. Face to face with the risen Christ, the Apostles expressed their natural expectation: "Lord, are you at this time going to restore the kingdom to Israel?" (Acts 1:6). Jesus told them to wait for the promise in Jerusalem.

Very soon, it came, and immediately they knew that the world had begun to accelerate towards its end. The Holy Spirit, promised by the prophets as a feature of the last days (Joel 2:29), descended mightily upon the sons and daughters of God, empowering them to prophesy and heal, interceding for them before the Father. The Spirit created a remarkable community of believers who devoted themselves to God and one another, sharing all things in common. In the face of the end-times, possessions, relationships, and political power were given a new twist as transformation settled in. The disciples held their possessions lightly, expressing the generosity that comes from the liberation of resurrection. They took care of one another, valuing and serving each other.

The success of the gospel was phenomenal. The message was spreading everywhere within a matter of a few years, received by Jew and Gentile alike. The peoples truly were streaming to the Lord's mountain (Micah 4:1; Isaiah 2:2). All the signs indicated that the post-resurrection days were indeed the last days, and the Apostles bathed their proclamation in language describing their own times as end-times: "Dear children, this is the last hour" (1 John 2.18; see Hebrews 1:2; 2 Timothy 3:1; 4:1; 2 Peter 3:3; Jude 18).

The resurrection also transformed their experience of fellowship. In their meals together, they anticipated a heavenly banquet, remembering the promise of Jesus that he would drink of the fruit of the vine anew with his disciples in the kingdom (Matthew 26:29). As believers gathered to celebrate the Lord's Supper, they anticipated the messianic feast that would one day come, looking forward to the time when people from east and west would gather to dine with Abraham, Isaac, and Jacob. The cup of thanksgiving they shared every Sunday was a sweet foretaste of the wedding celebration of the Lamb (Matthew 8:11; Revelation 19:6–8).

155

The time was short. The gospel message carried a sense of urgency: "The kingdom is at hand!" Jesus' own teaching counseled wary attentiveness, for the end could arrive at any moment. "Therefore, keep watch," Jesus had said. "The Son of Man will come at an hour when you do not expect him" (Matthew 24:42, 44). Wise virgins were always ready for the Bridegroom's sudden arrival. Paul warns, "The Day of the Lord will come like a thief in the night" (1 Thessalonians 5:2). In Revelation, the Lord declares, "Blessed are those who stay awake and keep their clothes with them, so that they may not go naked and be shamefully exposed" (Revelation 16:15).

Jesus' resurrection joins the horizon of our present day with the imminent horizon of the end-times, so that the Christian walks each day in the light of that first Lord's Day morning. Since Jesus' resurrection, the universe has begun to move as never before, and the implications for believers and for churches who are caught up in that transformation are staggering, as we shall see.

United with Him in His Resurrection

The resurrection body of Jesus was extraordinary. He was basically recognizable, yet he could also remain incognito when he wanted to (Luke 24:13–16; John 20:14–16). He was able to drift through walls and ascend into the air, but he also had fish and bread for breakfast, and the wounds of his crucifixion apparently remained with him, open to the inspection of prying fingers (John 20:26–27; 21:12–15). The resurrection body of Jesus shows both continuity and discontinuity with his state of existence before his resurrection. After leaving the tomb, he was the same, only different.

It may be that Jesus' resurrection body gives us a sense of what our bodies will

> "Death for the Christian, it is sometimes said, is like the old family servant who opens the door to welcome the children home.... For those who know God and who are trusting in Christ as their Saviour and Lord, there is nothing to fear, and it is sufficient to know that we shall be like him and perfectly with him. Nothing could be more wonderful than that. Never fear the worst. The best is yet to be. When I die, it is my firm belief that I shall be more alive than ever...."
>
> *David Watson (1984)*

be like in the resurrection at the last day, since Paul says that we shall "bear the likeness of the man from heaven" (1 Corinthians 15:49). A precious treasure that Christians have is the hope of resurrection according to the pattern laid down by Jesus. The sentiments of modern hymns like "Because He Lives" and "Arise, My Love" resonate with the ancient words that early Christians used to recite at their baptism: "I believe…in the resurrection of the body and in the life everlasting." The promise of resurrection is timeless.

The empty tomb of Jesus reminds us that God has the last word over all other powers—not crippling disease or mental illness or violent crime or the horrors of war and starvation—none of these gets the last word. A life on this earth may be long and blessed, or it may be a bitter experience of groaning and constant longing for the earthly tent to be clothed in its heavenly dwelling (2 Corinthians 5:1–5). Whatever ravages the hostile powers

> "We are buried with him in the element of water that we may rise again renewed by the Spirit. For in the water is the representation of death, in the Spirit is the pledge of life, that the body of sin may die through the water, which encloses the body as it were in a kind of tomb, that we, by the power of the Spirit, may be renewed from the death of sin being born again in God."
>
> *Ambrose of Milan (381)*

may inflict on our bodies or on the bodies of those we love, the resurrected body of Christ infuses the Christian with hope that the body "sown in weakness" will be "raised in power" (1 Corinthians 15:43). Like Jesus, after the resurrection of our bodies we will be ourselves, only transformed.

The transformation has already begun. Christians identify with Jesus' resurrection both because he is the first-fruits of the final resurrection for which we all hope and because the power of the resurrection is working in us now. "If anyone is in Christ, he is a new creation" (2 Corinthians 5:17). Baptism pictures this renewing and life-changing power at work. It forms special connections to Jesus, involving the disciple in Jesus' life and experience. Rising up out of the waters of baptism, the Christian dis-

157

covers that the same Spirit that accomplished Jesus' victory over death has taken up residence within, imparting new life to her own spirit and bestowing the pledge of the final resurrection of her body (Romans 8:10–11). In this way, the believer also mirrors Christ's incarnation, for the Spirit has become inextricably linked to her life and living. Of course, such an identity is not about status, nor is it a static achievement; it is an ongoing witness of God's promise.

It is the believers' participation in Jesus that saves them. The resurrection shows us what that participation looks like, because the resurrection actually links the believer to the fulfillment of end-times expectation, the ultimate goal toward which the universe is headed: conformity to the lordship of Jesus Christ (see Philippians 2:10–11; 1 Corinthians 15:25). Disciples arise from the waters of baptism to begin a new life, the Spirit-empowered journey towards Christlikeness.

As a result of his encounter with the risen Christ (Acts 9), Paul concluded that the "mystery" of God's plan had finally been revealed and was actually set in motion by Jesus' resurrection. God established Jesus as Lord. Having risen from the dead and ascended to his Father, he sits at the right hand of God, enthroned over the universe. Everything is now moving toward a single goal. When the times have been fulfilled, everything will fit snugly under the lordship of Christ (Ephesians 1:9–10). This is the Spirit's principal work in the world. Whether testifying to the truth of Christ or convicting the world of sin, the Spirit is moving to establish the lordship of Jesus (John 16:8–15).

> ### "WWJD": The Discipline of *Imitatio Christi*
>
> "Imitation of Christ" as the hallmark of discipleship is a recurring theme in spiritual writing....
>
> "Now I begin to be a disciple.... Let all the dreadful tortures of the devil come upon me; only let me get to Christ."
>
> *Ignatius of Antioch (c. 117)*
>
> "Whoever wishes to understand fully the words of Christ must try to pattern his whole life on that of Christ."
>
> *Thomas à Kempis (15th century)*

We see the Spirit's best work in that regard within the Christian life. The Spirit works to transform character and lifestyle so that the disciple is a picture of Jesus, exhibiting the fruit of the Spirit's presence (Galatians 5:16–26). The Spirit brings the resurrected Christ into the life of the believer. Having died to sin, disciples discover what it means to be united with Jesus in his resurrection—it means an opportunity to offer the parts of their bodies to God, "as those who have been brought from death to life," to be living sacrifices, transformed through the renewal of their minds (Romans 6:5, 13; 12:1–2). To confess Jesus as Lord is not merely to claim a relationship with him; it is to surrender to a very specific aim—being shaped according to Jesus' image. Transformation into the image of Christ is the chief aim of the Christian life, and it is growing maturity in Christlikeness that validates authentic Christian experience.

Our experience of resurrection in Christ helps us focus on the true aim of discipleship, equipping us with quality-control standards that guide our priorities. How should we judge whether our lives and our churches are on track? What measurements are appropriate? Precise accuracy in doctrinal thought and practice? Numerical growth, bringing people in and meeting their needs? Worship experiences that are stimulating and emotionally powerful? All are compelling gauges of success. Churches plan entire strategies around aims like these, hiring and firing staff based on their ability to deliver on them. Yet none of these provide appropriate measurements for the authenticity of a Christian experience, whether the experience be worship, one's church involvement, daily life, interpersonal relationships, devotional practices, or whatever.

> ### The Discipline of *Imitatio Christi*
>
> "Everyone wishes very much to be a servant of Christ, but no one wishes to be his follower.... No one can love Christ who does not follow the example of his holy life."
>
> *Johann Arndt (c. 1610)*
>
> "I felt a burning desire to be in every thing a complete Christian; and conformed to the blessed image of Christ."
>
> *Jonathan Edwards (relating events of c. 1720)*

159

Paul clarified the immediate purpose of our lives in 2 Corinthians 3:18—"we, who with unveiled faces, all reflect the Lord's glory, are being transformed into his likeness with ever-increasing glory, which comes from the Lord, who is the Spirit." True Christian experience involves having the image of God reclaimed within us. "Be perfect, as your heavenly Father is perfect," Jesus said simply (Matthew 5:48), stressing not the ideal of flawlessness so much as that of being like God, having his heart. As he makes clear in his Sermon, people after God's heart will forgive as he does, they will bless their enemies as he does, they will keep heart and actions united and consistent as he does, they will see clearly the truth about what is necessary for real life as he does. This is the perfection that disciples and their Lord are working towards together.

> **The Discipline of *Imitatio Christi***
>
> "The object of the Christian religion then is to make men and women like Jesus Christ. To the extent that it fails to make us like Christ in our whole character, to that extent it fails to benefit man…. The great end to be gained here through the religion he has given us is to make ourselves like him in all that we think, feel, purpose, and do."
>
> *David Lipscomb (1867)*
>
> "I want volunteers…who will pledge themselves earnestly and honestly for an entire year not to do anything without first asking the question, 'What would Jesus do?'"
>
> *Charles M. Sheldon (1896)*

In short, authentic Christian experience always leaves a person acting, speaking, thinking, looking more like Jesus. It may or may not bring people in—sometimes Jesus attracted people; sometimes he repelled them. It may or may not be pleasant and fulfilling—joy abounds in Christ, and yet sharing fellowship with Jesus' sufferings is never likely to be pleasant. It may or may not impart a sense of warm intimacy with Jesus—sometimes, walking with Jesus causes the disciple to cry out, "My God, why have you forsaken me!"

The only clear sign that a person is sharing true intimacy with Jesus is the evidence that he or she is genuinely being shaped according to his image. This is the image the apostles repeatedly hold up to our attention, and this is the standard by which they judge the appropriateness of Christian decisions and behavior. "Your attitude should be the same as that of the Lord Jesus..."; "imitate me as I imitate Christ..."; "be imitators of God" (Philippians 2:5; 1 Corinthians 11:1; Ephesians 5:1). No other indicator, no matter how emotionally rich or intellectually satisfying, fits the witness of scripture. Stephen's experience illustrates this. It was at a moment of intense pain that Stephen was granted an astounding degree of intimacy with his Savior, as he exclaimed just before his death, "Look! I see heaven open and the Son of Man standing at the right hand of God!" (Acts 7:56). His direct experience of Jesus here comes as no surprise, since the moment of his death was also the moment when he was most closely imitating Jesus.

This is what God has predestined for his people: "to be conformed to the likeness of his Son, that he might be the firstborn among many siblings" (Romans 8:29), and it is towards this particular end that "in all things God works for the good of those who love him" (Romans 8:28). In this sense, God's will for a believer's life is plain. By the power of the Spirit who raised Jesus from the dead, he is transforming people according to the image of Christ, thereby asserting his lordship and expanding his kingdom.

Conclusion: Practicing the Resurrection

In the gospel story, resurrection comes as an unexpected twist, an unlooked-for resolution to the tension and conflict of the plot. It is the transformation of darkness into light, death into life. It turns the mistakes of the disciples and all humanity into an opportunity for a renewed relationship with God. Resurrection provides a second chance.

The same resurrecting power is at work in our churches. Whatever struggles and grim situations our churches may face, the story we are living out is not a new one, and we ought to remember that it includes the element of resurrection. We may expect unlooked-for transformations of any situation as God acts to vindicate the faith of his chosen people. His Spirit is working among us even now to bring hope out of the ashes of wrecked lives and discouraged or conflict-torn churches. This calls for trust in God, the kind of trust Jesus modeled. Going to the cross, Jesus showed us the folly of trusting in ourselves. Like him, we must die to ourselves and learn to trust the one who raised Jesus from the dead.

Trusting in the God of resurrection involves engaging in the practices of resurrection. We must meditate often on Jesus' resurrection in our preaching and teaching, validating the ancient tradition of Lord's Day worship by celebrating resurrection in our assemblies. We ought to behave as if we truly believe that our Lord is risen and ruling, that he is drawing all things to himself, us first of all. If God's will for his reborn children is to re-create us in the image of Christ, we should surrender to his will by cooperating with him. This means that we will use the aim of growth in Christlikeness as a standard in our personal lives and in our church ministries. Wherever we find other, counterfeit goals driving the agenda, as they often do, we need to identify them as distractions and re-center our focus on God's real work.

A prerequisite for practicing the resurrection is dying to self. Christian behavior is risky. Extending hospitality to strangers, resisting the urge to retaliate against those who threaten to harm us, giving up our money—spiritual disciplines like these leave us vulnerable. When we cannot seem to find the courage to take these risks, it is because we have not grounded our trust in the hope of resurrection so that we may surrender ourselves up for the death to which Christ calls us.

Practicing resurrection also means treating each other right. As disciples take up their places in Christ's living body, the church, we offer one another opportunities for second chances and fresh starts and accept them when offered. Because we are disciples, we act towards one another as Christ would act, and we also see Christ in one other. The church should be the place where we experience the living Christ in each other. Then, even in this world, we can know the joy that comes with the words, "Christ is risen. He is risen indeed!"

162

8

Conclusion: Power & Weakness

He withdrew from our sight, so that we might return
to our own hearts and find him there. He withdrew, yet
look, here he is.

Augustine of Hippo (4th century)

"Are we there yet?" Every parent with small children
knows the question well. Whether it's on a quick run to
the grocery store or a 1500-mile road-trip to the grandparents' house, no question gets asked more relentlessly
from the back seat of the car than this one. Kids know
that cars are for getting places, that a trip is meant to
end at a destination. The whole point of traveling is to
arrive, they figure, so they start to get impatient as soon
as Mom or Dad has pulled out onto the road. By the
time the same question has been asked 20 times or so,
parents are getting pretty impatient, too. Before long, at
least children and parents are in agreement that they are
all ready for the trip to be over.

The Christian life feels like an extended road-trip
sometimes, long and slow. If the goal is to be re-created
into the image of Christ, why is it taking so long? Why
can't I make better progress? Why do I slip backwards
so often? Or even, why can't those other people grow
up? We don't want to seem like whiny children, but we
sincerely wonder, "How much farther?" The question
is a legitimate one. After all, we only want what Jesus
wants. We want to serve him and be like him. We want

163

what is best, for ourselves and for the people we love. We work to acquire habits of focusing upon Jesus, hoping to gaze upon him until he fills our vision. Like Paul, we can scarcely wait "until Christ is formed" in us—and in the other disciples around us (Galatians 4:19). We long to be transformed into the elegant butterfly, but many days we feel like a dormant chrysalis, dry, crusty, and lifeless. We feel incomplete and unfinished, a feeling the apostles knew well.

A Complex Picture

In spite of the apostles' confident belief that the final days had dawned on the morning of Christ's resurrection, it soon became evident that the whole picture was more complex than they had at first believed. The resurrection was a great victory, overturning despair and inaugurating the final days of God's ultimate triumph. Even more glorious was the spectacle of Jesus' ascension into heaven. He had promised them that he would be returning to his Father, and before their very eyes he was lifted up to take his place as ruler over all the universe (John 20:17; Matthew 28:18; Ephesians 1:20; Colossians 3:1). There could be no doubt that the kingdom of God had arrived.

Yet in a sense, the happy ending had not yet arrived, and the golden age of promise soon began to show some tarnish. Over time, many people had accepted Christ, yet many others had not. Large numbers of Jews seemed immune to the gospel's appeal, even incensed by it. Many Christians were being harassed and persecuted in the most cruel ways—even as they proclaimed the victory of Christ over all powers and authorities. Not all was well. Some churches were models of the ideal end-times community, brimming with love for God and one another, yet at times evil flourished even within the church. False teachers ravaged the sheep. The wealthy exploited the poor. Christian slaves were at risk of mistreatment at the hands of Christian masters. Faithful wives struggled to cope with the difficulty of living with their non-Christian spouses. Injustice continued to exist all around. Perhaps worst of all, even committed disciples continued to struggle with their own sinful habits and weaknesses, confirming by their experience that the victory over evil was incomplete at best. And time stretched on. Sickness continued to find a home in the world, and death. The world had not been set right. The supreme finale to God's plan began to seem distant indeed.

In other words, the church gradually came to experience the tension between the "already" and the "not yet" dimensions of living in the kingdom. The apostles' reflections on the exalted lordship of Christ respect this tension. With Jesus' resurrection and ascension, the end is already upon us; but it is not yet complete. We live "between the times," awkwardly situated between two moments in history, the moments of Jesus' comings, past and present. In one sense, the resurrection has accomplished its aims decisively. The power that raised Jesus from the dead also placed him at the right hand of God in the heavenly realms, establishing his reign over all things. That same power has "raised us up with Christ and seated us with him in the heavenly realms" (Ephesians 1:19–22; 2:6). It's a "done deal," and we experience the power of that victory in many ways: every time a hungry mouth is fed in the name of Jesus, whenever a young person confesses Christ as Lord, in every Christian marriage where love and service vitalize and preserve a peaceful home.

> **Jesus' Resurrection: Bringing Worlds Together**
>
> "I see the appearance events as resulting from some kind of temporary intersection between the worlds of the old and new creations, meeting places between the risen life of Christ, which is the seminal event giving birth to the new creation, and the continuing life of the disciples in the world of the old creation.... The empty tomb also tells us something of the connection between these two worlds.... The empty tomb is of great theological significance, for it testifies that in Christ there is a destiny for matter as well as for humanity."
>
> *John Polkinghorne (2001)*

165

But an even more complete experience awaits us. Though the resurrection vindicated Jesus and sealed a new order, we long for the full unveiling of God's glory when Jesus returns to gather us to him. God is preparing his final judgment and the full revelation of his righteousness. Jesus is

> "I am the Alpha and the Omega," says the Lord God, "who is, and who was, and who is to come, the Almighty."
>
> *Revelation 1:8*

preparing a place for us in his Father's house (John 14:2). Meanwhile, the creation groans along with our own spirits as we grieve over the present state of affairs, trusting his promise but also eagerly anticipating the moment when "the children of God will be revealed," and we experience final "adoption as children, the redemption of our bodies" (Romans 8:19, 24). Paul directs our attention to a point on the horizon, a future instant, when the trumpet shall sound, the dead shall rise, and we will all go up to meet the Lord in the air. "And so we will be with the Lord forever" (1 Thessalonians 4:16–17). Kingdom dreams will become the total reality one day.

Isaiah pictured a time when none would worship any but God, with all peoples converging on the Lord's mountain to honor him. Warfare and conflict would cease as people beat their swords into plowshares, turning to more peaceful and constructive activities (Isaiah 2:2–4). He called these "the last days," and he did not see them in his lifetime. In a sense, Jesus opened up the last days, and we see them fulfilled in his life. Yet Jesus and the apostles also teach us to look towards the distant horizon to see the clouds that are farther away and to look for the complete fulfillment of God's promises. Meanwhile, along with Isaiah, they invite us to "walk in the light of the Lord" (Isaiah 2:5), to live like people whose inner sight sees the truth about where things are headed.

166   The genius of the prayer that Jesus taught his disciples is its timeless applicability for people living between the times. Even while the signs of the kingdom's arrival were popping up all around, Jesus instructed his first disciples

to pray for the still fuller expression of God's rule that was about to break in on the world. Today, even under the lordship of the risen king, his disciples continue to pray for the very same thing. And in both eras, disciples pray, seeking to be transformed by that prayer into people

> "Our Father in heaven,
> hallowed be your name,
> your kingdom come,
> your will be done on earth as it is in heaven.
> Give us today our daily bread.
> Forgive us our debts, as we also have forgiven our debtors.
> And lead us not into temptation, but deliver us from the evil one."
>
> *Matthew 6:9–13*

who are not only content to live under his rule but are themselves living expressions of his will. Strong tension still exists between the world as it is and the world as it ought to be. God's work in Jesus is bridging the gap and transforming us into what God intends. Should we expect everything to be fixed in the here and now, or only after the final end to the present era? Scripture upholds both expectations. The doctrines of Jesus' resurrection and ascension enable us to hold simultaneously our ardent expectations for a glorious future and our hunger to experience the power of God in the here and now. The world-affirming and world-rejecting dimensions of Christian discipleship discussed in Chapters 1 and 3 find their interconnection in the events of the resurrection and the ascension.

"We are being saved..."

Christians feel the painful tension that exists between the "already" and the "not yet," not only in the world around them, but also deep within. Whereas our essential identity is clear—we are God's children, destined to be like Jesus—our final appearance remains intangible, since the Lord is not yet finished copying his portrait onto the canvas of our lives. "Dear friends, now we are children of God, and what we will be has not yet been made known. But we know that when he appears we shall be like him,

167

for we shall see him as he is" (1 John 3:2). Meanwhile, we feel doomed to "see but a poor reflection," unable to realize the vision fully (1 Corinthians 13:12). The birth pangs Paul spoke of never seem to let up. We crave a full surrender to the virtues of faith, hope, and love, but instead we continue to struggle with anger, pride, lust, laziness, and doubt. Our distress casts a shadow on the joy we feel at the Savior's resurrection.

Baptism and the resurrection once again share basic qualities here. As pictures of salvation, they convey the sense of a sudden, once-for-all event of rescue and transformation. In a moment, we are changed into something new. On the other hand, in being raised up from the waters, we have experienced only a beginning, the first step of a new journey. Every step in the right direction is one toward conformity to Jesus Christ, yet the journey can seem long and slow, with many obstacles and false turns. Beyond the verge of Jordan is a wide world, fraught with perils and griefs.

Disciples of Jesus quickly learn that, embedded within the dazzling glory of resurrection, is the harsh reality of death. Jesus illustrated this when he said, "Unless a kernel of wheat falls to the ground and dies, it remains only a single seed. But if it dies, it produces many seeds. The person who loves his life will lose it, while the person who hates his life in this world will keep it for eternal life" (John 12:24–25). Jesus' disciples often misunderstood this principle. At the transfiguration, they were basking in the revealed glory of the Lord, and they wanted to build shrines of honor. Yet the Father interrupted the scene, commanding them to listen to his Son's message and true mission: "the Son of Man is going to suffer" (Matthew 17:13). The life of discipleship, though trodden in the glorious light of the Lord's Day morning, is still one of continual sacrifice and self-denial. Out of the agony of that sacrifice, a new day springs to life.

168

As we have already seen, salvation is not just an object to possess. "We are being saved…," Paul says, reminding us that salvation is also an ongoing, dynamic experience

(1 Corinthians 1:18). To experience salvation is not simply to enjoy the status of having been forgiven or to become qualified for entry into heaven. Salvation is the experience of "being transformed into his likeness," bit by bit over time, as we contemplate glory with unveiled faces (2 Corinthians 3:18). Like the first disciples, who were fully com-

> **Spiritual Growth— a Treasure Worth the Investment**
>
> "It is not appropriate that things of great magnitude should fall easily into our hands; otherwise God's gift will be held in contempt.... Anything that is easily found is also easily lost, whereas what is found after much labor will be guarded with vigilance."
>
> *Isaac of Nineveh (7th century)*

mitted to Jesus from the beginning yet always had more to learn, we find ourselves on a journey of discovery and growth. We learn to expect progress, but deep progress takes time.

When Paul expressed his desire to "know" Jesus, he was voicing a desire to share in his every experience—"the power of his resurrection and the fellowship of sharing in his sufferings." Yet even Paul had to admit shortcomings: "not that I have already obtained all this, or have already been made perfect, but I press on...," he said (Philippians 3:10–12). Paul saw the Christian life as a race, an athletic contest. Each day he strained to take hold of that which was already his: total identification with his Lord. Through the combined efforts of Lord and disciple, the goal comes within reach, though perhaps it is not fully realized until the very end. Yet Paul was confident that he could count on God to complete the good work he had begun (Philippians 1:6). Meanwhile, Paul learned to embrace even his most annoying weaknesses as further evidence of Christ's power resting on him, since in spite of them, God continued to accomplish his will through Paul. The Lord had taught him, "My power is made perfect in weakness" (2 Corinthians 12:9).

A life lived in the power of resurrection is one of progress. At times, radical transformation occurs in our lives, watershed moments in which we are dramatically liberated from some sin or addiction or make great strides forward. But not everything is accomplished all at once. Most of the time, God chooses to work through the developmental processes that he created for us in the first place, which are slow but constant. Peter reminds us that "His divine power has given us everything we need for life and godliness," demonstrating its presence through the steady addition of goodness to faith, along with knowledge, self-control, perseverance, godliness, brotherly kindness, and love. The sequence of these virtues is not the point; the point is to "possess these qualities in increasing measure" (2 Peter 1:3, 5–8), to be engaged in a process of steady spiritual growth.

Over the years, many who have written on the spiritual life have pictured it as a ladder. Through commitment, spiritual discipline, and surrender to God's grace, disciples move up, perhaps in small steps, one rung at a time, towards their destination: an experience of unity with God in heart, mind, character, and virtuous life. We are on a journey. We have not yet arrived but are making progress. The picture of Christ within us is incomplete, but it is materializing. The resurrected body of Christ provides not only the target for this progress, but also the power of transformation necessary to complete the journey. On this journey, the Christian community becomes indispensable.

> **The Christian Life as an Ongoing Journey**
>
> "The perfection of human nature consists perhaps in its very growth in goodness... the continual development of life to what is better is the soul's way to perfection."
>
> *Gregory of Nyssa (c. 357)*

The Resurrection Body of Jesus

In the last chapter, we observed some fascinating aspects of Jesus' resurrection body. Perhaps its most striking feature after the ascension was the way that it grew to encompass the whole community of people who had been united to Christ's resurrection through baptism—the church. The resurrection created the church, for the very Spirit that accomplished the resurrection of Jesus and who does the same within the individual believer has now come to dwell in the community of faith as a whole.

John's Gospel presents Jesus as the fulfillment or replacement of various Jewish symbols: the Messianic wine of abundance for the water held in Jewish purification jars, the Bread of Life coming down from heaven for Moses' manna, and so forth. The exchange that gains the widest currency in the New Testament is that of Jesus' body for the temple itself: "Destroy this temple, and I will raise it again in three days.... The temple he had spoken of was his body" (John 2:19, 21). The church has a unique gathering place—the very body of Jesus. Within the temple of the church, the Spirit is hard at work to complete the task at hand: consolidating the lordship of Jesus and shaping his body according to his image.

Incorporation into the body has many implications. As different people come into Christ, they discover that, in his body, the dividing walls of animosity that segregated them from each other in the world are demolished, and they find themselves pressed into a relationship

> "We must think of the post-resurrection body of Christ as a new kind of body because, in Paul's theology, the body of Christ incorporates an entire community of members through their baptism into his death and resurrection."
>
> *Carl Braaten (2001)*

of unity with their fellow humans (Ephesians 2:14–18). Jesus' welcoming attitude is meant to translate into open hospitality within the church. On this side of Jesus' ascension, "neither circumcision nor uncircumcision means anything; what counts is a new creation" (Galatians 6:15). Drawing on the strength of its own unity with the One God, the Spirit of peace works to create a bond of peace within the church, combining the different elements of embattled humanity, of every race and age and gender and personality type, into a single body (Ephesians 4:3–6). The church is one. Each member serves the same Lord, which means that the old ways of separating people out

171

by such things as wealth or education or social status no longer have a place (James 2:1–13). Yet not everyone in the body is the same. In order that the church may carry out its mission, the Lord has bestowed gifts on his people, enabling and equipping them for many different good works (Ephesians 4:7–12; see 1 Corinthians 12; Romans 12).

The power of the resurrection creates the same thing for the church as for the individual: an experience of growing maturity in Christlikeness. Yet as we saw in Chapter 2, no individual can be everything that Jesus is. It is through each disciple's integration into a unified body that the body together is able to attain "to the whole measure of the fullness of Christ" (Ephesians 4:13). Church leaders must share with Paul a burden that aches like the pains of childbirth: the passionate ambition to see Christ formed in the people of the church (Galatians 4:19).

Bewildered and distracted by the assortment of activities, traditions, and commitments that make up church life, it's easy to forget that the church's real business is to foster growth in Christlikeness, both in individuals and in the community as a whole. Again, the test of the quality of a church's program will be its effectiveness in shaping people according to the image of Jesus. This transformation can happen only when each member is connected to the other members, like joints sewn together by their ligaments, growing and building themselves up. As the parts move together—in worship, fellowship, service, with each part doing its work—the church will "grow up into him who is the Head, that is Christ" (Ephesians 4:15–16).

> "Christianity, though the most perfect rule of life that ever was devised, is far from being barely a rule of life.... It is being transformed into the image of God. It is being like-minded with Christ."
>
> *Hannah More (1811)*

172

Consequently, churches and church leaders that want to be cooperating with the work of God need to "keep in step with the Spirit" by walking in the light of the resurrection, the life that the Spirit provides (Galatians 5:25). This is not just a flowery sentiment. It has specific aims. Genuine living by the Spirit focuses resolutely on the business of forming Christ in people. For this reason, the teaching, preaching, ministry, and worship agendas of any congregation should maintain an unwavering focus on spiritual formation.

The church brings people together, not just to dispense to them the commodity of salvation or to keep them busy or to mobilize workers who will do chores or to help lonely people find friends. It brings disciples together to create a "body ecology" within which Christlike transformation may be achieved. It will give attention to the growth of individual persons, but it will also struggle to keep its members closely linked to one another. Such a church measures the success of its teaching programs and its service projects by the degree to which Christ is formed in members. In this church, people who want good worship are aware that good worship is worship that brings people to greater levels of effective Christlikeness. In other words, the church's task is to testify to the resurrection, proclaiming

> "Jesus left few traces of himself on earth. He wrote no books or even pamphlets. A wanderer, he left no home or even belongings that could be enshrined in a museum. He did not marry, settle down, and begin a dynasty. We would, in fact, know nothing about him except for the traces he left in human beings."
>
> *Philip Yancy (1995)*

and celebrating it through the evidence of new life being made available in Christ to members of his body.

The gathered church celebrates Jesus' resurrection in many ways. When the church gathers, the power of Jesus' resurrection becomes visible when the assembly renews tired spirits or when people are rescued from the death of sin into new life because of the instruction they receive. The church offers its prayers and its service to God in Jesus' name, attesting to its belief that Jesus is not dead. He lives at the right hand of the Father and is active in a ministry of intercession. Jesus has never

173

stopped working for us. His priestly work of intercession goes on continuously in the heavenly sanctuary. At the altar, "he always lives to intercede" for us (Hebrews 7:25). When we teach our children to close their prayers with the simple formula, "in Jesus' name, amen," we are subtly planting within them an awareness that the crucified Lord is risen and continues to oversee the expanding work of the kingdom.

The church also administers baptism, thereby professing the full gospel story in a single act, as we have seen in Chapter 3. Just as Jesus was the passive recipient of resurrection power, so the candidate passively submits to being baptized and raised up into Christ to enjoy God's victory over the forces of evil. Yet the connection is not a vertical one only, for in baptism a person is also joined to the body of Jesus. When the members of a church gather around to witness the baptism, they rejoice since the person being baptized depicts what they themselves have become—integral members of Jesus' resurrected body. And ever after in life, we can call ourselves back to Christ, reclaiming the comfort and calling of our salvation by remembering, as Martin Luther put it, "I am baptized."

Even in the Lord's Supper, we catch a glimpse of the exalted body of Jesus. Early Christians felt that it was important to share the Lord's Supper together at least every first day of the week, the same day they celebrated Christ's resurrection. We have already noticed the end-times dimensions of the Supper, how it anticipates the heavenly feast awaiting us. Luke 24:13–35 follows this thread in a profound direction: on the road to Emmaus, two travelers encountered the risen Jesus, but at first they did not recognize him. However, once they were seated with him at the table—and at the very moment that he took the bread, gave thanks, and broke it—"their eyes were opened and they recognized him" (Luke 24:31). This story underscores an important theme in Luke-Acts: the risen Christ is present with his church. He has not abandoned it. When the congregation gathers, the Lord is there, hosting the celebratory meal.

In Luke-Acts, meals tend to be sacred moments. The vagueness of the expression "breaking bread" shows how difficult it can be for the reader to determine whether a meal in Luke-Acts is "normal" or "sacred" (see Acts 2:42, 46; 20:7). Perhaps the blurring is intentional, and when Christians gather around a table, they are to practice the resurrection by observing in that moment a fusion of the world that is and the world that is coming to be. For those who have eyes to see, the simple sight of bread and the fruit of the vine at the communion table becomes a vision of the resurrected Lord. For those with keen vision, a routine assembly of believers becomes an opportunity to share the blessings of heaven's peace and comfort with others at the table.

A church that is baptizing and celebrating the Lord's Supper is witnessing to the resurrection story as power-fully as the closing chapters of the Gospels do—and even more tangibly. Yet the church's most spectacular display of resurrection power occurs when it cooperates with the Spirit in the work of forming Christ in its members and in being Christ wherever it is. More than any historical evidences or logical argumentation, the transformation of Jesus' misguided and bickering early disciples into a potent and unified force for carrying out God's minis-try of reconciliation in the world was the most striking evidence for the truth of the resurrection. And so it is today. By faith, the church has certain knowledge of the event of Jesus' resurrection. Yet it is by the dynamic evi-dence of resurrection power at work in its midst that the church engenders faith in others. The church's compelling testimony to the resurrection is the display of ongoing transformation in the lives of its people.

"Blessed are those who have not seen..."

The doctrine of the resurrection reminds us that God's salvation actually brings Jesus' life and death together. Like Jesus' incarnation, the resurrection holds together the world-rejecting and world-affirming emphases of the Christian faith. On the one hand, God's raising Jesus from the dead represents an indicting judgment against the world order that crucified him, offering the hope of final escape from that world in the resurrection of our bodies after death. We look for a new heaven and a new earth (2 Peter 3:13).

On the other hand, Jesus' resurrection body is in some sense the one that walked the earth and ate and wept and was wounded. Jesus participates in humanity still. And his is the body that is transforming the world here and now, since, due to the resurrection, it has become the one into which we are incorporated through baptism. Having been "saved through the washing of rebirth and renewal by the Holy Spirit" (Titus 3:5), those who live in-between the times, who walk on the earth in newness of life, testify by their present lives and words that the world is already being made new. Jesus was not just speaking hypothetically about a new world; it is real. The resurrection shows us that world and actually involves us in it.

Yet the old spiritual song plaintively asks, "Were you there when he rose up from the grave?" We know the answer, and we regret it. We were born too far away and too late to be eyewitnesses. "If only I had been there!" we tell ourselves. "If only I could have run to the tomb that morning and seen it empty." Surely then it would have been easy to believe, easy to stand firm for the cause of Christ, easy to proclaim the gospel message boldly, easy to make the sacrifices necessary for spiritual growth. But this is wishful thinking. First-century skeptics were plentiful: the Jewish Sadducees did not believe in resurrection, and most of the Greek Areopagites at Athens scoffed at the notion. No, the resurrection was strange and frightening—even for Jesus' disciples who saw the empty tomb. In the very presence of the risen Christ, "they worshiped him; but some doubted" (Matthew 28:17). We need look no further than the proverbial doubter, Thomas, to realize that faith in the risen Lord was hard-won even for those close to the event. Once Thomas had finally confessed the truth, "My Lord and my God!"

176

Jesus spoke encouraging words for those of us who are far off: "Blessed are those who have not seen and yet have believed" (John 20:28–29).

By appearing to them after his resurrection, Jesus privileged a few of his disciples with incontrovertible proof that he was alive. Yet the fact of the matter is that we have the same evidence that most first-century believers had: the testimony of an empty tomb and a few eyewitnesses, the spectacle of changed lives, and the experience of our own transformation through a relationship with Jesus. And, like they, we also have reasons to ponder and doubt: even though we believe that Jesus has been exalted, the world has not yet been set right, prayers go seemingly unanswered, we still struggle with sin, and the Lord tarries. The laments of the Psalms and the outcry of the prophets against the Lord due to injustice still find appropriate venues. We confess Jesus as Lord, yet we know that not everything that occurs in the world happens according to the Lord's will.

Conclusion: Transformation & Testimony

Matthew's Gospel opens by telling of the advent of Immanuel, "God with us"; it concludes by inviting us to trust Jesus' parting promise, "and surely *I am with you always*, to the very end of the age" (Matthew 1:23; 28:20). The resurrection is an essential part of the gospel picture. It was not just a device for fixing the problem of Jesus' death so that the cross could go on being the main point of the gospel. Jesus' birth, life and ministry, death, res-

> ### Jesus' Companions
>
> "The Resurrection means above all just this, that Christians do not inherit their task from Christ; they share it with him. We are not the successors of Jesus, but his companions."
>
> *T. W. Manson (1953)*

urrection, and ascension—all of them hold together as a unity, and it is through the resurrection and ascension that they all come to be a living and present reality among us, not just facts of history.

The early disciples did not come to trust in the resurrection just because they could visit an empty tomb or because they knew someone who knew someone that once did. They came to trust in it because God himself, by his Holy Spirit, made the resurrection of his Son real to them from the inside out. "If the Spirit of him who raised Jesus from the dead is living in you, he who raised Christ from the dead will also give life to your mortal bodies through his Spirit, who lives in you" (Romans 8:11). Their main testimony to God's power was the transformation occurring in their midst.

Each morning we set out on the pathway of eternal life. This road leads finally to heaven, but it also shines with the light of resurrection in the here and now. The words that we speak, the appointments we keep, our budget planning and our career priorities—everything ought to show that we walk each step in both the "already" and the "not yet." Christ's presence is active within us, alive and working, not to overwhelm us, but to remake us slowly from within. It can be a frustrating journey. Our goals for spiritual maturity often seem to keep moving just beyond our reach. We experience relapses into our old ways. We may even become impatient with the slow-moving immaturity of our church. It is right to be dissatisfied and long for greater growth. At the same time, processes of development are normal. Maturity takes time. Life is meant to unfold and take its shape in season. The goal may be Christlikeness, but the journey involves growth.

These are the last days. Yet they are also the first days, since a new creation has already begun to emerge among us. We are living a resurrection paradigm, in-between the times. We want God's power and love to visit us now and do its work among us, but we also long for him to bring about his final great coming. So we utter the prayer of early Christians to a living Lord: "*Marana, tha!*" Our Lord, come. Come to us. Repair your world. Heal your church. Transform us, every one, into the image of Christ. And bring us home.

178

Study Guide

This study guide has three sections: a section of chapter discussion questions, a section of scenarios, and a section of case studies.

Discussion questions for each chapter are designed to assist readers in processing the material in the book and also to challenge them to deeper reflection and prayer. These questions can be used by individuals to enhance personal insight or by groups in various settings to improve sharing and discussion.

Following this section, three scenarios offer readers an opportunity to begin exploring the implications of *Unveiling Glory* in true-to-life situations. After each scenario, discussion questions are included to assist readers in probing the issues presented. The scenarios provide models for individuals or churches to use in framing some of their own unique situations and in exploring how the material from this book might be used to address them.

Finally, the last section offers two case studies that provide readers with more comprehensive opportunities to enter real circumstances and discuss issues of christology vital to the community of faith. Teaching notes are included with each case to aid readers in its processing. For further information about case teaching, the Association for Case Teaching offers a useful website at <www.caseteaching.org>.

Jeanene Reese

Chapter Discussion Questions

Introduction

For Study & Analysis

1) Describe one way you see or hear a love for Jesus being openly declared in your life or in the lives of others. Are these experiences similar to or different from those you experienced growing up? Why do you think so?

2) In sculpture, painting, and film, Jesus has been pictured in many different ways. Of all the ways Jesus has been portrayed, which most appeals to you? Share this image with others. What is important to you about this image? What would it mean for you to reexamine this image? What thoughts and feelings do you have about engaging in a deeper examination of the person of Jesus—even if it means altering the image that you cherish?

3) According to the authors, what is the reason Jesus spoke to his disciples in parables? What significance does this insight carry for believers today? What role has in-depth study of Christ's nature and person played in your spiritual growth up to this point?

4) How is "christological reflection" different from looking for direct answers to specific questions? What is a "christological lens?" Why do you think christological reflection might be especially critical at this time in the history of Churches of Christ?

5) On a scale of 1 to 5 (1 is strongly disagree, 5 is strongly agree) rate your assessment of this statement: "Ultimately, then, the aim of christology is the same as that of our salvation: transformation" (p. 6). How does the authors' statement fit your understanding of salvation's purpose?

6) The metaphor of "unveiling glory" is rich with significance. What are some of the promises and

possibilities it holds for our relationships: **a** · with Christ; **b** · with one another in the church; **c** · with the unbelieving world?

7) Imagine an unveiling. What thoughts, experiences, and feelings do you bring to it? How do these translate into what you anticipate in reading the rest of *Unveiling Glory*?

For Reflection & Prayer

1) Since "God's solution to the world's problems is to offer himself" (p. 9), which of the following best reflects what you need in Christ? **a** · a relationship with him; **b** · healing from him; **c** · a redirected purpose with him; **d** · The power to live for him.

2) What does your choice above say about your current relationship with Jesus? How would you describe the environment in which you are currently living your spiritual life? What would it take to create the kind of healthy environment you need to have a full and meaningful relationship with Christ?

3) Spend time reflecting about your answers to the two questions above. Pray for your relationship with Christ, with the church in which you worship and serve, and with the world to whom you bear witness for the Lord.

Chapter 1

For Study & Analysis

1) What is the relevance of Jesus Christ for your daily life? How did you come to these conclusions?

2) On a scale of 1 to 5 (1 is strongly disagree, 5 is strongly agree), rate your response to the authors' observation that much of the traditional preaching in Churches of Christ has focused on our heavenly reward in a way that severs salvation from creation (pp. 18–19). Explain your answer.

3) The authors claim that God came to earth in order to show us how to be human. Why then are we tempted to adopt the following flawed and narrow views? a · that to sin is merely to be human; b · that everything human and earthly is sad and worthless; c · that a call to Christlikeness is a call to be superhuman.

4) Which has been more important to the way you understand and practice your Christianity: the journey or the destination? Think about the world-affirming and the world-rejecting attributes of Jesus. Which side appeals to you most? Be prepared to explain your response and to discuss how these understandings affect your discipleship.

5) The authors speak of our Christian walk as filled with life-transforming experiences that lead us to our heavenly destination. Share an experience that has changed your life in recent years. What did you learn about God's nature from it? What did you learn about your humanity?

6) How do you think Jesus' call to discipleship, his invitation to "come home," is both reorienting and disorienting at the same time? What can the church do to help people in their reorientation or disorientation?

7) Describe 2 or 3 ways in which your belief in the incarnation should translate into actions when you follow Christ's model as one who accepts the role of collaborator with God.

8) How does an appreciation for the incarnation affect our approach to many of the either/or questions about faith that we are prone to ask?

182

9) Compare the house in which you live with the church building in which you worship. How are the styles, the art, and the architecture similar? How are they different? What values are expressed by each building? What does this comparison show

you about your understanding of the relationship between creation, daily life, and religion?

10) After reading this chapter, what would you now say is the relevance of Jesus Christ for everyday life? What impact do these insights have on your life in Christ?

For Reflection & Prayer

1) Looking through the lens of the incarnation, reflect on what it means for your life that God, through Jesus Christ, calls us to be unflinchingly holy while also being truly human?

2) What does Christ want to "re-educate" (p. 25) you about in terms of the nature, purpose and goal of human existence? Why is it necessary for you to learn these lessons? What must you give up in order for this transformation to take place?

3) Consider your daily occupation. List some ways in which it is (or could be) a collaboration with God.

4) What does it mean for your faith that "living like Jesus is not something we do to get salvation—it is our salvation" (p. 26)?

5) Spend time in prayer asking God to work his transformation in you and through you.

Chapter 2

For Study & Analysis

1) Name some of the common descriptions you use when trying to tell others about God. Select 2 or 3 of these that you think are most commonly used and share why we tend to favor them.

2) Contrast these descriptions of God with the statement that "He is a humble God, and his ways are humble" (p. 39). What similarities and differences do you see between these common descriptions and the description in this chapter? What insights

do you gain about yourself from exploring these descriptions? about God? about the birth of Jesus?

3) The authors state that the birth of Jesus "affirm[s] our neediness, nakedness, and dependence" (p. 40). What do you think this means? Why would God want to affirm this? Why is understanding Christ's birth so critical to our understanding of God and the purpose of Jesus' life?

4) Look at the complexities of human life present at the nativity and choose the one which most resonates with you: **a**·the slaughter of innocent children; **b**·Mary's willing surrender to a shocking revelation; **c**·Zechariah's doubtful questioning; **d**·wise nobles from afar bringing expensive gifts. Why did you choose as you did? What do you think your choice says about your own experience with the transforming picture of Jesus' birth?

5) The authors describe two commonly-held views of God's involvement in our lives (pp. 44–48). With which of these are you generally most comfortable and why? **a**·in his foreknowledge, God has predetermined a precise flow of events; **b**·God designed the world to follow a natural order, and he trusts human beings to make their own choices. What alternative view is suggested in *Unveiling Glory*? What does it mean for us to "collaborate" with God, to serve as his partners?

6) How does the church need to change in order to portray more effectively the "inclusive family picture" (pp. 52–56) described in this chapter of *Unveiling Glory*? Determine 4 or 5 specific goals your congregation could have to achieve this inclusivity.

184

For Reflection & Prayer

1) The authors describe the following transformative possibilities. Identify the area in which you most need to grow and describe why this area is so impor-

tant for you: **a** · imitating the Lord's peaceful, humble ways; **b** · trusting God more completely; **c** · assuming personal responsibilities in relation to God's actions and rejoicing in doing so; **d** · growing in wisdom as well as in physical well-being; **e** · investing in the hard work of spiritual discipline.

2) We often speak of the ground at the cross being "level," meaning accessible to all people. In the closing section of this chapter, the authors are saying the ground is also level at the manger. Reflect on what this means in your life. What challenges or blessings does it present for your Christian walk?

3) Which of the following challenges pose the greatest difficulties for you and your church? **a** · meeting and accepting people where they are; **b** · covering up neediness with an accumulation of things or accomplishments; **c** · getting your hands dirty in the messiness of human sin and pain. What help does the nativity provide for dealing with these challenges?

4) Pray about your response to these questions and about how you may continue to learn and grow from the nativity.

Chapter 3

For Study & Analysis

1) The authors suggest that our churches have spent more time debating the essentials of baptism than discussing its essence. On a scale of 1 to 5 (1 is strongly disagree, 5 is strongly agree) how would you respond to their assessment? Explain your response.

2) What do you find significant about the fact that Jesus' ministry and our Christian discipleship share the same beginning point: his baptism? Briefly share your baptismal story, describing what you remember most about it. In what ways does your baptism echo his?

3) Examine each of the following points in baptism through which we connect with Jesus and enact the meaning of salvation. Which one is most meaningful for you and why? a · being reborn of water and Spirit; b · joining Jesus in the Jordan River; c · entering the tomb with him.

4) How does knowing that baptism, like salvation and the Christian life, requires our collaboration with God change your view of it?

5) Looking at the sidebar on p. 67, "The Meaning of Baptism," answer the following questions: In what ways can your church enhance an individual's preparation for baptism? How can you enrich the baptismal event? What can your congregation do to accompany and support the newly baptized in their faith walk in more effective ways?

6) Why do you think we are often tempted to "domesticate" Jesus' call to discipleship? What are the results when we do?

For Reflection & Prayer

1) Reflect on the ways that baptism invites us to share with Jesus in the whole life of God as Father, Son and Spirit.

2) How would your Christian life be the same or different if you focused each day on the freshness of your baptism and the promise of continual transformation into the image of the Lord?

3) Reflect on the authors' statement "The death that comes with discipleship is difficult, but it is also liberating" (p. 73).

186 4) Examine and respond to each of the following questions, remembering to frame your responses in terms of changes you can make rather than what others need to do: What would it mean in your life if you relinquished your grudges and laid aside your

differences with others? Where do you need to be lavish in forgiveness? How could you learn to be more focused on your common life in Christ rather than on peripheral issues? As a follow-up, imagine that everyone in your congregation was actively engaged in the practices you described in your responses. How might life in the church be different if this were so?

5) Examine each of the following demands Jesus makes. Choose one that is especially challenging to you and ask others to hold you accountable as you seek to incorporate it more fully into your life. a · denying yourself, taking up your cross and following Jesus (Matthew 16:28); b · finding life by losing it (Luke 9:24); c · hating father, mother, wife and children, even your own life (Luke 14:26); d · serving instead of being served (Matthew 20:28); e · giving up everything (Luke 14:33).

6) Choose one of your responses above and pray about it.

Chapter 4

For Study & Analysis

1) Describe how you think Jesus accomplishes his great work of reconciliation. Examine the sidebar on p. 80, "The Picture of Health" that outlines Christ's three antidotes for brokenness. How does your description of reconciliation fit this diagram? How does this picture challenge your understanding of reconciliation?

2) Why do you think that the institutional developments of the past several centuries have led Christians frequently to equate God's kingdom with the church alone? What is at stake in this understanding? How is this challenged by Jesus' teaching that God's kingdom equates to his reign or rule?   187

3) When John the Baptist's followers ask Jesus if he is the one they've been expecting (Matthew 11:3–6), how

does Jesus respond? If asked today in your church for evidence of God's rule or reign, to what events, people, or actions would Jesus point? What do you learn about your community of faith from this evidence of God's reign? What do you learn about yourself?

4) The authors note several world-rejecting practices that they see as characteristic of Churches of Christ over the years (pp. 83–84). They also observe some current practices that could be described as world-affirming, such as singing fewer songs about heaven and showing a preference for teaching and ministries that enrich daily life (p. 87). One a scale of 1 to 5 (1 is strongly disagree, 5 is strongly agree) how do you respond to these categorizations? Do you feel that your congregation is balancing these characteristics in productive ways? Explain your response.

5) How does it affect you to view Jesus' miracles as his business of restoring the world to the way God intended it to be? How does this view expand your understanding of his serving and suffering nature? of your discipleship?

6) Name a person you know who exemplifies hospitality. What about this person is distinctive? How might the authors' understanding of the ministry of hospitality differ from our traditional views? What impact would the authors' definition have on your own practice of hospitality?

7) Several common distortions of Jesus' image that can lead churches away from practicing his ministry are cited in *Unveiling Glory* (pp. 93–97). List these and brainstorm others of which you are aware. What makes these distortions alluring? What are some possible safeguards against each?

For Reflection & Prayer

1) Reflect on what it means for you fully to focus your attention on Jesus. What senses and approaches do

you use most effectively to help you focus? Imagine an encounter where Jesus reveals to you more deeply the foolishness of his wisdom (1 Corinthians 1:21–25; 2:14). How might this encounter reshape how you live as a disciple of Jesus Christ?

2) Does it bother you that God chooses not to wave a "magic wand…over the world's hurts" (p. 90)? How do you feel about God's chosen way of resolving the world's problems?

3) If you could invite anyone—past, present, or future—to the Lord's table, who would it be? Why would you choose this person? What experience would you share there?

4) Spend time in prayer asking God to help you see him through Christ and through your fellow Christians more fully.

Chapter 5

For Study & Analysis

1) When you think of Jesus as Teacher, what comes to mind?

2) How do Jesus' methods of teaching reveal what he wanted from his students? Do you think these approaches still have these effects? Explain your answer.

3) What are the three traits of a learner suggested by the authors of *Unveiling Glory*? Which of these qualities do you feel are strongest in you? Which one is still a struggle for you? What other qualities do you think are essential for people to have in order to learn from the great Teacher? Why?

189

4) Do you agree that there is a connection between students' level of understanding and their depth of personal relationship with the teacher? Why do you think Jesus wants to keep understanding and rela-

tionship clearly connected? What happens when they get separated? What do you think the authors mean when they argue that "Christ's teaching starts in the heart" (p. 111)? How does this perspective change the way we view ourselves as learners and teachers?

5) How does Jesus embody what he teaches? What difference do you think this makes in his role as Teacher? to those who are learning? to those who teach today? to the content of the message?

6) Why is Jesus' example of washing the disciples' feet an important picture to keep in mind when reflecting on his role as teacher? on his teaching?

7) The authors discuss how our communion provides a basic teaching opportunity for the church. Consider how your church currently practices the Lord's Supper. What are these practices teaching? What are your communion practices proclaiming about Christ? Brainstorm ways that you could better learn and teach through this important celebration.

8) Look at the sidebar on p. 118. In your experience, in which area has your congregation excelled? a · teaching Christianity as doctrine; b · teaching Christianity "as a life, an ethic, a mode of behavior." What are some ways your church might find and institute a balanced curriculum that connects faith and life?

For Reflection & Prayer

1) Think about the most effective Bible teacher you have ever had. What made this person a great teacher? How do you think he or she became such a significant teacher? What can the church do to ensure excellence in teaching for future generations?

190   2) Imagine yourself as a disciple at the Last Supper. What expectations do you think you would have about sharing the Passover with Jesus and the others? How do you think you would respond when Jesus

connected the Passover bread and wine with his own body and blood? How might your responses impact your current participation in the Lord's Supper? What effect does it have for you to think of the Lord's Supper through the world-denying and world-affirming elements of Christ's story?

3) Are you more attracted to "head-knowledge" or "heart-knowledge?" Why is this particular kind of knowledge appealing to you? What specifically can you do to achieve or maintain a balanced spiritual diet?

4) Reflect on this statement: "We have only one lesson to learn—Jesus Christ—but that lesson is as big as God's heart and as deep as a fully transformed life" (p. 118). What impact does this lesson have on your desire to learn? What lessons do you think God has been trying to teach you recently? What means is he using to teach you? What do you need to pray about this lesson and your life?

Chapter 6

For Study & Analysis

1) In what ways did your becoming a Christian give you a new world to inhabit? What challenges or blessings did you experience in learning a new language and new practices? How are you currently struggling to grow into this new way of life?

2) If you had to use one image to describe the gift of your salvation, what would you choose? Why?

3) What impact does the image of the cross have on your understanding of salvation? of God? of Jesus?

4) The authors use four key images that run through scripture to describe God's work of salvation in Christ. Briefly review each of these, describing them in your own words and indicating the strengths and weaknesses of each: **a** · salvation as satisfaction;

b · salvation as victory; **c** · salvation as moral example; **d** · salvation as new creation.

5) Which of the four images is/are most prominent in your church's preaching, teaching, singing, and religious language?

6) How has it been helpful to examine these views of salvation with their strengths and weaknesses? What are the potential dangers of such an examination?

7) The authors assert that in our heritage we have tended to see salvation as static—as an accurate understanding of facts, as a correct awareness of rituals and forms, and as the upkeep of faithful church membership. How do you think this view has enhanced or inhibited our understanding of salvation? What do you see as the effect of more current trends toward the experiential nature of our salvation? In what ways is this current approach likely to create the same sort of problems as our earlier view?

For Reflection & Prayer

1) The authors state that "justification (God's declaration of forgiveness) and sanctification (the process of God's transforming work in our lives), though distinct, are richly woven into the larger scheme of God's life" (p. 146). What obstacles still remain in your life that keep you from living out your salvation with this full understanding? How effective is your church in encouraging you to fulfill the call to be like God? What could your congregation do to help its members be more like God?

2) What are some ways you could more purposefully enact the story of Christ in your daily life? Be specific.

192

3) Reflect on which of the four images of salvation have been most meaningful for you and consider how your image of salvation has changed over time. Pray about these responses, asking God to increase

your understanding of and participation in his work of salvation.

Chapter 7

For Study & Analysis

1) On a scale of 1 to 5 (1 is strongly disagree, 5 is strongly agree), how do you assess the authors' assertion that much of our present day preaching and teaching focuses on the pressing affairs of Christians in daily life rather than on heavenly themes and the resurrection? Why do you think this is so?

2) The authors depict the resurrection of Christ in each of the following ways. Choose one depiction with which you most closely identify and share with others why this portrayal is crucial to your life of faith: a · as a new beginning, not a final conclusion; b · as a means of empowerment and transformation; c · as a cause for bold witnessing to others; d · as a hope for continual resurrection; e · as a transition from this age to the age to come; f · as a radical transformation of fellowship.

3) What do you think it means that because of Jesus' death, burial, and resurrection, God has the last word over all powers? What hope do you take from this thought? What effect does it have on your life today?

4) How is the gift of the Holy Spirit that you received at baptism an ongoing witness of God's promise in your life? What does it mean for you to be filled with the indwelling Spirit?

5) What is the true aim of Christian discipleship? What does the resurrection have to do with it? How will you know if you are achieving this aim in your life? in your church?

6) What role does suffering and pain play in our participation in Jesus' resurrection? How do you think most

193

Christians generally deal with pain and suffering in their lives? Why?

7) What can the church do to equip all believers more effectively and more fully to participate in the death, burial and resurrection of Jesus?

For Reflection & Prayer

1) Imagine yourself as the first disciple at the empty tomb. What do you imagine you would see? How would it feel? What would you do? How would you explain what you found there to others? What specific concerns and challenges would being at the tomb present to your faith?

2) Reflect on the authors' suggestion that true intimacy with Jesus is marked by a person's being transformed into Christ's image. How does this standard compare with the standards of intimacy you or others have been using?

3) The authors state in the conclusion of this chapter that "[t]rusting in the God of resurrection involves engaging in the practices of resurrection" (p. 162). What would it take for you to practice the resurrection in your marriage? with your children? in your friendships? at your work? in your church's life and worship?

4) Pray about your need to practice the resurrection in each of these situations.

Chapter 8

For Study & Analysis

1) Living with the "already" and the "not yet" dimensions of the kingdom can be difficult. With which of the following challenges do you struggle most? a · evil is still present in the church; b · false teachers still ravage the sheep; c · the wealthy exploit the poor; d · the disadvantaged are mistreated by the advantaged; e · Christians live with unbelieving spouses;

f · injustice can be seen everywhere; g · committed disciples continue to struggle with sinful behaviors; h · sickness and disease affect us all.

2) How do you live in the tension between "already" and the "not yet" like "people whose inner sight sees the truth about where things are headed" (p. 166)? How can you live in triumph without being triumphalistic—one who always seems to have the quick, easy answer to complex, difficult circumstances?

3) When you pray for God's kingdom to be more fully realized on the earth, for what specifically are you praying? What does that kingdom look like? Where would you like to see a fuller expression of God's rule in the world? in the church? in your life?

4) Realizing that a "life lived in the power of resurrection is one of progress" (p. 169), share the progress you have seen evident in your Christian walk recently. What are the areas in which you continue to struggle? How can your brothers and sisters in Christ help you with these in the days ahead?

5) In what specific ways do you see your church growing in Christian maturity? What are some areas in which you would like to see more growth?

For Reflection & Prayer

1) In what area of your personal life are you tempted to ask God, "How much farther?" (or "Why is it taking so long?" or "Why can't I make better progress?"). In what area of your congregational life are you tempted to ask the same questions? How has reading *Unveiling Glory* affected you in addressing these concerns?

2) As you reflect on where you are in your journey of faith, how would you describe your present status? **195** a · at the beginning of the journey, enthusiastic about what lies ahead; b · at a crossroads, unsure of what direction to take next; c · pretty far on the way but

growing stale and discouraged; **d** · a seasoned traveler, headed in the right direction; **e** · one who is near the end, almost able to see home. How would others close to you describe your status? What do you think Jesus would say to you about your status and about how you are making the journey?

3) According to this chapter, what does it mean to keep in step with the Spirit? How could your congregation become more adept at keeping in step with the Spirit? What part could you play in making that happen?

4) How can you be an eyewitness of Jesus' resurrection to those around you? How can your life in the church give testimony of the resurrection? What difference would it make if we saw ourselves as those who are set out on the pathway of eternal life?

5) Close with a period of reflection, meditation, and prayer about your spiritual journey, thanking God for those who have helped you along the way and asking God to give you the opportunity to help others.

Scenarios & Discussion Questions

Read the following scenarios (each is followed by a set of possible discussion questions). All of them are fictional, but they represent congregational issues that many will find familiar. These situations are not based on any one specific congregation but rather are composites of people and churches that have struggled in various ways. The purpose of each scenario is to draw learners into true-to-life situations that will assist in processing what they have read in *Unveiling Glory*. Remember that, while these incidents have no single conclusion or "right" answer, they provide opportunities for individuals to decide what they would do in these situations and why they would make particular choices.

The main task of the teacher in using scenarios (as well as the case studies in the following section) is to serve as a facilitator by fostering meaningful discussion, highlighting significant insights, and assisting in the examination of the ramifications of actions and attitudes. The teacher serves as a guide, leading the participants to discover their own insights rather than being one who supplies all the information or who coaches participants to arrive at predetermined conclusions. Preparation for teaching a scenario demands that the teacher assume a learning stance alongside class participants. More—rather than less—study, analysis, and preparation are required to teach a scenario effectively.

The first step in preparing to teach a scenario is to read it thoroughly. The teacher may choose to list the central issues presented, the main characters portrayed, or the major events or dates indicated—any details that help "flesh out" the situation.

The second step involves exploring the various paths that a scenario or case might take. Given the make-up of the class and the teaching situation, the teacher should determine which issues posed by the scenario would be most useful to explore. The teacher then decides on a possible direction and selects teaching tools (role playing, voting, small groups, video clips or other visual aids, etc.) that will best facilitate the discussion. The teacher should develop questions that involve the participants in reviewing the basic details of the scenario, clarifying key issues, and formulating possible solutions.

Finally, the teacher should prepare a wrap-up of the discussion. This might include summarizing what participants have shared or asking them to list what they have learned. The leader might want to share personal insights about the scenario or case at this point but must be careful not to trump the learning process or invalidate the contribution of others.

Scenario 1: "Where Are Your Loyalties?"

The Situation

197

Bill Knowles shook his head again as he walked into the church building. He had hoped to slip quietly into the office this morning for some prayer and reflection time. But as he had crossed the parking lot, he ran into one of the college students hurrying to his 8:00 AM class.

"What happened at that business meeting last night?" Jim asked. "I had to study for an exam, but some of the students came in and said that things got really heated—they thought there was going to be a fist fight at church. Boy, I wish I could have seen that!" he exclaimed before rushing off to campus.

It was only Monday morning, and already Bill felt the tension mounting. He felt concern about how Jim, a recent convert, would process all that was going on. As he sat down in his chair, he thought back to the business meeting. "How had things gotten so out of hand," he wondered?

Just then the phone rang, and the caller ID let Bill know that it was Sue Renshaw, one of the vocal community leaders. He braced himself and answered the phone.

"Good morning, Bill," she began. "I thought you might want to know that some of us met last night after the business meeting to discuss the situation further. We don't want to see this church divided, but we feel it is imperative that we hold the line on these so-called 'innovations.' Some of us aren't sure where you place your loyalties, and we'd like to schedule an appointment with you on Wednesday to talk about it."

Bill set the appointment and hung up the phone. His heart was heavy, and he found it difficult to know exactly how to pray in this situation. He had served as the pulpit minister and only full-time staff person at the University Church for the past thirteen years.

Although the church had recently appointed elders, they were still new at the task and generally looked to Bill for direction. Like many churches in university settings, there had always been something of a separation between "town" and "gown," between those from the community and the ones who were part of the university. Bill had always felt that he ministered as a bridge between these two entities.

Only recently, however, had the differences centered on any specific issue. "Ironically," Bill reflected, "this church is no different from many others I've read and heard about."

The current debate centered around how the church would conduct its worship. The townspeople were interested in keeping it mostly traditional with only a few changes here and there. The university group, however, wanted more freedom to "experience" their worship with contemporary songs, hand-raising, clapping, and worship teams.

Obviously the situation was tearing them apart, and Bill had to decide what he should do to help maintain unity in the current crisis.

For Discussion

Ask participants to gather in groups of 4 or 5 to answer the following questions, making sure each group is as diverse as possible. Groups should be prepared to share the details of their discussion with the larger class as time permits.

1) On a scale of 1 to 5 (1 is extremely dissimilar, 5 is extremely similar), how does this situation compare with those you know about in churches today? Without giving away any names or identities, are there any examples you would like to share? How are these churches handling their difficulties? What lessons might Bill glean from these churches?

2) In the introduction of *Unveiling Glory*, the authors suggest that we need to acquire a "christological lens" through which we can look at our problems and find God's resources for help. What does it mean to have a christological lens? How does one go about developing it? What are the resources that God offers to help Christians in situations like this one?

199

3) What would you suggest should be Bill's first course of action? Whom should he contact? What should he say? How should he proceed? What does scripture have to say about situations like this one?

4) What would you do about the meeting on Wednesday? How would you respond to the various factions, or what would you advise them to do? What attitudes and actions must the congregation adopt in this situation? What are the specific challenges you think they will face?

5) How does the church care for those who are young in the faith, like Jim, in difficult circumstances? What should Bill do regarding Jim?

After gathering the class back together and discussing each group's responses to the above questions, ask the class to answer the following questions:

1) What situations do you see in your own congregation that are similar to this one?

2) How are you going about developing a christological lens through which to see these conflicts? What resources from God are you utilizing in them?

Finally, spend time together in prayer for your church and its unity.

Scenario 2: "Service or Sacrifice"
The Situation

For four years, ever since the time he had entered college, Peter Murphy had planned to go into the Peace Corps when he graduated. Now the pressure was building on him to take a different option.

Peter and Jane had married during the Christmas break of their senior year. With graduation only a few weeks away, Peter's father was hesitant about the Peace Corps decision. He had been very clear about including both Peter and Jane in his concern for their future.

"You and Jane need time to get settled and to get to know one another in your own environment without taking on the additional stress of learning to live in another country. Now that you're married, you must assume an added sense of responsibility. A solid marriage is invaluable to both of you in order for you to be able to give your own talents to other people in need.

"Several companies have approached you, Peter, with solid offers which won't be there for long. With the summer experience you've had and your degree in business, you're perfectly suited for a number of those jobs. If you leave the country for several years and are out of touch with the business world, it will be difficult to get a job on your return.

"Get a few years' experience behind you. Begin to get established. Then you can make a much more valuable and lasting contribution to those around you. After all, there are always struggling businesses getting started that could benefit from sound management advice. This is a volunteer service you could give to your own community. You don't have to go half-way around the world to help someone else."

Peter knew that his father was genuinely concerned about helping others. He knew that his father had served on the school board, that he was a deacon in the church, and that his active involvement in community affairs was a reflection of his own understanding of ministry.

Peter and Jane had talked about their decision for over a week. This past spring, they had been to the Peace Corps' "preliminary staging," and they each had a pretty good idea about what their work would be like. They had both been accepted into the program, but they would have to submit their response to Washington by the following morning in order to be included in the next training cycle.

Peter asked Jane to be as honest about her own feelings as possible. Her family had expressed doubts

201

about the decision as well, but Jane's response was clear. "We're mature enough to make up our own minds." However, she had expressed some uncertainty to Peter. "I'm very excited about traveling and seeing new places, but it would also be pretty good to settle down for awhile. I want most of all to teach school, but I'll be able to do that in South America or the United States. Peter, you've got a much greater conflict about this than I do. To be content with the final decision, you really have to sort out what's most important for *you*."

Peter tried to summarize his feelings about his father's suggestions and his own reactions. "I've always had a deep sense of wanting to give what I could to someone in need. There's a great sense of satisfaction in that for me, but there's a lot more to it than that. The idea of 'loving your neighbor' doesn't make any sense to me unless I'm really committed to *doing* that. Where is the line between being responsible for myself, for *our*selves, and being responsible for other people? I've prayed about this and realized that basically the issue is getting my priorities straight. I'd like to talk to the people in our mentoring group about this decision, if that's okay with you."

For Discussion

Ask participants to gather in groups of 5 to 7 people to roleplay the situation. Prior to roleplaying, the groups should briefly discuss the following questions. One person in each group should serve as a facilitator and another should record the group's discussion.

1) If you had to sum up the central issue in this situation in one sentence, what would it be?

2) What do you see as the primary issues of discipleship that Peter and Jane are facing?

3) As you consider these issues, do you see them as primarily world-affirming or world-rejecting? Why?

4) How would you advise this young couple to make their decision about service and sacrifice based on your understanding of the collaboration we have with God in incarnational ministry?

5) How should Peter and Jane address the concerns of their parents in this situation so that they reflect honor and holiness? How should the parents respond to reflect these same attributes?

6) What role should the mentoring group have now and in the future to aid Peter and Jane? To help their parents?

Now, roleplay the scenario. Two people in each group should take on the roles of Peter and Jane while the rest serve as the mentoring group. Once the groups have worked through the scenario, bring the class back together and ask them to summarize what happened in each of their groups as time permits. Pay particular attention to what the groups saw as the primary issues and what they advised Peter and Jane to do. When each group has reported about its roleplaying, the class should address the following questions:

1) On a scale of 1 to 5 (1 is very dissimilar, 5 is very similar), rate how the decision Peter and Jane are facing compares to decisions you are facing. What lessons might you glean from the example of Peter and Jane for your own decision-making?

2) What tensions do you feel in these situations between Jesus' world-affirming and world-rejecting tendencies? What bearing do they have on your sense of discipleship?

3) List 2 or 3 insights you have gained from this discussion that will assist you and others in living incarnational lives of service and sacrifice.

203

To conclude, close with a prayer asking God to guide you personally and corporately as you serve him.

Scenario 3: "Help Me, Lord"

The Situation

Charles Gibson closed his Bible, finished scribbling some notes, took off his glasses, and sat back with a smile. He was almost ready for an important conversation with his fourteen-year-old grandson, Adam. He just needed some quiet time for reflection and prayer.

It seemed like only yesterday that the family had celebrated Adam's arrival as the first grandchild. "Where had the time gone?" wondered Charles. "It's hard to believe that the boy's already in his teens and facing the most important decision of his life." He bowed his head and prayed simply,

"Help me, Lord, to know what to say and how to say it to Adam. You've been teaching me patience these past several years, and I may need it now. I need the patience, not with Adam, Father, but with myself. Sometimes I can't keep my thoughts straight and this conversation is really important to me. I know it's important to you, too."

Charles' daughter Sarah, Adam's mother, had called just two nights ago to ask if she and her husband, David, could bring Adam to spend the weekend with his grandparents. She had explained that Adam was at a critical juncture in his life of faith. Apparently, the youth group had just finished a faith-decisions class, and several of Adam's friends were baptized as a result. When Sarah and David had talked to Adam, he expressed uncertainty about why he needed to be baptized since he already lived a Christian life and was a faithful participant in almost every youth activity.

Sarah and David had been hesitant to pressure Adam about baptism; they wanted it to be his decision and not something he did simply to please them. Sarah remembered that her dad had mentioned his work with the Seekers class at his church and had talked about how responsive some of those people had been to his fresh insights on baptism.

"I just thought it might be helpful for him to hear your perspective on these things, Dad," she had commented on the phone. "I just know Adam will listen to you. You guys have always had such a special relationship. Do you mind if we bring him for a visit?"

Charles chuckled to himself at that last question. What grandparent ever minded having a grandchild visit? But this trip would be different, he mused. He had shared his recent experience thinking and teaching about baptism when the kids last visited, but he hadn't been sure anyone was really listening then. Now he needed to get ready for this important visit.

He got up from the porch, put his study materials away, and began to look down the road for a familiar mini-van.

For Discussion

Ask participants to gather in groups of 4 or 5 to answer the following questions, making sure each group is as diverse as possible. Groups should be prepared to share the details of their discussion with the larger class as time permits.

1) How has your understanding of baptism grown and deepened as you have lived as Christians? Why has your perspective changed over time?

2) Where would you begin the conversation with Adam if you were Charles? Why would you choose this starting point?

3) What are some of the important dimensions of baptism that you would like to share with someone like Adam? How have you come to these understandings? Do they reflect your own experience, your further studies, or your theological reflection on baptism?

4) What would you be careful to avoid in the conversation? Why?

205

5) How do you determine if a 14-year-old is old enough and mature enough to make a decision as important as this one?

6) How would you work with parents like Sarah and David to equip them to deal with their children's important faith decisions?

After gathering the class back together and discussing each group's responses to the above questions, ask the class to answer the following questions either in writing or verbally (these responses may give you insight into areas that need further discussion):

1) What I found most enlightening about our discussion was...

2) What I wish we would talk more about is...

If the class wants to talk about certain issues further, do so. Then, ask the group to respond to the following:

1) How has working through this scenario affected your understanding of baptism?

2) How has your perspective changed or developed as you've worked through this scenario?

3) How might what you've learned from working through this scenario affect how you will teach others in the future about baptism?

Conclude by praying for your congregation's unity and role in teaching others about this.

Case Studies & Teaching Notes

206   Two cases are included in this section. The first one, "Not in My Back Yard," reflects an urban church setting and many of the natural struggles experienced there. The characters and settings have been renamed to protect privacy, but the events described are taken from an actual church situation.

The second case, "Peace Child," examines a missions situation, asking readers seriously to rethink how we present Christ in cross-cultural settings. The names and places in this case have not been changed at the insistence of Don Richardson, the author of the book from which this case is adapted.

Following each case are suggested teaching notes that may help in preparing the case for presentation. You may also wish to reexamine the directions that precede the congregational scenario section for helpful suggestions on how to maximize teaching effectiveness.

Case Study 1: "Not in My Back Yard"

This was a particularly anguish-filled morning for Fred Washington as he drove to his office at 7:00 AM. At age forty-five, he was serving his fourth congregation. He considered himself to be a pretty savvy urban minister. He had seen it all.

In his last church in Pittsburgh, he had organized a community development corporation that had built 156 houses for low- to moderate-income first-time homeowners, had organized a well-baby clinic to address the high incidence of infant mortality in the neighborhood, and had organized a charter school focusing on the crisis of young African-American males in third through seventh grades. His ministry motto had been, "If you have no passion, you have no project."

As he drove into the church parking lot, Washington felt a knot tightening in the pit of his stomach. His mind was riddled with all the logistics for the big community meeting that would take place that night—a meeting that would demand every ounce of his leadership skills in the West End Church of Christ in Cincinnati.

Since 1945, the church had prided itself on being an integrated congregation. Now, however, its 250 members came mainly from outside the community, with only a small percentage from the immediate neighborhood, these latter consisting principally of children. The present attitude of members presumed

207

that city officials lacked the capacity and know-how to respond to the crisis of neglect.

Once the home of the wealthy of Cincinnati, this aging neighborhood of three- and four-story houses near the downtown business district (the West End) was a predominantly black and increasingly poor community. "How do I put into practice what I have preached and worked so hard for all these years—in building a bridge between the church and the community about issues of homelessness?" Fred asked himself as he put on his pastoral care hat. It was his dubious task each morning to gently remove a group of homeless men who found the church's rear steps a refuge in which to rest during the night.

This particular morning, Jim, a thirty-six-year-old African-American man, greeted the minister with a groggy hello. Fred was hooked by Jim's greeting: "The Lord provided me with a stone for a pillow to lay my head on in the same way He provided one for Jacob. God watched over me, allowing me to see another day."

Jim, a divorced glass-factory worker, had lost his job due to a plant closing and the relocation of the work to Mexico as part of the NAFTA agreement. "I thank God for this church," he exclaimed as he gathered up all of his worldly possessions and put them into a shopping cart from the nearby A&P. "Minister," Jim mumbled, still groggy and stiff from the hard, cold steps that substituted for a bed, "I can tell you're a good person; I said a prayer for you last night that God would bless your work in this community in a special way."

Impressed but not surprised by the theological language coming from Jim, Fred's thoughts were more about his congregation and why they refused to acknowledge the inhuman treatment of people like Jim. Fred was well aware that several of the homeless demonstrated a theological understanding and level of faith that would put many in his congregation to shame. In fact, they had taught him more than he had learned in seminary.

Somehow, though, Jim's God-talk seemed foreign to both the church and the community. By this time Fred was anticipating the next sentence out of Jim's mouth: "Brother Fred, can you spare some change for a sausage-and-biscuit sandwich and a cup of coffee?" Fred's decision to give or not to give in response to Jim's request was not based on Jim's need or on any philosophical discourse about "teaching a person to fish...." Rather, it was based on his relationship with Jim. He didn't see himself perpetuating Jim's dependency or admitting any sense of guilt on his own part. He was more interested in getting to the root problem of homelessness.

The one thing Fred could say with confidence after giving Jim all of his spare change was that he was not intimidated by this everyday encounter with "panhandling." Some in the neighborhood—and more particularly around the church—had become so alarmed at the increased number of panhandlers that all evening activities had virtually stopped for fear of encountering these men. As far as Fred was concerned, everyone in the church and the community seemed more concerned about moving the problem somewhere else rather than dealing with its root causes. "The church has a 'NIMBY' attitude—'not in my back yard,'" Fred mused to himself.

As he left Jim and entered the church, the office phone rang. It was Chuck Glenn, deacon over property management.

"Good morning, Fred," Chuck said, "I'm just calling to check in with you to see if we're on the same page for the meeting tonight. You know I'm obligated to carry out the congregation's mandate of announcing our intent to evict these unsightly people from around our church. They're an impediment to the revitalizing efforts to recruit new families for the church."

"It doesn't help our recruitment efforts for new families," Fred thought silently with disgust. The church and the others in the community haven't heard a word I've said. Haven't I been clear that we need to hear God's calling to address the homeless situation as a witness to God's presence in the city?"

The neighborhood block council had called an emergency meeting for that night in the auditorium for the purpose of petitioning city hall. They wanted to obtain police protection and have the homeless men evicted from the area. Fred felt deeply torn. He had a pastoral responsibility to respond to the concerns of the church while he continued to address their reluctance to demonstrate compassion for the homeless. Yet his desire to seek justice and decent shelter for the homeless ran deep. For three years now he had been trying to encourage the congregation to take seriously the systemic plight of the homeless. By all accounts, the problem of homeless men sleeping on the church's steps was not the real problem, but rather the tip of the socio-economic iceberg.

That night, the Deputy Mayor, the Assistant Chief of Police, and the Director of Human Relations showed up for the meeting, along with the lead organizer of the homeless coalition who was mounting a campaign for a homeless shelter in the community. Fred knew the homeless coalition was going to conduct a direct action to disrupt the meeting.

As he walked into the room for the meeting, he pondered his choices: "How do I raise the issue of root causes without alienating my congregation while still maintaining a peaceful exchange?" He could not get rid of the image of Jim's using the steps of the church as a pillow. "How can I be passionate about issues of justice, be an advocate for the homeless, and be a minister to my congregation?" he wondered...

Teaching Notes

Preparation

Before addressing the issues of this case, read the following passages: Matthew 8:18–20, Luke 6:17–36, Mark 12:38–44, Matthew 25:31–46, and Acts 6:1–7.

Goals

1) To frame a discussion about current issues that challenge our christology;

2) To explore issues of class and race through a christological lens;

3) To examine systemic poverty and homelessness and to explore how they might be more effectively addressed by communities of faith;

4) To discuss the possibilities of churches working with communities for social action;

5) To explore the dynamics of pastoral leadership in challenging situations.

Preliminary Activities

1) Ask the class to read the case aloud together or allow them time to read it quietly. Remember that individuals who are sight-impaired may struggle with this last option.

2) Begin the discussion by asking participants what thoughts or feelings this case initially invokes. Write their responses in a list for everyone to see.

3) Identify the main characters in the case. As the facilitator, you may allow this process to be done exclusively by the participants, or you may have made copies of this information in advance for their review:

> *Fred Washington*, the savvy urban minister. He is serving his fourth congregation and has organized a community development corporation with one of his congregations. He has a passion for working in the city and is deeply concerned about the plight of the homeless;
>
> *Jim*, a thirty-six-year-old African-American man, is currently divorced, unemployed, and homeless. He is a man of faith and has astute theology. He sleeps near Washington's church and panhandles from him;

Chuck Glenn, the deacon in charge of property management who calls about the meeting. He feels obligated
to carry out the congregation's mandate about their
intention to evict the homeless from around the
church. He shows special concern about the church's
ability to attract new families;

The neighborhood block council, which has called an
emergency meeting at the church to petition city hall
for police protection in evicting the homeless men
from the area.

4) Identify the minor characters:

The Deputy Mayor, who shows up at the meeting;

The Assistant Chief of Police, who also shows up unex-
pectedly;

The Director of Human Relations, also at the meeting;

The lead organizer of the homeless coalition, who is
mounting a campaign for a homeless shelter in the
community. The coalition is planning a direct action
to disrupt the meeting.

5) Identify the key issues you see in the case. Again, as
facilitator, you may allow an open forum in which
the class identifies the issues or may want to specify
what issues are of greatest interest for your context:

The problem of homelessness in the community;

The church's reaction to the homeless situation;

The disparity between the church's membership and the
neighborhood's inhabitants;

The gap between the theological understanding and
insight reflected by some of the homeless individuals compared to the lack of this kind of theological
understanding in the congregation;

The impending meeting that evening with various sides
being represented;

The tension over ministerial responsibilities to the various parties;

The unwillingness to address the systemic problems of
poverty and homelessness in this urban setting.

Detailed Questions & Activities

Several possibilities exist for processing this case. One involves the use of groups consisting of 4 or 5 members to discuss the following questions. You might assign the groups any or all of the scriptures listed in the preparation section to help them gain perspective on these questions.

1) What do you think are the main characters' interests? What are their feelings? What is at stake for each of them in this discussion?

2) How would you suggest that Fred Washington proceed in leading the meeting at the church that night? What is most important for him to keep in mind?

3) What would it take to help this group put on christological lenses through which to see the situation? What difference would seeing the situation through these lenses make?

4) What do you see in the case that is world-affirming? What do you see that is world-rejecting? Explain your responses.

5) Where do you see possibilities for incarnational ministry in this setting? How would you proceed in implementing it?

6) What possibilities does this situation hold for the church to be more inclusive? What are the specific challenges that will have to be addressed for this to happen?

Another way to process this case involves inviting different participants to represent each of the major and minor characters in roleplaying. You might initially roleplay the scene as it is likely to happen based on what you know about the case. Allow this "meeting" to go on for 10 to 15 minutes. Next, roleplay the discussion again using a christological lens to shape the discussion. Again, allow this meeting to take 10 to 15 minutes. Finally, invite participants to dialogue in groups of 4 or 5 about the differences they saw in the two meetings.

Making Applications

1) With either of the activities listed above, conclude by leading the group in formulating insights they have gained that would be useful to all Christians faced with these difficult circumstances.

2) Brainstorm situations in your church that are similar to those in this case, and discuss ways to minister like Christ more effectively in these settings.

3) Close with a prayer for wisdom in your spiritual service to the congregation and the community.

Case Study 2: "Peace Child"

Don Richardson sat cross-legged facing the elders of a Sawi (*Să´·wē*) village deep in the interior of West Irian in early 1963. These long-isolated people were headhunters and cannibals. Don had spent much time pressing them to make peace, despite their training for violence, and urging them to accept Jesus Christ as their Lord and peacemaker. In the past few months, Don had come close to despair of ever reaching his goals, however, so pervasive was their hostility. Now he had another chance…

The Sawi

In June, 1962, Don Richardson had established a camp in Sawi territory. He built a house and moved into it with his wife and young son. For the next seven months, Don worked to learn their language and customs. During this period, the people of two Sawi villages relocated nearby. He believed that the novelty of the new family and the practicality of things like nylon fishing line, machetes, mirrors, and so forth had drawn them and overcome the villagers' normally warlike ways. Soon, though, Don realized that this initial optimism was unfounded; fourteen fierce, inter-village battles were fought within sight of his house during the first two months he lived among them. After that, he lost count of the hostilities.

214

As Don lived among them, he began to realize how pervasive hostility was in Sawi culture. A Sawi child is trained to get his way by sheer force of violence and temper. He is goaded constantly to take revenge for every hurt or insult. Parents give examples as they carry out violent retaliation for anything that offends them. The Sawi hear a constant recitation of stories and legends exalting violence and treachery as traditional obligations. Those devising new forms of treachery insure that their names will be passed down in honor in the main body of Sawi legends.

In the peaceful times between fighting, Don Richardson tried to teach the Sawi men stories from the Bible. They were generally uninterested. Only once did his presentation get a ringing response from the Sawi. He reported afterward: "I was describing Judas' betrayal of Jesus. About half-way through the description, I noticed they were all listening intently. They seemed fascinated to learn how Judas had kept close company with Jesus for three years, sharing the same food, traveling the same road...

"At the climax of the story, Maum (*Măūm*) whistled a birdcall of admiration. Kani (*Kă·nē´*) and several others touched their fingertips to their chests in awe. Others chuckled. Kani leaned forward and exclaimed, 'That was a real *tuwi asonai man*' (*tū´·wē ă·sō·nī´ măn*)." It took Richardson some time to understand the phrase. He later understood it to mean "to fatten him with friendship for an unsuspected slaughter." He knew that the Sawi idealized treachery as a virtue—a goal in life—and suddenly realized that they were reacting to the story of Judas with great admiration. Judas, to them, was a super-Sawi!

Don and his wife, Carol, discussed the problem over lunch as they always did. They had hoped together to bring the gospel to the Sawi while respecting the Sawi culture. Now it seemed almost hopeless.

"God always has a way," Carol said. "There must be a way." They agreed to hope and pray for a key to

215

the situation. Then, the next day, really serious fighting broke out again between the villages of Haenam (*Hĭ·năm'*) and Kamur (*Kă·mŭr'*).

Reluctantly, the Richardsons concluded that their coming and drawing two villages together had deprived these violent people of the mutual isolation they needed to survive in relative peace. The Richardsons determined that, for the good of the people, they would leave. Don told his decision to the chief men of each village. "Since you cannot make peace with each other, it is clear to us that we ought to leave. If we stay here, it is only a matter of time until more are killed, and then you will be locked in a blood-feud which may take still more lives."

That evening a delegation of leading men from each of the villages came to the Richardson's home. "Don't leave us," one of them pleaded solemnly. "But I don't want you to kill each other," Richardson replied. "We are not going to kill each other," the speaker said. Then, steeling himself, he continued, "Tomorrow, we are going to make peace."

The Peace Child

On the following day, the Richardsons watched as all the people of the two villages gathered. Emotions were at a high pitch and women were crying as two men from the different villages approached each other, each with a tiny baby—a son—in his arms. Kaiyo (*Kĭ·yō'*) and Mahor (*Mă·chŏr'*) stood face to face. "Mahor," Kaiyo challenged, "will you plead the words of the village of Kamur among your people?"

"Yes," Mahor responded, "I will plead the words of Kamur among my people." Kaiyo held forth his little son: "Then, I give you my son and with him, my name." Mahor received him gently into his arms: "Eehaa! It is enough! I will surely plead for peace between us."

People of both villages thundered forth with shouts of triumph. People now began calling Mahor by Kaiyo's name. A man named Mahaen (*Mă·hīn'*),

216

from Mahor's village, appeared at the front of the crowed. He presented his baby son to Kaiyo. Again the exchange of a child and names took place. The shouts of triumph from the two villages were mixed with anguished cries from the mothers and close relatives of the children who were being exchanged.

The ceremony continued. Mahor shouted an invitation to people of both villages: "Those who accept this child as a basis for peace, come and lay hands on him." Men and women, young and old, filed past the two newly exchanged babies and laid their hands on them. Then the children were carried to the man-houses of their respective villages and adorned for a peace celebration.

A leading woman of each village next held her village's child, while rows of former enemies passed by the children to confront each other. They moved to the throb of drums, meeting each other and exchanging names and gifts. After the trade, a wild dance ensued, indicating that the people of the two villages had now embraced each other. As long as the peace-children lived, no one who had here laid his hand on one could work violence against those of the village who gave him.

Richardson was moved and puzzled at first by this sudden reversal of warlike patterns. All his efforts to urge peace in the name of his God had failed. Yet this tribal ceremony had apparently succeeded and held great power. Should he now go or stay? Was there a way of sharing the gospel he believed with people whose traditions were so alien to his own, without compromising what he believed or destroying them and their culture?

The Christian Message in West Irian

After two months of reflection and questioning to learn more about the peace-child custom, Richardson now sat before the elders of the Sawi villages. "When I saw you exchanging children, at first I

217

was horrified," he began. "I kept saying to myself, 'Couldn't they make peace without this painful giving of a son?' But you kept telling me, 'There is no other way.'" He leaned forward and, in accordance with Sawi custom, placed his right hand palm down on the floor. "You were right," he said.

Every eye in the man-house was fixed on him as he continued. "When I stopped to think about it, I realized you and your ancestors are not the only ones who found that peace required a peace child. *Myao Kodon* (*Mē·ow′ Kō·dōn′*), the Spirit whose message I bear, has declared the same thing—true peace can never come without a peace child." There was silence. "Because *Myao Kodon* wants men to find peace with him and each other, he decided to choose a once-for-all peace child to establish peace forever."

"Whom did he choose?" asked Mahaen.

Richardson answered with another question, "Did Kaiyo give another man's son or his own?"

"His own," they replied.

"And Mahaen, did you give another man's son or your own?"

"I gave my own," he replied, remembering the pain.

"So did God," Richardson replied, looking sideways at the wall with a Sawi gesture meaning 'think about that.' He opened an English Bible and read a part of Isaiah's prophecy in Sawi: "Unto us a child is born, unto us a son is given; and the government shall be upon his shoulders, and his name shall be called Wonderful, Counselor, the Mighty God, the Everlasting Father, the Prince of peace. Of the increase of this government there shall be no end."

Mahaen looked at Richardson. "Is he the one you've been telling us about?"

218

"He is," Richardson replied softly.

"But you said a friend betrayed him. If Jesus was a peace child, it was the worst thing anyone could do to betray him," Mahaen continued. The room was quiet.

As he walked away, Richardson wondered about the future. He wanted to believe the Sawi could incorporate his message about Jesus Christ into their own traditions. Would the message of a once-for-all peace child be effective in changing the Sawi tendency toward violence? And if it was, would the message be distorted beyond recognition?

Teaching Notes

Preparation

Unlike most case studies where the identity of the main characters are hidden, the people in this case have retained their true identity—Don Richardson insisted upon it when Jack Rogers adapted the case.

Before actually planning to teach this case, it may be helpful to realize why it is included in *Unveiling Glory*. It is a missions case, but one that is so unusual that it will have little benefit for most American Christians if processed solely from that vantage. It does, however, offer some cultural distance which may prove helpful in examining our own experiences and understanding of the gospel and the development of our christology.

Goals

1) To examine our common images of Christ and their application to people of different languages, symbols, and culture;

2) To explore how Christ can be presented in every culture in a way that can be received without distorting the central message of Christ's life, ministry, and teaching;

3) To recognize the transforming power of Jesus Christ in even the most difficult of circumstances.

219

Preliminary Activities

1) Ask the class to read the case aloud together or allow them time to read it quietly. Remember that

individuals who are sight-impaired may struggle with this last option.

2) Begin the discussion by asking participants what they found most surprising (or appealing) in this case. Write their responses in a list for everyone to see.

3) Identify the main characters in the case. As the facilitator, you may allow this process to be done exclusively by the participants, or you may have made copies of this information in advance for their review:

> *Don Richardson*, the newly arrived missionary who has spent seven months in West Irian with his wife and child. He has drawn the attention of two villages and is intent on learning about the language and the culture;
> *Carol Richardson*, Don's wife. She and her young son moved to West Irian with Don to serve as missionaries. She is a supportive spouse who trusts in God;
> *Kaiyo*, the village chief who gave up his son to attain peace;
> *Mahaen*, the man from the other village who also gave his son to attain peace.

4) Identify the minor characters:

> The Richardsons' infant son;
> *Maum*, who admires Judas when the story is told;
> *Kane*, who proclaims Judas a hero, a super-Sawi;
> *Mahor*, who receives Kaiyo's child on behalf of the village.

Detailed Questions & Activities

Divide the class into groups of 4 or 5 and ask them to discuss all or some of the following questions together:

1) What do you think is the biggest problem that Don and Carol Richardson are facing in this situation?

2) Have you ever experienced a circumstance where you were frustrated and unsure about the direction you should take next in your walk with Christ? Share the details with the others in your group.

3) Where in your world do you find people who are unable to hear the message of Jesus Christ, no matter how clearly it is presented?

4) What does this case teach you about teaching and living Christ in an alien and strange world? How might what you've learned affect how you approach others?

5) What do you think it felt like to be in Kaiyo's or Maehan's place as leaders who must make such huge sacrifices? Have you ever been in a situation where you had to give up what was most precious to you? Share that situation with the others.

6) What fresh insights do you gather from this case on what it meant for God to send his Son to live among us? What effects do these insights have on your faith?

7) Identify 1 or 2 things from your small group discussion you would like to share with the larger gathering.

Draw the larger group back together and allow all of the groups to present their insights, focusing especially on how this exercise has enriched their perspectives. Continue sharing until everyone has had a chance to participate.

Making Applications

1) Spend time in prayer together for each of the following: **a** · those who are serving as missionaries around the world; **b** · the leaders of churches everywhere; **c** · the lost who do not know Jesus; **d** · those unsure of their direction who are struggling and discouraged; **e** · your congregation and the need for every member to grow in Christ; **f** · the specific situations of your daily lives in which each of you witness and serve.

2) End the time together by reading Luke 1:67–80.

Works Cited

Introduction

Kathryn Lindskoog, *C. S. Lewis: Mere Christian*, 3d ed. (Wheaton, IL: Harold Shaw, 1987): 46–7.

Augustine of Hippo, *Confessions* 1.1.1. In Maria Boulding, trans., *The Confessions: Saint Augustine* (New York: Random House, 1998): 3.

Allen, C. Leonard and Danny Gray Swick, *Participating in God's Life: Two Crossroads for Churches of Christ* (Orange, CA; New Leaf Books, 2001): 155–6.

Robert Richardson, *Communings in the Sanctuary*, ed. C. Leonard Allen (Orange, CA: New Leaf Books, 2000): 46.

David Lipscomb, in *Gospel Advocate* 11/21 (May 27, 1869): 495.

Chapter 1

"Nicene Creed." In Henry Bettenson and Chris Maunder, eds., *Documents of the Christian Church*, 3d ed. (Oxford: University Press, 1999): 27–28.

"This World is not my Home." In Alton H. Howard, ed., *Songs of the Church* (West Monroe: LA, Howard Publishing, 1975): no. 957.

Kallistos Ware, *The Orthodox Way* (Crestwood, NY: St. Vladimir's Seminary Press, 1979): 74.

Desiderius Erasmus. In John P. Dolan, trans., *The Essential Erasmus* (New York: New American Library, 1964): 58.

John Sanders, *The God Who Risks: A Theology of Providence*, (Downers Grove, IL: IVP, 1998): 174.

A.W. Tozer, *The Pursuit of God* (Camp Hill, PA: Christian Publications, 1993): 111, 113.

Chapter 2

Mary Elizabeth Coleridge. In Robert Atwan and Laurance Wieder, eds., *Chapters into Verse: Poetry In English Inspired by the Bible. Volume One: Gospels to Revelation* (New York: Oxford University Press, 1993): 26.

Ephrem the Syrian, *Hymn on the Nativity* 8. In Kathleen McVey, trans., *Ephrem the Syrian: Hymns* (New York: Paulist, 1989): 119.

John Neville Figgis, *The Gospel and Human Needs* (New York: Longmans, Green & Co., 1909): 11.

William C. Placher, *Jesus the Savior. The Meaning of Jesus Christ for Christian Faith* (Louisville: Westminster John Knox, 2001): 57.

Olivier Clément, *Taizé: A Meaning to Life* (Chicago: GIA Publications, 1997): 60.

Halford E. Luccock, "Whoops! It's Christmas—in Which the Old Order of Seating Changeth." In Herbert W. Luthin, ed., *The Abbot Christmas Book* (Garden City, NY: Doubleday, 1960): 39.

Thérèse of Lisieux, *The Autobiography of St. Thérèse of Lisieux: The Story of a Soul*, trans. John Beevers (New York: Doubleday, 1957): 19.

Chapter 3

Alexander Campbell, *The Christian System* (Cincinnati: H.S. Bosworth, 1866): 58.

A. J. Gossip, *From the Edge of the Crowd: Being Musings of a Pagan Mind on Jesus Christ* (Edinburgh: T. & T. Clark, 1924): 230–31.

Martin Luther, *Larg Catechism* 13. In F. Bente and W. H. T. Dau, trans., *The Large Catechism by Martin Luther* (St. Louis: Concordia Publishing House, 1921).

Alexander Campbell, *The Christian System* (Cincinnati: H. S. Bosworth, 1866): 266.

Michael Card, "Scandalon," from album *Scandalon* (Birdwing Music, 1985).

Dietrich Bonhoeffer, *The Cost of Discipleship*, trans. R. H. Fuller, 2nd ed. (New York: Macmillan, 1963): 99.

Dietrich Bonhoeffer, *The Cost of Discipleship*, trans. R. H. Fuller, 2nd ed. (New York: Macmillan, 1963): 46–7.

Robert E. Webber, *Ancient-Future Faith. Rethinking Evangelicalism for a Postmodern World* (Grand Rapids: Baker, 1999): 110.

Jean Vanier, *Community and Growth* (Darton, Longman & Todd, 1979): 10.

Thomas Aquinas, *Summa Theologica* 3.66.7. In Fathers of the English Dominican Province, trans., *The Summa Theologica of St. Thomas Aquinas*, 2nd ed. (1920). Online edition copyright 2001. <http://www.newadvent.org/summa>.

Chapter 4

Mother Theresa, *A Gift for God: Prayers and Meditations* (New York: Harper & Row, 1975): 19.

Maltbie D. Babcock, "This is My Father's World." In Alton H. Howard, ed., *Songs of Faith and Praise* (West Monroe: LA, Howard Publishing, 1994): no. 991.

Tillit S. Teddlie, "Heaven Holds All to Me." In Alton H. Howard, ed., *Songs of the Church* (West Monroe: LA, Howard Publishing, 1975): no. 95.

Epistle to Diognetus, 5–6. In A. Roberts and J. Donaldson, eds., *The Ante-Nicene Fathers: Translations of the Writings of the Fathers Down to* AD *325* (Buffalo, NY: Christian Literature, 1885–96; reprinted Peabody: Hendrickson, 1994): 1.26–7.

Clement of Alexandria, *Paedogogos* 1.2 (*The Instructor*). In A. Roberts and J. Donaldson, eds., *The Ante-Nicene Fathers: Translations of the Writings of the Fathers Down to* AD *325* (Buffalo, NY: Christian Literature, 1885–96; reprinted Peabody: Hendrickson, 1994): 2.210.

Marjorie J. Thompson, *Soul Feast: An Invitation to the Christian Spiritual Life* (Louisville: Westminster John Knox, 1995): 122.

E. G. Sewell, *Gospel Advocate* 51/50 (December 16, 1909): 1575.

David Lipscomb, "Aid to Christians in Need—How Shall it Be Administered," *Gospel Advocate* 12/11 (March 17, 1870): 253; and "The Destitution South," *Gospel Advocate* 9/9 (February 28, 1867): 171–2.

Christine D. Pohl, *Making Room: Recovering Hospitality as a Christian Tradition* (Grand Rapids: Eerdmans, 1999): 73.

Chapter 5

Parker J. Palmer, *To Know as We Are Known: Education as a Spiritual Journey* (New York: HarperSanFrancisco, 1993): 47.

Parker J. Palmer, *The Courage to Teach: Exploring the Inner Landscape of a Teacher's Life* (San Francisco: Jossey-Bass, 1998): 115.

Herbert Kohl, *The Discipline of Hope: Learning from a Lifetime of Teaching* (New York: New Press, 1998): 13.

T. W. Manson, *The Teaching of Jesus*, 2nd ed. reprint (New York: Cambridge University Press, 1959): 19.

Herbert Kohl, *Growing Minds: On Becoming a Teacher* (New York: Harper Torchbooks, 1988): 64.

Newman, John Henry, Cardinal, *The Idea of a University*, ed. Martin J. Svaglic (Notre Dame, IN: University of Notre Dame Press, 1982), Discourse 7.1.

Günther Bornkamm, *Jesus of Nazareth*, trans. Irene and Fraser McLuskey, with James M. Robinson (New York: Harper & Row, 1960): 56–7.

Alfie Kohn, *What to Look For in a Classroom...and Other Essays* (New York: Jossey-Bass, 2000): 5.

Thomas C. Oden, *Pastoral Theology: Essentials of Ministry* (San Francisco: Harper Collins, 1983): 141.

Basil of Caesarea, *Epistle* 150.4. In P. Schaff, et al., eds., *A Select Library of Nicene and Post-Nicene Fathers of the Christian Church*, 2nd series (New York: Christian Literature, 1887–94; reprinted Peabody: Hendrickson, 1994): 8.208.

Chapter 6

Bernard of Clairvaux, *On Loving God*, 4.5. In G.R. Evans, trans., *Bernard of Clairvaux. Selected Works* (New York: Paulist, 1987): 186.

Anselm of Canterbury, *Cur deus homo?* (*Why the God-Man?*), 1.11; 2.6, 19. In Eugene R. Fairweather, ed., *A Scholastic Miscellany: Anselm to Ockham* (Philadelphia: Westminster Press, 1956): 119, 151, 180–81.

Max Lucado, *No Wonder They Call Him the Savior* (Portland, OR: Multnomah, 1986): 67.

Gregory of Nyssa, *Address on Religious Instruction*, 24. Quoted in Edward Roche Hardy and Cyril C. Richardson, eds., *Christology of the Later Fathers* (*Library of Christian Classics* 3; Philadelphia: Westminster, 1954): 301.

Melito of Sardis, *Peri Pascha*, 102. In Stuart George Hall, ed., *Melito of Sardis. On Pascha, and Fragments* (Oxford: Clarendon Press, 1979): 59.

Jamie Owens-Collins, "The Battle Belongs to the Lord." Copyright 1985. In Alton H. Howard, ed., *Songs of Faith and Praise* (West Monroe, LA: Howard Publishing, 1994): no. 749.

Peter Lombard, *Libra sententiarum* 3.19.1 (*Book of Sentences*). Quoted in Hastings Rashdall, *The Idea of Atonement in Christian Theology* (New York: Macmillan, 1919): 371.

Hastings Rashdall, "The Abelardian Doctrine of the Atonement." Quoted in Alister E. McGrath, ed., *The Christian Theology Reader* (Oxford: Blackwell, 1995): 197.

Athanasius of Alexandria, *De incarnatione*, 54 (*On the Incarnation*). In Penelope Lawson, trans., *On the Incarnation: The Treatise* De Incarnatione Verbi Dei *by St. Athanasius* (New York: Macmillan, 1981).

Robert Richardson, *Communings in the Sanctuary*, ed. C. Leonard Allen (Orange, CA: New Leaf Books, 2000): 102.

Robert Milligan, *The Scheme of Redemption* (St. Louis: Christian Board of Publication, 1869): 226–54.

Chapter 7

Philip Yancy, *The Jesus I Never Knew* (Grand Rapids: Zondervan, 1995): 211.

C.S. Lewis, *Miracles* (New York: Macmillan, 1978): 143–4.

David Watson, *Fear No Evil: A Personal Struggle with Cancer* (London: Hodder & Stoughton, 1984): 168.

Ambrose of Milan, *De Spiritu Sancto*, 1.6.76 (*On the Holy Spirit*). In P. Schaff, et al., eds., *A Select Library of Nicene and Post-Nicene Fathers of the Christian Church*, 2nd series (New York: Christian Literature: 1887–94; reprinted Peabody: Hendrickson, 1994): 10.103.

Ignatius of Antioch, *Epistle to the Romans*, 5. In A. Roberts and J. Donaldson, eds., *The Ante-Nicene Fathers: Translations of the Writings of the Fathers down to AD 325* (Buffalo, NY: Christian Literature, 1885–96; reprinted Peabody: Hendrickson, 1994): 1.76.

Thomas à Kempis, *Imitatio Christi*, 1.1 (*The Imitation of Christ*) (Grand Rapids: Zondervan, 1983): 3.

Johann Arndt, in *Johann Arndt: True Christianity*, trans. Peter Erb (New York: Paulist Press, 1979): 22.

Jonathan Edwards, in *The Works of President Edwards in Four Volumes: A Reprint of the Worcester Edition* (New York: Leavitt, Trow, and Co., 1844): 1.11.

David Lipscomb, "Like Christ," *Gospel Advocate* 9/21 (May 23, 1867): 416.

Charles M. Sheldon, *In His Steps* (Chicago: John C. Winston, 1937): 25.

Chapter 8

Augustine of Hippo, *Confessions* 4.12.19. In Maria Boulding, trans., *The Confessions: Saint Augustine* (New York: Random House, 1998): 66.

John Polkinghorne, "Opening Windows onto Reality," *Theology Today* 58 (2001): 153.

Isaac of Nineveh, *Part* I, *Discourse* III. In S. P. Brock, trans., *The Syriac Fathers on Prayer and the Spiritual Life* (Kalamazoo, MI: Cistercian, 1987): 247–8.

Gregory of Nyssa, *Life of Moses*, 1.10; 2.306. In Abraham J. Malherbe and Everett Ferguson, trans., *Gregory of Nyssa: The Life of Moses* (New York: Paulist, 1978): 31.

Carl Braaten, "The Reality of the Resurrection." In Christopher R. Seitz, ed., *Nicene Christianity: The Future for a New Ecumenism* (Grand Rapids: Brazos, 2001): 115.

Hannah More, *Practical Piety: or The Influence of the Religion of the Heart on the Conduct of Life* (New York: American Tract Society, 1811): 12.

Philip Yancy, *The Jesus I Never Knew* (Grand Rapids: Zondervan, 1995): 228.

Martin Luther. See Roland H. Bainton, *Here I Stand* (Nashville: Abingdon-Cokesbury, 1950): 367.

T. W. Manson, *The Servant Messiah: A Study of the Public Ministry of Jesus* (Cambridge: Cambridge University Press 1953): 98.

Recommended Reading

Books about Jesus Christ abound. Some are properly christological, dealing with various topics relating to the significance of Christ for faith and life, as he is presented in scripture or experienced in the church of yesterday and today. Others focus on Jesus' life, employing scripture and historical data in an attempt to understand him and his teaching in his first-century Jewish context. Still others have a more devotional purpose, adapting some of the insights of the former two types of books in order to nurture personal faith in Christ. With the vast number of books and articles that deal with Jesus, the following list can only be very selective. It includes a few titles for further reading, mostly from the first category of books mentioned above. The list could easily be multiplied. Though it should not be assumed that the authors of the present volume fully endorse everything the books in this list say, they believe that these would be useful starting points for anyone wanting further conversation on the meaning of Christ for faith and life.

Allen, C. Leonard and Danny Gray Swick, *Participating in God's Life: Two Crossroads for Churches of Christ* (Orange, CA: New Leaf Books, 2001).

> The authors revisit a 19th-century moment in the history of the Restoration Movement, when the Movement "chose" to follow Tolbert Fanning's emphasis on the rationalistic and materialistic dimensions of the

Christian faith, rather than Robert Richardson's emphasis on relationship and transformation. Believing that Churches of Christ face a similar crossroads today, the authors suggest that we choose the way upheld by Richardson this time, grounding our beliefs and practices in a fuller appreciation of what it means to participate in the life of God the Father, the Son, and the Spirit.

Aquino, Frederick, "The Incarnation: The Dignity and Honor of Human Personhood." *Restoration Quarterly* 42 (2000): 39–46.

This article explores the connection between the doctrine of the incarnation and the ministerial task of the church. It shows how the incarnation addresses the question of whether Christian faith promotes the dignity and honor of human personhood. The author suggests that the Incarnation serves as an important theological resource for addressing the moral dimension of Christian faith, for nurturing people in the life of the church, and for extending the church's ministerial task to surrounding communities.

Fiddes, Paul, *Past Event and Present Salvation: The Christian Idea of Atonement* (Louisville, KY: Westminster/John Knox, 1989).

This book explores the question of how salvation as a past event is relevant to human experience in the present. In a readable style, the book surveys different biblical, theological, and historical understandings of atonement while probing their relevance for practical areas such as forgiveness, liberation, and suffering. The authors shows how different images of salvation relate to different historical and political realities.

McGrath, Alister, *Understanding Jesus: Who Jesus Christ Is and Why He Matters* (Grand Rapids: Zondervan, 1987).

This introductory investigation of Jesus Christ sees his person and his (ongoing) work as inseparably bound together. Though the book focuses specifically on the cross, the author takes pains to show how a cross-centered atonement must also be seen as integrally connected to the incarnation, Jesus' teaching and ministry, and his resurrection. Especially pertinent for today's multi-cultural contexts, the book illuminates ways in which a Christ-centered approach to the world and human problems differs from the approaches of other belief systems in fundamental ways. But in order for Christianity's distinct resources in Christ to enter the life of the church, Christians must engage in deliberate processes of doctrinal formation within the church family. This in turn requires that Christians never stop returning to their sources of knowledge about Christ, always sharpening their skills in using them responsibly and applying them to real-world problems.

Milligan, Robert, *The Scheme of Redemption* (St. Louis: Christian Board of Publication, 1869).

Within the Restoration Movement, this 582-page tome is the classic presentation of the traditional understanding of Jesus' saving work. Rather than applying philosophical or speculative methods for understanding Christ, the author confines himself rigorously to the language, categories, and images of the biblical text. Yet, in keeping with many other modern Protestant treatments, he chooses to focus particularly on the substitutionary/sacrifice function of the cross, neglecting other key images in scripture. Nevertheless, within this limited framework, his treatment of the topic of salvation is systematic, logical, and exhaustively comprehensive. It gives the reader a thorough look at the theological background underlying many of the traditional assumptions about salvation that exist within Churches of Christ and, for that matter, in many other groups today.

Pelikan, Jaroslav, *Jesus through the Centuries: His Place in the History of Culture* (New Haven, CT: Yale University Press, 1985).

This book surveys the various ways in which Jesus has been understood and depicted throughout the history of Christianity. Written by a historian of doctrine, the book challenges readers to recognize that, as the issues, questions, and modes of thinking have changed over the years, so have notions about the meaning of Jesus and the nature of his mission. The illustrated edition, though textually abridged, includes marvelous plates illustrating changing fashions in the popular conception of Jesus.

233

Placher, William C., *Jesus the Savior: The Meaning of Jesus Christ for Christian Faith* (Louisville: Westminster/John Knox, 2001).

> This book presents the four major parts of Jesus' story that have shown up consistently in theological treatments of his significance—incarnation, ministry, the cross, and resurrection. In a readable style, the author thoughtfully explores the relevance of each of these topics within three contexts: Jesus' first-century Jewish context, that of the church's ongoing faith, and that of the daily life of Christians. Though not all his conclusions regarding controversial issues are likely to meet with the reader's agreement, his methods for discussing contemporary issues in light of Jesus' story provide the reader with a useful model.

Wilson, Jonathan R., *God So Loved the World: A Christology for Disciples* (Grand Rapids: Baker, 2001).

> The author crafts a lively series of reflections on Christ that effectively "connect believing with living." He deals with (1) the story of Jesus Christ, (2) biblical images that aid us in understanding how Jesus' saves (e.g. victor, sacrifice, example), and (3) Christian practices in the world and the church that grow out of the story and its dominant images. Throughout the book, Wilson considers each subject according to its biblical basis and historical development, followed by an effort to synthesize doctrines through systematic reflection.

Wright, N. T., *The Challenge of Jesus: Rediscovering Who Jesus Was and Is* (Downers Grove, IL: IVP, 1999).

> This concise presentation of the main elements of Jesus' life and work not only does a masterful job of helping the reader situate Jesus within his original setting but also provokes deep thought about his ongoing significance for the people of God today. Wright is well-known for his ability to unveil startling insights gleaned from the ancient texts in ways that flexibly address contemporary needs, while fitting them into a grand theological vision and respecting the basic commitments of conservative, traditional Christianity. This book presents in brief form many of the key points to be found in his magisterial *Jesus and the Victory of God* (Minneapolis: Fortress, 1996) and *The Resurrection of*

the Son of God (Minneapolis: Fortress, 2003), focusing on what it means to announce the gospel message of new creation, as people encountering Jesus afresh on the Emmaus road of 21st-century postmodernity. He suggests ways that a fuller appreciation for Christ will deeply impact daily life, for example in transforming how we see our careers and how we conduct ourselves in them.

Yancy, Philip, *The Jesus I Never Knew* (Grand Rapids: Zondervan, 1995).

In this book, the author explores the life and teachings of Jesus during the major phases of his life, focusing on the provocative and often startling features of the narrative often overlooked in "Sunday School" presentations of Jesus. Though many of his basic insights will not be new to those acquainted with academic studies of the Gospels, Yancy's engaging style and his knack for relating Christ to our contemporary world challenge readers to rethink their understandings of who Jesus is and what his followers should look like.

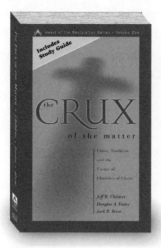

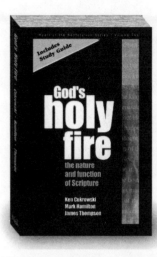